What Happened? Re-presenting Traumas, Uncovering Recoveries

At the Interface/Probing the Boundaries

VOLUME 113

The titles published in this series are listed at *brill.com/aipb*

What Happened? Re-presenting Traumas, Uncovering Recoveries

Processing Individual and Collective Trauma

Edited by

Elspeth McInnes
Danielle Schaub

BRILL
RODOPI

LEIDEN | BOSTON

Cover illustration: The image conveys both the constraints of traumatic experiences and the light beyond and is of the required resolution. Photographer: Danielle Schaub. Used with permission.

The Library of Congress Cataloging-in-Publication Data is available online at http://catalog.loc.gov

Typeface for the Latin, Greek, and Cyrillic scripts: "Brill". See and download: brill.com/brill-typeface.

ISSN 1570-7113
ISBN 978-90-04-38319-7 (paperback)
ISBN 978-90-04-38593-1 (e-book)

This book is printed on acid-free paper and produced in a sustainable manner.

Contents

Illustrations

Notes on Contributors

Svetlana Antropova

currently a full-time professor at Centro Universitario Villanueva, affiliated with the Complutense University of Madrid, Spain – completed her PhD in English and North-American Literature at the Autonomous University of Madrid. Her doctoral thesis was entitled 'Staging Memory and Trauma: Past Voices and Bodies Haunting the Present in the Theatre of Samuel Beckett.' While interested in English literature, especially theatre, she currently devotes her research and writing to the artistic representation of memory and trauma in postmodern theatre.

Peter Bray

PhD, Senior Lecturer and Programme Leader for Counsellor Education at the University of Auckland – has recently co-edited a number of interdisciplinary volumes including *At the Crossroads of Crisis and Opportunity: Interdisciplinary Conversations* (2015); *Beyond Present Patient Realities: Collaboration, Care and Identity* (2015) and *Beyond Diagnosis: Relating the Person to the Patient – the Patient to the Person* (2014); *Voicing Trauma and Truth: Narratives of Disruption and Transformation'* (2013) and *The strangled Cry: The Communication and Experience of Trauma* (2013), which reflect his research interest in spirituality, heroic identity and the transformational aspects of loss and trauma.

Kate Burton

is a registered psychotherapist in private practice in Perth, Western Australia. She holds a PhD from Murdoch University. Her doctoral research was funded by an Australian Postgraduate Award and examined giftedness in relation to trauma theory, addiction and self-destructive behaviour. Prior to entering private practice, Kate lectured in the Department of Interdisciplinary Studies at Manchester Metropolitan University and the Faculty of Arts and Social Sciences at The Open University. Kate's current research focuses on optimal learning environments and mitigating trauma in educational settings.

Mark Callaghan

a former Art History Lecturer for the Highgate Institution and Associate Tutor at Birkbeck College, University of London – completed his PhD thesis on *Trauma, Memory and Aesthetics: The Berlin Holocaust Memorial Competition and the Representation of Negative History*. He graduated from Oxford University and the University of Manchester, and served as General Editor and Art

History Editor of the academic journal *Dandelion*. His research interests include Holocaust memorialization, cultural memory and trauma studies.

Marie France Forcier
a Canadian dance artist and writer, has produced choreographic work seen internationally. She acts as the artistic director for *Forcier Stage Works* and co-artistic director for *Hub 14*. She completed her Master of Fine Arts in Dance at York University in 2014 and is currently on faculty as Assistant Professor in the School of Creative and Performing Arts at the University of Calgary, Canada.

Monica Hinton
a registered clinical social worker – is currently completing her PhD at the University of South Australia. Her dissertation research focuses on the process of resiliency despite childhood trauma, an extension of her MSW research. Her 15 years of clinical experience includes work in both non-profit & government agencies in the area of mental health and her workshop presentations include local, national and international venues. Her presentations focus on helping individuals foster resiliency in themselves and their clients.

Gen'ichiro Itakura
an Associate Professor at the Faculty of Letters, Kansai University, Japan – has published several books including *Daigaku de yomu Harii Pottā* [*Reading Harry Potter at University*] (2012), and his articles ('On Beauty and Doing Justice to Art: Aesthetics and Ethics in Zadie Smith's *On Beauty*,' etc.) have appeared in journals including *ARIEL*.

Elspeth McInnes
is a sociologist and Senior Lecturer and researcher in the School of Education at the University of South Australia. Her research engages with family violence and child abuse, child abuse recovery and prevention. She co-edited, also with Danielle Schaub, the book *Trauma and Meaning Making* (2016), and has published numerous journal articles and book chapters relating to family-generated trauma.

Danielle Schaub
an Associate Professor at Oranim Academic College of Education, Israel, and Adjunct Professor at the University of Alberta, Canada, as well as a poet, short-story writer, photographer and bibliotherapist – has published a monograph on Mavis Gallant (1998), *Interior Views: Photopoetry* (2009), and collections such as *Mapping Canadian Cultural Space: Essays on Canadian Literature*

(2000) and *Reading Writers Reading: Canadian Authors' Reflections* (2006). She has co-edited *Precarious Present, Promising Future? Ethnicity and Identities in Canadian Literature* (1996), *Identity, Community, Nation: Essays on Canadian Literature* (2004), *Tissage et métissage dans l'oeuvre de Gérard Etienne* (2014) and, also with Elspeth McInnes, *Trauma and Meaning Making* (2016).

Zeina Tarraf
completed her PhD in the Department of English and Film Studies at the University of Alberta in Edmonton, Canada. Her research and teaching interests focus on situating visual and literary texts from the Global South within larger mediascapes and theoretical frameworks to track how cultural representations are productively entangled with global and local power dynamics and discourses.

Paul Vivian
an artist and academic – currently works as Course Leader for Fine Art and Arts and Media at the University for the Creative Arts in Farnham, Surrey. His practice as an artist encompasses explorations in re-contextualising the functions of imagery through found objects and collage. He has presented papers regarding theories of collage at conferences in Cambridge, Prague and Berlin.

Introduction

Elspeth McInnes and Danielle Schaub

Traumatising experiences galvanise every sense of the body. Asked to describe a traumatic or highly stressful event, witnesses can often identify the smallest details – smells, tastes, sights, sounds and touch – related to the traumatic event. While gathering all information, the body can encode the experience, leaving the survivor with detailed physical recall, but often with gaps in the story of 'what happened'. Each survivor lives in their world of survival, sometimes coping, sometimes stuck in the experience, sometimes learning and growing into new ways to function in the world. How each survivor knows 'what happened' begins with their sensate world but expands into other understandings with trauma re-presented and shared with others.

Representing trauma, the first of the two key themes of this volume, can vary between a voyeuristic exploitation, a cultural accommodation of a preferred reality, a searing powerful uncomfortable truth, a pathway to personal growth or even a re-hiding of the barely known. The representation of trauma thus carries a politics of power and an ethics of care, always necessarily socially mediated. How representations of traumatic events are interpreted and understood presupposes the presence of a witness, viewer, reader or interpreter. The individual perspectives comprising the audience for representations of trauma includes those of direct and indirect victims, of survivors and of the broader population willing to address the represented trauma, be it in a text, play, film, memorial, photography or other medium.

One of the many complexities of encounters with trauma includes the absence of fixity and thus an enforced degree of tolerance variously of disintegration and fragmentation, suppression, intrusive expression, re-integration and re-covery, where recovery stands for a new encounter with a re-formed self, no longer separated or defined by trauma. For those who have been exposed to trauma, no single state of post-traumatic being is inevitable or even necessarily possible. The experience of trauma interacts with the multiplicities of individuals' and communities' pasts, presents and futures and the ways traumatic experience reverberates in each context.

The personalised meaning of trauma for survivors also contributes to shared cultural narratives, embedding a politics of meaning in the ways that trauma is talked about and represented at a cultural level. Visual and expressive arts, cinema and television, still images and written texts provide the means of creating dialogue between conflicted perspectives and modes of expressive codes to explore reified moral questions of power, conflict, wrongdoing and blame haunting survivors. Viewers can engage with the politics behind representations of trauma with the intermediary technology creating a distance from 'what happened'.

The theme of representing trauma featured in this volume reflects on such questions across arenas of war, culture and performance as well as interpersonal relationships. It brings together a range of disciplinary perspectives, including cultural and cinema studies, to reflect on the ways that trauma is re-presented, re-written and re-enacted, and in turn interpreted and understood by its audience.

For example, in remembering their war dead, families carry their trauma of loss through memory and the artefacts of the person's life. What do war memorials mean to the families who live with the losses of war? The grandeur of a national statement concerning memory cannot approximate the meaning of daily living without a family member lost to a national conflict project. The connections between personal loss and national war agendas are forged in the intersections of meaning created in the encounter between those with memories and the memorialised.

The second key theme of this volume relates to the role of creativity in trauma recovery. The fragmenting disintegration of the self intrinsic to trauma experiences has the capacity to trap victims in a vortex of annihilation, sometimes endlessly repeating reactions to traumas of the past, sometimes partially perceived through a fragment of surviving self. Finding a way to wholeness which integrates the lived experience of 'what happened' necessitates the formation of a new kind of self, beyond the scars and scraps of memory. Scriptotherapy, phototherapy, autobiographical writing and performance, resilience work and breathing therapies include some of the ways in which survivors have created new ways to live in their own minds and bodies.

The role of memory in re-presenting trauma acts as a central stage in forming individual and collective spectres of trauma – ghosts of the past stalking the present. The re-membering can variously surface as an absence, a form of denial, disjointed fragments, an intrusive and compulsive claim on the present, or a way of coming to terms with the past to enable a different kind of present and future. Transforming everyday objects and routines into tropes of trauma provides a method that at once depicts, and disposes of, memories haunting the survivor of traumatic experiences.

Therapeutic approaches to trauma recovery come in many forms, inviting survivors to engage with and process their painful experience into a new way of being, re-presenting trauma as a pathway to its transcendence. Finding adequate ways to respond to traumatic memories to enable recovery in place of endless pain and echoes from the harrowing experience presents a challenge to every traumatised being. Creative visual and expressive arts stand in place of, re-present and re-cover trauma with different forms, moving on and discarding the frozen chrysalis of 'what happened' to release a new incarnation of the present. Alongside conscious healing strategies, trauma survivors' search for a way to live well emerges in sub-conscious expression of creative impulses, finding pathways for re-integration of emergent fragments of a new whole self, not the self left pinned in the pain of relived experience.

This volume brings together the creative, critical and cultural expression of trauma alongside survivors' search for a life beyond the scarifying obliteration of trauma experiences. Alongside new and non-catastrophic life narratives, releasing and growing through trauma requires ways of releasing the body's remembered hold on trauma. How to thrive beyond trauma matters evermore strongly as individuals, families, communities and countries, struggle to deal with natural and human-made disasters or brutality made universally pervasive through the media and individual electronic coverage circulated on the net.

This volume has addressed the ways in which individual and collective survivors encode, re-present, transmit and transform trauma in search for recovery. The terror of trauma, both to individuals, families, communities and countries at once unspeakable and unforgettable creates the necessity to find ways of answering vital questions, such as 'What happened?' What story counts? How can it be told? Whose truths are real? How do we know? How do we safely leave such harrowing experience/s in the past? How do we remember?

The chapters in this volume have addressed these questions in various ways drawing on personal memory, film, photographs, written texts, everyday objects, public memorials, bodies, movements, breath and belief. The power of memory, narratives, and shared cultural meanings create new canvasses for working beyond trauma and survival. The intersections of the disciplinary perspectives represented in this volume hopefully invite the reader to engage with new ways of working with trauma.

PART 1

Representing Trauma

CHAPTER 1

Reflections on the Wall: Artefacts and Valediction at the Vietnam Veterans' Memorial

Mark Callaghan

1 Introduction

In 2012, managers of a Maryland storage facility estimated that their warehouse contained some 400,000 objects.[1] A collection that began in 1982 consists of mostly vernacular items made personal. Jewellery, bottles of beer, baseball gloves, photographs, cigarettes, cheerleaders' pompoms, and a helmet with a peace sign, are just some of the articles carefully stored but rarely made available for viewing.[2] Items that became unseen artefacts were originally, in most cases, mass-produced goods purchased for or by a soldier, and left, as a consequence of that person's death in combat, as a gift at the base of a memorial – the *Vietnam Veterans Memorial*, Washington D.C, a black minimalist cenotaph also known as 'The Wall'. As people bring their own memorials to the *Wall*, the memorial is protean, appearing different each day, sometimes each hour. The leaving of such items changes the meaning of the object, the meaning of the memorial, and, as a result, the meaning of the war itself.

For reasons I shall explore, a minimalist memorial that lists the 58,282[3] names of men and women killed in action caused, right from its unveiling, unexpected reactions, sometimes prepared, sometimes spontaneous. Be it the leaving of dog tags, photographs, or messages hastily written onto hotel stationery, a darkly reflective wall of coarse granite has inspired responses never envisaged by its designer, Maya Lin, or by those who commissioned the radical

1 Rachel Manteuffel. *The Things They Leave Behind: Artifacts from the Vietnam Veterans Memorial.* Washingtonian.com. The storage facility is entitled The Museum and Archaeological Regional Storage Facility. All items are stored by category, though there are currently, as of 24.10.2012, 200,000 objects awaiting classification.

2 In October 1992, the first sample for five hundred of these offerings was put on display at the Smithsonian Institution's National Museum of American History in Washington, DC, followed by exhibitions at the Museum of Out National Heritage in Lexington, Massachusetts, the Gerald R. Ford Museum in Ann Arbor, Michigan, and a number of other sites.

3 The memorial originally listed 57,939 veterans, but a further 343 names have been added between 1983 and 2011.

 | DOI:10.1163/9789004385931_002

mnemonic form.[4] The gifts are, for the most part, offered to the memorial by friends and family of deceased veterans, including veterans who survived the Vietnam War. Little is known about the donors except that they felt strongly enough to leave their keepsakes in a public setting. It is often impossible to know even for whom they left an object.[5] We know for certain, though, that the person leaving the item knew they would never see it again, that they were placing a highly personal memento, such as cowboy boots and a wedding ring, knowing the item could only be imagined from then on and returned to memory. As mainstream funerary and memorial traditions in American culture do not involve the practice of offering objects – medals and personal items usually adorn mantels and attics – several questions emanate from this ritual of remembrance.[6] I ask whether this abstract memorial needs completing in some way, hence the leaving of personal items? Or does minimalism serve as a conduit for such acts of remembrance? Is the listing of names a sufficient form of commemoration? How does the temporary placement of an object at the memorial change its meaning, and how do the numerous objects change the meaning of the memorial in tandem?

2 Encounters with the Vietnam Veterans Wall

Maya Lin's design was favoured, not only for its daring colour and its modernist simplicity, but also for its interactive possibilities. Visitors can see themselves in the memorial's highly reflective veneer, and each carved name invites corporeal interaction; the names have a physical presence, they ask to be touched. Though the competition guidelines called for a listing of the veteran's names,[7] Lin organised the death-toll in a unique manner, presenting the names chronologically, and not alphabetically, so the reader must search for a specific name according to the specific moment of loss. Each name, therefore, locates the meaning of war in the lived individual experience of a specific casualty, whose absence from social discourse extends the meaning of war to the community. Each name is a sign of an injured body, a life lost at a specific moment in

4 Surreal items also left at the Wall include a large sliding glass door, left at the memorial in November 1990.

5 Kristen Ann Hass, *Carried to The Wall: American Memory and the Vietnam Veterans Memorial* (Los Angeles: University of California Press, 1998) 23.

6 Ibid., 8.

7 The competition had several criteria including, item 3) "Contain the names of those who had died in the conflict or are still missing". Ibid., 36.

time.[8] The list of names makes it possible for the memorial to simultaneously comfort the visitor while evoking an interpretation of profound loss. Finding a loved one's name can generate an urge to write to that person, as though they can still read it. Lin also wanted visitors to take something of the *Wall* away with them – a rubbing of a veteran's name.[9] Cards made available enabled visitors to carry out this process, though visitors more likely brought items to the memorial rather than taking something away.

Despite the innovative qualities of Lin's design, the memorial aroused considerable controversy. There were inevitable objections to the memorial given that its aesthetic is completely at odds with the white neo-classical monuments of the capital. Lin took an apolitical stance[10] designing a memorial that contravened political memory, defined by Aleida Assmann as a type of commemorative work that tends towards 'homogenous unity and self-contained closure'.[11] Though designed as impartial, the memorial's colour struck critics as non-heroic, and they expressed disdain regarding the *Wall's* V-shape, which some interpreted as a peace sign, or alarmingly, a symbol of the Vietcong, America's nemesis in the war.[12] The memorial conveyed a conception of the war and a comprehension of the soldier that ran counter to those of many Americans. These Americans, responded Jan Scruggs, the memorial's founder, 'wanted the Memorial to make Vietnam what it had never been in reality: a good, clean, glorious war, seen as necessary and supported by a united country'.[13] Hostility toward the design ultimately led to the commissioning of two supplementary and notably figurative memorials shoehorned close to Lin's *Wall* in 1984 and 1993 respectively.[14] However, amongst the plethora of interpretations, the

8 Harry W. Haines, 'Disputing the Wreckage: Ideological Struggle at the Vietnam Veterans Memorial', *Historical Memory and Representations of the Vietnam War,* ed. Walter L. Hixon, (New York: Routledge,. 2000), 8.

9 Hass, *Carried to The Wall,* 36.

10 In imagining her design, Lin made a clear decision not to study the history of the war, or to enmesh herself in the controversies surrounding it.

11 Aleida Assmann, 'Four Formats of Memory: From Individual to Collective Constructions of the Past', *Cultural Memory and Historical Consciousness in the German Speaking World since 1500, eds.* Christian Emden, and David Midgley (Bern: Peter Lang. 2000), 14.

12 Siobhan Kattago, *Ambiguous Memory: The Nazi Past and German National Identity* (London, New York: Praeger, 2001), 16.

13 Robin Wagner-Pacifici and Barry Schwartz, *The Vietnam Veterans Memorial: Commemorating a Difficult Past* (Chicago: University of Chicago Press, 1991), 37.

14 Conservative politicians such as James Webb, who was part of the Reagan Administration, and Ross Perot who would be a presidential candidate in 1992, wanted something more traditional, figurative, heroic, and something more overtly about the Vietnam War. In the *Moral Majority Weekly* Phyllis Schlafly called it a 'tribute to Jane Fonda'. *National Review* described it as an 'Orwellian glob'. In an open letter to President Reagan, Republican

majority of veterans favoured Lin's design. To the veterans, the *Wall* offered atonement for their treatment since the war; and to the families and friends of those who died, it officially recognised their sorrow and gave them an opportunity to express a grief not previously sanctioned.[15] That grief, however, did not find an expression purely by the erection of the memorial, but also by the reactions to it, specially the leaving of personal items.

Regardless of objections to, and misunderstandings of, the design, one should acknowledge that Lin recognised the inherent power of the minimalist genre, particularly when accompanied with an overwhelming list of names. As Dori Laub states: 'The predominant view is that massive trauma precludes all representation because the ordinary mechanisms of consciousness and memory are temporally destroyed. It is an encounter that is inaccessible to understanding and imagery'.[16] This substantiates an argument in favour of minimalist abstraction, as trauma cannot be represented by 'normal', accessible means and must instead be depicted in such a way that the viewer can approach the work autonomously. In front of abstract artworks, the lack of a depicted image tends to heighten our awareness of materials, of compositional (or anti-compositional) structures, of the process of looking itself.[17] Abstraction can therefore help to develop aesthetics, not just by moving away from centuries of work largely based on figuration, but also because in order to understand the artwork the viewer has to consider the memorial with different noetic processes. Without an image corresponding to empirical reality, the viewer has to read an abstract minimalist work with questions more founded on the conveyance of a mood, state or atmosphere. This inclination works well for remembering the Vietnam War, as the observers can develop their own interpretation, one that arguably allows the spectators' emotional involvement, as well as keeping a cognitive distance. Yet, as I shall elucidate, the decoration of the memorial by associates of the deceased suggests the constant existence of an impulse to adorn the *Wall* with imagery, which suggests the abstract

---

Representative Henry Hyde complained about its 'political statement of shame and dishonour'. Its implicit admission that the war was disastrous, of course, is precisely what others loved about the design. A great many Vietnam veterans reacted with cautious approval. Hass, *Carried to The Wall*, 16. Prior to this President Carter approved Congress's resolution and expressed his belief that the formal honouring of the veteran would also promote the healing of a nation divided by war. Wagner-Pacifici and Schwartz, *The Vietnam Veterans Memorial*, 33.

15 Marita Sturken, *Tangled Memories: The Vietnam War, the AIDS Epidemic, and the Politics of Remembering* (Los Angeles: University of California Press, 1997), 80.

16 Dori Laub 'Truth and Testimony: The Process and the Struggle' *Trauma and Cinema: Cross-Cultural Explorations*, edited by Ann Kaplan (Hong Kong: Hong Kong University Press, 2004), 3.

17 Mark Godfrey, *Abstraction and the Holocaust* (New Haven: Yale University Press, 2007), 4.

memorial is considered as being either insufficient or in some way responsible for stimulating these reactions.

Though I describe the memorial as 'minimalist, abstract' the leaving of gifts moves it toward a hybrid of genres, or perhaps, for its time, a genus of its own. Where abstract, minimalist designs might be criticised for their lack of specificity, the alternative is to produce figurative memorials that are potentially instructional and efficient in doing our memory work for us. This situation has been witnessed at the memorial site since 1984 when objections to the radical nature of Lin's *Wall* – primarily its mournful colour, its lack of ornamentation, and its V-shape – led to the commissioning of two figurative memorials: Frederick Hart's bronze figurative, *Three Soldiers*, and in 1993, Glenda Goodacre's *Vietnam Women's Memorial*. The two supplementary memorials, situated close to Lin's *Wall*, provide a contrast of styles and verify the differing needs of mourners, visitors and commissioners.

Hart's *Three Soldiers* focuses memorialisation on a specific aspect of the war, namely the soldiers, depicted as exhausted though defiant.[18] Unlike the black wall of names, however, *Three Soldiers* memorialises a need to remember the veterans as manly and heroic, as this memorial tries to evoke very explicit emotions of pride and acceptance for the soldiers' efforts and sacrifice. The use of a specific image to memorialise an event can, however, often limit the form and extent of the memory evoked in the memorialisation process. Lin in her criticism of the ancillary statues argues that, 'a specific image would be limiting. A realistic sculpture would be only one interpretation of that time. I wanted something that all people could relate to on a personal level'.[19] Thus, while the representative statue presents an arguably more patriotic and sympathetic view towards the war, it limits its ability to evoke a diverse spread of memories and arguably de-personalises the memorialisation process.[20]

As part of any debate concerning the representation of mass death, names are inevitably and increasingly present when analysing contemporary memory culture in order to represent pain, violence, trauma and loss, as opposed to more traditional imagery, with the *9/11 Memorial*, New York City, and *The Survivors Wall*, Oklahoma City, as recent examples of a commemorative strategy

18 Marita Sturken argues that Frederick Hart's sculpture memorialises a need to remember these veterans as manly and heroic, whereas Glenda Goodacre's sculpture memorialises a victory for women veterans over the perceived threat to patriotism posed by the idea of making any memory of war that is not singular and masculine. Sturken, *Tangled Memories*, 84.

19 Maya Ying Lin, 'Design Competition: Winning Designer's Statement' (Washington D.C: Vietnam Veterans Memorial Fund, 1982), 6.

20 Julianne Corbin, *Memory and Form: An Analysis of the Vietnam Veterans Memorial* (Boston: University of Boston, 2009), 8.

to list the dead without accompanying imagery – an approach traceable to the *Menin Gate*, Ypres. This causes one to wonder whether the simple use of words – the naming of people, dates, and basic facts – is all that is required. One might also wonder whether this form of commemoration signifies the remembrance of the person not only as part of a collective tragedy, but also as an individual. Furthermore, without accompanying figuration (which arguably represents the generic victim rather than the individual), the use of names can also mean remembering a person outside of the circumstances in which they died due to the lack of supporting imagery, so that, in some respects, the victim's life is being commemorated as opposed to their death. One should acknowledge though that memorials of any style have limitations, and can only convey aspects of history. Memorials often attempt to elide complex events in a single ambitious and ultimately not viable mnemonic form, yet Lin's *Wall* and its subsequent reception, suggest that it has become the canvas for multiple expressions that convey the wider context of the conflict and its aftermath.

Memorials and museums both function selectively in their representations of the past. They play a role in circumscribing the contours of historic events. Memorials affirm what their creators and commissioners deem as essential and what we might understand as less relevant or even unimportant. Abstract memorials are also selective, including Lin's memorial, which omits the names of combatants who died after the war and those suffering from Post-Traumatic Stress Disorder. Yet, the *Vietnam Veterans' Memorial* does not dictate the narrative of memory but instead promotes personal reflection, leaving visitors to consider and interpret their memories as they will. Many people would posit that only minimalism can do this. Michael Kimmelman at the New York Times argues that Lin exploited the inherent theatricality and ambiguity of Minimalist abstraction, linking it with the most literal kind of descriptive device – a list: a list that represents every person who died, not through some generalised image of a soldier holding a gun or a flag, but specifically, by name. Lin grasped the modern memorial sublime, the way Minimalist art, precisely because of its stripped-down, elemental forms, evokes a kind of long-lost grandeur.[21] Lin herself argues that:

> The use of names is a way to bring back everything someone could remember about a person .... The ability of a name to bring back every single memory you have of that person is far more realistic and specific than a still photograph.[22]

21 Hass, *Carried to The Wall*, 18.

22 Maya Ying Lin, 'Design Competition', 3.

Responses to the Wall do not correspond to other abstract memorials though; the leaving of gifts is not typical. The memorial's reception has been adorned with imagery since its inauguration, so despite Lin's cogent case for abstraction, the public has never been entirely satisfied with the black wall's mnemonic index as originally conceived.[23] Visitors have always felt the need to intervene. One explanation for this might lie in the minimalist approach to the names and how, despite their ability to be personal and evocative, their lack of specifics, including fundamental details such as age, and place of civilian residence, actually reduces their individuality. Whilst no symbolic reference to the cause or country for which they died, immediately *highlights* the individual, Lin's naming criterion dissolves the individual's uniqueness into a homogenising sequence of death dates.[24] Here I posit that the friends and families of deceased veterans have been compelled to fill this gap and re-appropriate the names to something more specific to the person commemorated, the person that they knew.

3 The Human Dimension

Whilst *The Vietnam Veterans Memorial* has not become a place of national celebration it arguably relates to heroism. In spite of its intended neutral character, it has become, by the leaving of mementos, a memorial with an apparently collective drive to remember the individual through public displays, often relating to moments in a soldier's life that only the giver can fully understand. This gap between representation of the individual and the need for more specific, though temporary, markers is illustrated by the *Wall*'s assortment of objects. The jovial or juvenile mementoes are, for the most part, unambiguous when compared to the photographs and letters that often line the base of the memorial. Toys clearly signal nostalgia for a time in the fallen soldier's boyhood. The people who leave these objects – presumably parents – are drawn to reflect upon a time of innocence not far removed from their son or daughter's departure to Vietnam. The average age of the soldiers killed in the conflict

---

23 When Glenda Goodacre's *Vietnam Women's Memorial* was dedicated, it was festooned with many bouquets and wreaths – conventional markers of mourning and chivalrous tributes to female recipients. This, the third memorial, had been commissioned because Frederick Hart's design, unveiled in 1993, depicted an African American soldier, a Hispanic Soldier and a Caucasian marine, but omitted to represent the women who served and died in the conflict too.

24 Wagner-Pacifici and Schwartz, *The Vietnam Veterans Memorial*, 42.

was, after all, just nineteen.[25] Such objects can, however, evince a demonstration of protest or despair concerning the loss of so many young lives, and, like many objects, childhood mementoes have been placed at the *Wall* accompanied by symbols or placards protesting against the conflict. The placement of photographs, which can also relate to demonstrations against the war, is more complex.

Lin's argument that the carved names are more realistic than a photograph is contested by the regularity of portraits left at the foot of the memorial. Whether one interprets this as an inclination to complete the representation of a veteran, or whether the names and design have inspired such offerings, is open to conjecture, but there is certainly a heightened expectation that this national memorial should demonstrate a desire for more imagery.[26] Here we might see that the proclivity for bringing photographs to the *Wall* relates to the respective person's mourning process. In his groundbreaking study of grieving, Erich Lindemann claims preoccupation with the image of the deceased characterises the grieving process.[27] The placement of photographs at the *Wall* suggests that relatives of the deceased need more than the sight of their loved one's name to enact a process of remembrance; that seeing the soldier's faces has a cathartic role in their healing. Furthermore, given that the photographs normally represent the soldiers whilst in uniform, an additional reading can be proffered. The representation of the deceased as living, healthy and proud human beings draws parallels to Gil Pasternak's study of photographs that supplement Jewish soldier's graves in Israel. Writing of one such image, Pasternak argues that its appearance on the tombstone evokes a sense of identification between the dead subject and the social role he played at the moment of his death: 'After all, the pose enacted is of a proud, obedient soldier, a soldier at the service of the state and its military commanders'.[28] The photographs offered to the *Vietnam Veterans Memorial* do, like those on the Israeli soldier's graves, re-contextualise the site, representing not just a place of commemoration and

---

25 Michael Hunt, *A Vietnam War Reader: American and Vietnamese Perspectives* (Penguin: London, 2006), 4.

26 Hass, *Carried to The Wall*, 26.

27 Erich Lindemann, 'Symptomology and Management of Acute Grief', *American Journal of Psychiatry* 101 (1944): 141–148. This also draws parallels to Paul Vivian's chapter where he argues that Collage represents a mediated trauma and a case where the photograph relates to a destructive act that mirrors the traumatic event. At the *Vietnam Veterans Memorial*, the leaving of a photograph by a friend or family member, knowing they will never see it again, also functions as a destructive act, symbolising the loss of the soldier.

28 Gil Pasternak, 'Posthumous Interruptions: The Political Life of Family Photographs in Israeli Military Cemeteries', *Photography and Culture* 3. 1 (2010): 47.

death, but also a monument to pride and dignity, thus confronting prevailing attitudes toward veterans who were often, particularly in the 1980s, portrayed as being malcontents or worse.[29] The fillip to bring photographs to the *Wall* might emanate, then, not just from the visceral need to see the face of a loved one, but also to remind the public that veterans died whilst serving their country. Regardless of how one might feel about the war and its atrocities, the images insist they were humans, usually teenagers, and that those who returned from Vietnam faced the complexities of reintegration in a society that often disparaged their contribution to the nation. As surviving veterans find the photographs particularly welcome, we might observe that this form of commemoration gives a voice to veterans not otherwise part of Lin's apolitical concept.

A closer analysis of the notes and letters reveals multifarious reasons for them being written and donated to the *Wall*. Notes are commonly written as though the soldier could read it, as though still alive, thus confirming Patrick Hagopian's assertion that dynamic public responses to the *Wall* – which include the touching of names – allow families to have contact with the person.[30] Such offerings can sustain personal relationships with the dead. A note left with a can of Colt 45 reads, 'Hey Bro, Here's the beer I owe you – 24 yrs late'. In the late 1980s, the progenies of dead veterans began to make their pilgrimage to Washington D.C., leaving gifts and notes. A photo was left with a note: 'Hi Dad. I'm grown up now',[31] and in more recent times, sonogram images of soldier's grandchildren have also been found at the *Wall*.

Many of the letters left in the early years of the memorial's existence seemed intended to achieve closure and purge the nation's grief, stressing the heroism and sacrifice of those who died, or decrying the waste of their lives so that the nation would avoid unnecessary wars in the future. Other offerings bespeak irremediable pain that cannot be compensated by recognition or assuaged by the promised comforts of 'healing'.[32] A note left at the memorial accompanied a wedding band and engagement ring and explained that the widow of a young

29 As Veteran George Swiers writes in regard to popular fictional portrayals of Vietnam Veterans in the 1980s: The message sent from national leadership and embraced by the public was clear. Vietnam veterans were liars, wackos, losers. Hollywood, ever bizarre in its efforts to mirror life, discovered a marketable villain – the standard vet: a psychotic, axe-wielding rapist. Hass, *Carried to the Wall.*, 76.

30 Patrick Hagopian, *The Vietnam War in American Memory: Veterans, Memorials, and the Politics of Healing* (Boston: University of Massachusetts Press, 2009), 358.

31 Ibid., 362.

32 A regular at the memorial, Jeffrey Davis, had seen almost his entire company of 160 men wiped out in a single night of fighting in Vietnam. The Washington police officer became increasingly preoccupied with that night, unable to eat or sleep. He became the first Vietnam veteran to kill himself at the memorial in September 1984. Ibid., 365.

man who died in Vietnam no longer wanted to keep the rings when she remarried because she 'chooses to forget this part of her life'.[33] Letters that could have been left, in many cases, at a veteran's graveside were instead brought to the *Wall*, suggesting this cenotaph holds more poignancy and power than the veteran's burial place.[34]

By contributing their private representations to a public space, those leaving mementoes cross a boundary between the private and the public, between the nation and the citizen powerfully claiming the memorial as their own.[35] They also transform, what was already an experience-based design into a co-authored memorial where the dedications represent a ritual of remembrance that might help relatives to work through their trauma. Here routine practices of memory are circumvented due to the tactility and tangibility of experiencing the *Wall* in this way, thus encouraging the visitor to emotionally and physically participate in the memory.[36] Equally, those who leave gifts at the *Wall* might be trying to reconcile their trauma through the assertion of higher, more positive ideals, interpreting Lin's black *Wall* as mournful, which correlates to the political objections to the design, only by appropriating the memorial with personal narratives instead of petitions.

Whatever the motivation, those leaving messages and dedications must be aware that others will see their words, that this acts as a public work of art, an open and accessible memorial space. The messages and dedications amplify the memorial's work, by offering public testimony to the war's losses, making evident enduring grief and testifying to the importance of the individual about, or to whom, the note was written. During the first years of the memorial's existence this drew sympathetic visitors into a community of feeling and brought survivors out of their isolation.[37] A memorial was always desideratum

33 Ibid., 370.

34 Similar responses occurred at the replica Vietnam veterans' memorials built around the country where the practice of leaving offerings became part of a commemorative tradition, spread from the national Vietnam Veterans' Memorial to these monuments. Ibid., 375.

35 Hass, *Carried to The Wall,* 20–21.

36 Kirsten Harjes, 'Stumbling Stones: Holocaust Memorials, National Identity, and Democratic Inclusion in Berlin', *German Politics and Society*, 23.1 (2005): 5.

37 Hagopian, *The Vietnam War in American Memory,* 362. In her chapter on Beckett's *Eh* Joe, Svetlana Antopova writes of the separation between voice and body and how this can be an artistic technique for staging trauma as well as its symptom. In this example we become a witness to protagonist Joe's torture through the voice he endures each night. On the contrary, at the *Vietnam Veterans Memorial*, we 'hear' the voice of the bereaved through their letters and notes left at the base of the *Wall*, thus making us witnesses to their suffering through a different, though not envisaged device by its designer Maya

to the veterans and the soldier's families, but it fast became a social production, sometimes enigmatic, sometimes so intimate that only the provider or the deceased could understand the story behind an object. But the *Wall* and its objects have always been germane and perhaps, in some cases, mollifying.

The collection of gifts at the base of the memorial changes the memorial experience for other visitors too, including those who have no personal connection to the war, and might instead be curious to see the details of such public shows of affection, or wish to vicariously partake in the emotions of the bereaved. Most of the offerings left at the *Wall* seem to make a memory of a name on the *Wall* or the experience of a specific veteran, and yet taken together, the objects, which I see as a response to a crisis of public memory, articulate a struggle on the part of the ordinary American to participate in a conversation about how to remember the war and, therefore, partake of a conversation about the shape of the nation.

Seeing the display of such personal items signifies empathetic identification with the soldier's grieving friends and family, thereby providing a more profound, personal encounter with the memorial even for those not directly affected by the Vietnam war and its consequences. Empathy, especially as constructed out of mimesis, is not an emotional self-pitying identification with victims, but a way of both feeling for, while different from, the subject of enquiry.[38] On this critical point, comes an important strand of trauma studies that promotes a significant and self-reflective *empathy* as the most appropriate from of engagement with trauma imagery. Dominick LaCapra, in his various studies on the representation of Holocaust experience, distinguishes empathy in the spectator (the third party, seeing, testimony delivered) from the primary experience of trauma. To that end, he proposes the concept of *empathic unsettlement* to describe the aesthetic experience of simultaneously *feeling for* another and becoming aware of a distinction between one's own perceptions and the experience of the other.[39]

Lin. Additionally, Gen'ichiro Itakura's chapter focuses on ways in which trauma is predicated on the de-humanisation of victims, or the transformation of the human into the non-human. In the example of the *Vietnam Veterans Memorial*, there has been a drive to make the victims more human despite an original design that did not intend to dehumanise victims at all.

38 Alison Landsberg, 'America, the Holocaust, and the Mass Culture of Memory: Towards a Radical Politics of Memory', *The New German Critique* 71 (1997): 82.

39 Jill Bennett, *Empathic Vision: Affect, Trauma and Contemporary Art* (Redwood City: Stanford University Press, 2005): 80.

Though, as LaCapra warns, one must be conscious of intrusively arrogating ourselves to the victim's experience or undergoing surrogate victimage,[40] one should, nevertheless, consider empathetic identification's transformational impact.[41] In Washington D.C., such viewers face an unanticipated row of personal messages to the dead, which convey the resonating effects of the loss and insights into the plight of the bereaved. Kaja Silverman's distinction between idiopathic and heteropathic identification goes some way to illuminating the nature of empathic relationships in this instance. Whereas heteropathic identification implies identification with an alien body or experience, idiopathic identification is essentially self-referential, grounded on shared identity. In the latter mode, which appears to apply in this case, one evaluates the trauma of the other simply by asking, 'I wonder what I would be like if this happened to me?'. Thus unfamiliar experience is not encountered on its own terms but assimilated to the self.[42] By seeing the numerous letters, the viewer might become part of the mourning process itself, feeling themselves as the writer, rather than the reader, of a letter written to a deceased veteran, imagining themselves in the position of the bereaved. The ordinary American is therefore drawn into the experience of the bereaved, into their thoughts and emotions, into a normally private, usually withheld encounter of a war's resonating effects for friends and family, be they politically-related statements or not. In this respect, Lin's design has been transformed from an already evocative tomb of names into a temporary shrine, not only to individual victims of war, but also to expressions of loss that might have the dual effect of being cathartic for the writer and empathetic to the reader.

Trauma, whether individual or collective, often triggers the impulse to commemorate, but at the *Vietnam Veterans' Memorial* the merits, inadequacies and political context of the design, combine to initiate further, more visible layers of memory. Be it teddy bears or dog tags, photographs or letters, the objects are unified by their ability to further personalise a memorial, proclaiming the characteristics of lost soldiers, resulting in a modification of Lin's intention to individualise the veterans by simply listing the names on a black elegiac slab. The personalisation of the memorial continues what began with the emotive listing of names, that memory of the war became humanised and subsequently the veteran became a more sympathetic and suitably complex figure.

40 Dominic LaCapra, *History & Memory After Auschwitz* (Ithaca: Cornell University Press, 1998): 162.

41 David Bathrick, et al., *Visualizing the Holocaust: Documents, Aesthetics, Memory* (London: Camden House, 2012): 76.

42 Judith Greenberg, *Trauma at Home After 9/11* (New York: Bison, 2003): 4.

The objects might conjure memories of a veteran's childhood, their marriage, their interests or their disposition. But whatever the items might be, and whatever specific memories they might evoke, they cause an abstract memorial to be figurative and they politicise an apolitical memorial by giving insights into the lives of the lost, reminding the onlooker that the Vietnam Veteran had a character and was human.

National memory is receptive to historical moments of triumph and trauma provided they can be integrated into the semantics of a heroic narrative.[43] The figurative supplementary memorials correspond more to this tradition than Lin's *Wall* of names. Yet the *Wall* is the memorial that evokes such responses and has come to represent, not just a social mirror, but also a place where the bereaved humanise the previously disrespected veteran. But as the deeply personal objects cannot be recovered, the process of offering a gift to the *Wall* relates to a further, even more emotive aspect of commemoration. To leave an item so unique, so charged with meaning, represents more than a personalisation of the memorial. For the individual who places the object at the base of the *Wall*, the donation to the *Wall* represents a process of letting go. What we see, then, is a valedictory act.

4 Changes to the Memorial Site from 2018

In 2018, some of these keepsakes will be displayed in a museum setting rather than being temporary public exhibits previously intended as ephemeral–items collected at the end of each day and subsequently dispatched to the storage facility in Maryland. The proposed *Education Centre at the Wall* will be a subterranean exhibit space occupying 20,000 square feet.[44] It has already caused controversy due to concerns that it will reduce the narrative of the conflict and present a less nuanced, more singular view of veterans as heroic and the war as just and almost without objections by the American public, including some returning veterans. As the *Education Centre* will feature numerous artefacts left at the *Wall* during its three decades of existence, the presentation of these items is especially pertinent here.

Though designed as apolitical, Lin's memorial was interpreted by some critics as non-patriotic, non-heroic. It conveyed a conception of the war and a comprehension of the soldier that ran counter to those of many Americans. Returning to memorial founder Jan Scruggs' response to this reading, for these

43 Aleida Assmann, 'Four Formats of Memory', 28.
44 Meredith Lair, 'Memorialization: The Education Centre at The Wall and the re-Writing of History', *The Public Historian* 34.1 (2012): 40.

Americans, Scruggs felt, the ideal memorial would make Vietnam what it had never been in reality: a good, clean, glorious war, supported by a united country. As we have also seen, the leaving of personal items transformed the meaning of the war still further, and, in tandem, an interpretation of Lin's *Wall*. As surviving veterans find the photographs, protest statements, and personal messages particularly welcome, we have also observed that this form of commemoration gave a voice to veterans not otherwise part of Lin's apolitical concept. Yet despite the approval of Lin's design and, further still, the humanisation and personalisation of veterans by way of families leaving keepsakes, Scruggs led the recent initiative to build *The Education Centre at the Wall*.

Reflecting on her role as exhibition script advisor, Meredith Lair posits that proponents of *The Education Centre at the Wall* seek to advance a sanitised narrative of the Vietnam War. An idealised militarised version of citizenship could be represented due to the *Education Centre's* forthcoming concentration on the heroism of veterans by way of displaying numerous artefacts that were never intended for permanent display.[45] Within the exhibit spaces dissenting views will be marginalised, as the anti-war movement, or any artefacts suggesting support for its stance, will not feature. As Lair goes on to write: 'Unless something dramatic changes in the design and implementation of exhibits in *The Education Centre at the Wall*, these ideas will be almost edited from national memory, marking a decisive turn in the public's understanding of the Vietnam War',[46] thereby using what Jeshajahu Weinberg describes as the 'authoritative voice of a federal museum' to illuminate one aspect of history whilst suggesting that other viewpoints are secondary or without merit.[47] This also raises the issue of authority and authenticity, as, by being selected for placement in a museum, an object is immediately deemed worthy of appreciation and gravitas, meaning the museum's authority can suffice to re-direct the narrative without too many objections.[48] Whilst some museum-goers might well ask about the master narrative and who formulated it, I am more inclined to agree with Susan Crane's point that the individual museum-goer will far more likely seek to be impressed by the spoils of war, be drawn to objects and meanings that s/he expected to find, or is perhaps expecting to be initiated into.[49]

The authority of a museum, situated in prominent location in the nation's capital, arguably manipulates the command and trust that we might

45 Ibid., 35.

46 Ibid., 36.

47 Jeshajahu Weinberg, *The Holocaust Museum in Washington* (Rizzoli. Washington D.C.: Rizzoli, 1995), 48.

48 Daniel Buren, 'Function of the Museum', *Theories of Contemporary Art*, ed. Richard Hertz (New Jersey: Prentice-Hall Inc., 1993), 19.

49 Susan Crane, *Museums and Memory* (City of Redwood: Stanford University Press, 2000): 21.

automatically associate with such institutions. Furthermore, when one considers that a similar 'veteran as hero' message is already part of what emanates by the leaving of personal items at the *Wall*, one necessarily asks why a museum is required? Whilst the *Education Centre's* various media will apparently convey the message of the veteran as defender of liberty, and almost erase the war's many controversies (including the actions of many veterans), the re-use of artefacts previously left at the memorial is apparently central to the *Education Centre's* forthcoming communiqué. The motive, whether recognised by Scruggs or not, is arguably to cement that same heroic narrative for future generations, employing the blueprint of a museum with its established sense of reliance in order to present what could be, in effect, a narrowed, re-write of history, which ironically mirrors Scruggs' earlier opposition to many American's perception of Vietnam as a 'good, clean, glorious war'.

Bibliography

Assmann, Aleida. 'Four Formats of Memory: From Individual to Collective Constructions of the Past'. *Cultural Memory and Historical Consciousness in the German Speaking World since 1500,* edited by Christian Emden and David Midgley, 24–41. Bern: Peter Lang. 2000.

Bathrick, David, Brad Prager, D. Richardson and D. Michael. *Visualizing the Holocaust: Documents, Aesthetics, Memory*. Rochester: Camden House, 2012.

Bennett, Jill. *Empathic Vision: Affect, Trauma and Contemporary Art*. City of Redwood: Stanford University Press, 2005.

Buren, Daniel. 'Function of the Museum'. *Theories of Contemporary Art*, edited by Richard Hetz. New Jersey: Prentice-Hall Inc., 1993.

Corbin, Julianne. *Memory and Form: An Analysis of the Vietnam Veterans Memorial.* Boston: University of Boston Press, 2009.

Crane, Susan. *Museums and Memory*. City of Redwood: Stanford University Press, 2000.

Forty, Adrian and Susanne Kuchler. *The Art of Forgetting*. Oxford and New York: Berg, 1999.

Godfrey, Mark. *Abstraction and the Holocaust.* New Haven: Yale University Press, 2007.

Greenberg, Judith. *Trauma at Home After 9/11*. New York: Bison, 2003.

Hagopian, Patrick. *The Vietnam War in American Memory: Veterans, Memorials, and the Politics of Healing.* Boston: University of Massachusetts Press, 2009.

Hunt, Michael. *A Vietnam War Reader: American and Vietnamese Perspectives*. London: Penguin, 2006.

Haines, Harry W. 'Disputing the Wreckage: Ideological Struggle at the Vietnam Veterans Memorial'. *Historical Memory and Representations of the Vietnam War*, edited by Walter L. Hixon, 6–20. New York: Routledge, 2000.

Harjes, Kirsten. 'Stumbling Stones: Holocaust Memorials, National Identity, and Democratic Inclusion in Berlin'. *German Politics and Society* 23.1 (2005): 4–17.

Hass, Kristin Ann. *Carried to the Wall: American Memory and the Vietnam Veterans Memorial.* Los Angeles: University of California Press, 1998.

Kattago, Siobhan. *Ambiguous Memory: The Nazi Past and German National Identity.* Westport CT: Praeger, 2001.

Landsberg, Alison'. America, the Holocaust, and the Mass Culture of Memory: Towards a Radical Politics of Memory', *The New German Critique.* 71 (1997): 63–86.

LaCapra, Dominic. *History & Memory After Auschwitz.* Ithaca: Cornell University Press, 1998.

Lair, Meredith. 'Memorialization: The Education Centre at The Wall and the re-Writing of History'. *The Public Historian* 34. 1 (2012): 34–60.

Laub, Dori. 'Truth and testimony: the process and the struggle' *Trauma and Cinema: Cross-Cultural Explorations*, edited by Ann E. Kaplan, 3–26. Hong Kong: Hong Kong University Press, 2004.

Lin, Maya Ying. *Design Competition: Winning Designer's Statement.* Washington D.C: Vietnam Veterans Memorial Fund, 1982.

Lindemann, Erich. 'Symptomology and Management of Acute Grief'. *American Journal of Psychiatry* 101 (1944): 141–148.

Manteuffel, Rachel. *The Things They Leave Behind: Artifacts From the Vietnam Veterans Memorial* www.Washingtonian.com (Viewed 10 January 2014).

Pasternak, Gil. 'Posthumous Interruptions: The Political Life of Family Photographs in Israeli Military Cemeteries'. *Photography and Culture* 3.1 (20 The Art of Forgetting 10): 38–52.

Sturken, Marita. *Tangled Memories: The Vietnam War, the AIDS Epidemic, and the Politics of Remembering.* Los Angeles: University of California Press, 1997.

Wagner-Pacifici, Robin and Barry Schwartz. *The Vietnam Veterans Memorial: Commemorating a Difficult Past.* Chicago: University of Chicago Press, 1991.

CHAPTER 2

The Attack: Doueiry's Depoliticisation of Trauma in the Transposition from Literature to Film

Zeina Tarraf

In late 2012 and early 2013, Ziad Doueiry's *The Attack*, swept international film festivals and Western cinemas, moving audiences with what many saw as its politically sensitive and powerfully affecting content. The film which follows the experience of Amin, an Arab Israeli surgeon whose wife turns out to be a suicide bomber offers a visually exceptional yet understated vision that touchingly represents the complexities and tragedies of the Palestinian Israeli conflict through the eyes of a man plagued and confused by his own loss – the loss of his wife. Upon my own initial viewing, the film resounded powerfully through its tragically woven narrative that speaks forcefully about the impossibilities that characterise a deeply implicated political conflict. Amin's subject position between two opposing worlds and the irreconcilability of their respective tragedies seemed a successful vantage point from which to capture the complexities of the Palestinian-Israeli conflict.

After my initial exposure to the film, however, as I reflected further on the piece and observed its critical success among Western audiences particularly, I began to feel increasingly unsettled about the film's contents and polemic character. Worth noting here, while Doueiry's film has received international acclaim for its balanced and nuanced depiction of Israeli and Palestinian suffering, the Arab world banned it for its sympathetic portrayal of Israelis. My own growing reservations about the movie had less to do with the empathetic depiction of Israelis in the aftermath of a suicide bombing attack, and more with the sense of balance that viewers remain with at the end of the film. Doueiry himself has defended the neutral position that the film takes as a 'moral duty' that 'bridge[s] the gap between two sides.'[1] He says, in reaction to news about the film's ban in the Arab world, 'I believe there are two points of view in any conflict. And I tried to explain to the Arab League that the role of the artist is to articulate both.' Doueiry adds,

1 Katherine Monk, 'Ziad Doueiry's the Attack Banned in the Arab World,' *Canada.com*, August 8, 2013. Viewed 13 January 2015, http://www.canada.com/entertainment/Ziad+Doueiri+Attack+banned+Arab+world/8763477/story.html.

 | DOI:10.1163/9789004385931_003

> I don't want to put 350 million Arabs in the same boat, but they said the fact the film was balanced made it unfair because it put the oppressor and the oppressed on the same level. I tried to have a discussion with them about it, but it was futile.[2]

It is precisely, then, this issue of balance that Doueiry argues reflects the *moral* responsibility that the artist has in representing political conflict; and it is precisely this appeal to the ethical that concerns and troubles me the most. No doubt when it comes to representations of trauma and suffering, particularly those of a political kind, the question of ethics is essential. In Shoshana Felman and Dori Laub's foundational book *Testimony: Crises of Witnessing in Literature, Psychoanalysis, and History*, Felman cites the words of the French writer Albert Camus upon reception of the Nobel Prize for literature awarded to him for 'illuminating… "the problems of the human conscience of our time."'[3] Camus claims that, 'The writer's function…is not without its arduous duties. By definition, he cannot serve today those who make history; he must serve those who are subject to it.'[4] It is not entirely clear who Camus means by those subject to history – in Felman's interpretation, subjects of history as holocaust specifically are 'neither its perpetrators nor its most immediate and most devastated victims, but its historic *onlookers*: its *witnesses*.'[5] In any case, clearly embedded in Camus' idea of the writer's function is an awareness of a particular power relationship that needs to be approached critically and responsibly.

Doueiry's quite problematic defence of the balanced nature of his film, I argue, proves even unethical despite his appeals to the moral character of his representation. For one thing, a balanced representation of trauma and suffering is arguably unethical in a highly asymmetrical conflict in which one side experiences a very structural and embedded form of traumatising violence. The everydayness of trauma in the Palestinian context is depicted to some degree in Doueiry's film and yet the political work that the piece performs overall does not do justice to the asymmetry of the conflict and the larger power relations that structure both Palestinian and Israeli traumas. Leading trauma theorist, Dominick LaCapra makes a similar claim in relation to representing the German experience of World War II. He states,

2 Ibid.

3 Shoshana Felman and Dori Laub, *Testimony* (New York: Routledge, 1992), 96.

4 Ibid.

5 Ibid.

> The Germans…did suffer losses on the eastern front and in the bombing of Dresden and other cities. But everything hinges on how the presentation of such losses proceeds and the larger framework in which it takes place, including the sociopolitical implications it may be argued to have.[6]

For LaCapra, therefore, at stake in the representation of German losses during World War II is an ethical commitment to a bigger picture that contextualises the presentation of these losses. Similarly, while one must acknowledge Israeli losses in the face of suicide bombing attacks, one must also necessarily view these tragedies not as isolated incidents but in terms of a larger framework of power relations. It would be unfair to say that Doueiry's film does not attempt to structure Palestinian and Israeli suffering in terms of one another. After all through Amin's own trauma of losing his wife, Sihem, does he venture out from his comfortable assimilated position in Tel Aviv to the rugged outskirts of the West Bank only to discover his increasing isolation from each of these worlds. From his point of view Doueiry manages to skilfully portray the irreconcilability of two national narratives and the impossibility that underlies Amin's tragic position between both of these worlds. Despite these attempts, however, the film does not fulfil an ethical responsibility to the larger power structures that frame its events. In this regard, through striving for universal appeal, the film depoliticises the very issues at the heart of its plot. This point bears pertinently when comparing the film to Yasmina Khadra's book *The Attack*. In contrast to the film, while the book shows both sides, it simultaneously 'renders the Palestinian frustration and fury'[7] that Amin once managed to ignore, and leaves readers 'questioning how the oppressed manage to even hold on to their dreams.'[8]

In what follows I demonstrate how the film achieves a sense of balance through the structuring of the various traumas at the centre of the its plot, particularly the trauma of the suicide bombing attack, Amin's own traumatic loss of his wife, and the trauma that the Palestinians experience.[9] Fundamental

---

6 Dominick LaCapra, 'Traumatopisms: From Trauma via Witnessing to the Sublime?' in *History and its Limits: Human, animal, violence* (Ithaca: Cornell University Press, 2009), 77.

7 Janet Maslin, 'In 'The Attack,' an Arab-Israeli learns too late of a terrorist stranger in the family,' review of *The Attack*, by Yasmina Khadra, *New York Times*, May 15, 2006, Sunday Book Review. Viewed 13 January 2015, http://www.nytimes.com/2006/05/15/books/15masl.html?_r=0.

8 Amal Awad, 'Book Review: The Attack: A Novel,' review of *The Attack* by Yasmina Khadra, *Electronic Intifada*, December 18, 2006. Viewed 13 January 2015 http://electronicintifada.net/content/book-review-attack-novel/3509.

9 The scope of this paper does not allow me to fully reflect on how the traumatic content affects the formal qualities of the film and novel, although a consideration of this significant

differences exist in the nature of each of these traumas, differences often not accounted for in mainstream trauma theory. By highlighting the different nature of traumatic experiences in the film, I do not necessarily seek to reproduce a hierarchy of suffering; rather, my attention to these differences in the nature of experiences seeks to expose a power discrepancy that the balanced representation of suffering in the film does not do justice to, and that contributes to the film's unethical quality. I aim, furthermore, to draw on Khadra's novel to reveal how certain omissions and subtle/obvious alterations in Doueiry's film account for its problematic nature. Here I am not so much concerned with the issue of fidelity to the original piece as representation is clearly always an unstable entity;[10] rather, I am interested in how the emphasis on affect in Doueiry's film reorients Khadra's narrative into a politically diluted piece that diverts attention away from the ethical imperatives of the novel.[11] Trauma itself is a useful concept for thinking about these issues particularly since identity becomes so embedded in the traumatic experience. As Michael Roth puts it, 'In trauma, the recollected past causes suffering, and the traumatic event has a magnetic appeal that pulls a wide constellation of experience (often, an individual's whole life) into its orbit.'[12] Considering the identity politics at stake in the Palestinian-Israeli conflict, then, one needs to think about how to conceptualise identities in terms of the respective traumas that each of these populations experience and endure.

---

issue would no doubt certainly contribute to fascinating findings, as both Svetlana Antropova's and Paul Vivian's chapters in this volume reveal. Antropova and Vivian have each prompted me to consider the ways in which trauma affects the formal features of a text. Antropova's compelling reading of Beckett's *Eh Joe* reveals how the disembodied voice acts as a cinematographic device that interconnects past and present in complicated ways. Seen in light of Antropova's argument, Doueiry's occasional use of voice-overs in representing images of Sihem interrupts the chronology of the film just as trauma commonly creates temporal ruptures between past and present. While not quite as disembodied as in *Eh Joe*, the voice-overs still recreate the aftermath of trauma in effective ways. Similarly, Vivian's argument that collage "functions as a metaphor for traumatic experiences encountered by the body" reveals how trauma can powerfully shape form. The lack of closure in Doueiry's film, for instance, contributes to a traumatic aesthetic experience because trauma complicates the self-containment of narratives.

10 Christa Albrecht-Crane and Dennis Cutchins, ed., *Adaptation Studies: New Approaches* (Madison: Fairleigh Dickinson Univesity, 2010), 17.

11 I do not mean to imply here that affect and politics are diametrically opposed; rather, in Doueiry's case, his use of affect works largely as a mechanism to render his film universally appealing – a quality that I argue depoliticises in its diversion from the issues at the heart of the film's plot.

12 Michael Roth, *Trauma, Memory, and History: Essays on Living with the Past* (New York: Columbia University Press, 2012), xvii.

While implicated in these larger political questions, the film, which switches between Hebrew and Arabic, centres on Amin's character and his quest to understand his wife's motives behind the suicide bombing attack. Sihem herself is never shown in real time in the film; rather, images of her appear in flashbacks or as figments of Amin's imagination. In the novel too, Sihem is presented through Amin's perspective. Sihem's ghostly presence haunts Amin throughout the film as he works through the traumatic loss. Gabrielle Schwab suggests that,

> The ghost is not simply a dead or a missing person, but a social figure, and investigating it can lead to that dense site where history and subjectivity make social life.[13]

Similarly, Sihem's ghost appears at the centre of the frame in the film and Amin's investigation of her death contributes to his own subjective transformation as well as to the complication of the initial act of violence that sparks the film's events. The first half of the film takes place in Tel Aviv where Amin lives as a fully assimilated and successful surgeon. In the scene before the credits, Sihem and Amin are shown at a train station in an embrace with Sihem's face to the camera and their voices heard in a voice-over. Amin asks, 'Sihem, why are you crying my love?' She answers, 'Because every time you leave a part of me dies.' This dialogue is repeated in the final scene of the movie but with Amin standing alone at the station and in reverse, as Sihem poses the question and Amin answers. The opening scene reveals a ceremony in which Amin receives an award for his work as a surgeon. The picture that this scene evokes is one of tolerance and acceptance, a paradigm of coexistence in which Arabs and Israelis interact collegially and their common humanity is appealed to. Before Amin goes on stage to accept his award, he receives a phone call from Sihem in which he abruptly tells her that he cannot talk. At the end of the movie, this phone call is replayed for us however this time it is from Sihem's end in the final moments before she blows herself up. There are several issues about these opening and closing scenes that are worth bearing reflection on, particularly because they are not included in the novel and therefore reframe the narrative in significant ways. The poignant circularity that Doueiry utilizises in these four scenes works on the one hand to highlight the tragic love story that is at the centre of his plot and on the other hand to emphasizise the tragic gap that exists between Amin and Sihem: Amin on the one hand being honoured by Israelis and Sihem on the other preparing to explode

13 Gabrielle Schwab, *Haunting Legacies* (New York: Columbia University Press, 2010), 8.

at a children's birthday party. Indeed this gap can also be read in light of the Palestinian-Israeli conflict, as it signifies the unbreachable chasm that Doueiry insists on portraying throughout the film. This circularity, however, also problematically reframes the emphasis of the novel and displaces affect in a move that depoliticises the issues in Khadra's account. The novel, like the film, uses circularity, but the opening and closing passages differ radically from those of Doueiry's. In Khadra's book, the opening scene describes an unidentified dead man still processing his death in the immediate aftermath of an explosion. The final scenes reveal this man as Amin finally recognising that he has passed on. The novel closes with Amin imagining a child running (most likely himself), 'swept away by his father's voice':

> *They can take everything you own–your property, your best years, all your joys, all your good works, everything down to your last shirt–but you'll always have your dreams, so you can reinvent your stolen world* (original emphasis).[14]

This final sequence follows a section of the novel in which Amin has returned to his childhood home and is surrounded by friends and extended family right before the destruction of their home by the occupying forces. The explosion occurs as Amin attempts to find his niece who has gone off to join the resistance after this destruction. This stark difference between the novel and the film, then, reveals how Doueiry shifts the focus and reframes the original narrative. The poignancy of Doueiry's circularity and the subsequent affective investment that viewers likely achieve by the end of Doueiry's film result from placing the love story between Amin and Sihem at the centre of the plot. This reframing ultimately depoliticises the narrative of oppression that Khadra's novel recounts because it individualises the issues instead of focussing on the larger context in which this particular case unfolds. Arguably problematic, such depoliticisation of trauma forsakes the issues of suffering and oppression – and the power relations that frame them – in favour of universal appeal.

The final sequence in Doueiry's film, in which Sihem phones Amin before she blows herself up, proves problematic too. This scene – mediated to us via Amin's television screen as he watches the video Adel, his nephew and Sihem's conspirator, gave to him – provides the viewers with a snapshot of Sihem's psyche before she commits her murderous act. As she sits presumably in the back of a van surrounded by devices and wires, Sihem appears distraught and uncertain. She tells her collaborator that she does not want to make a

14 Yasmina Khadra, *The Attack*, trans. John Cullen (New York: Anchor Books, 2007), 257.

statement. He softly asks her, 'Shall we go over this one more time?' She responds that it is not necessary, but asks if he could show her how to deactivate the device 'just in case something happens.' In these moments, as Sihem chokes back tears and asks to speak to her husband, she appears doubtful and childlike. In an attempt, perhaps, to humanise Sihem and make her more sympathetic, Doueiry's imagination of this scene infantilises her and thus offsets the effectiveness and conviction of her statement. These creative liberties that Doueiry takes serve to reorient the political focus of the film and ultimately reveal troubling issues about the conditions for the film's success. For one thing, Douery changes the background of many characters. The novel depicts Sihem as a moderate Muslim who drinks, does not pray, yet observes Ramadan, while the film depicts her as Christian. Similarly, another Palestinian character in the novel with whom Amin converses becomes a priest in the film. These changes are likely undertaken in order to distance the Palestinian cause from an Islamic one and therefore to show how the issue transcends that of religion. In doing so, however, Doueiry once again depoliticises the issues at the root of the conflict because by utilising Christian figures to render characters more sympathetic and universal, he implicitly maintains and reinforces the idea that Palestinian issues relating to Islam are not worthy of sympathy or at the very least not to the same degree.

As I mentioned earlier, in discussing the filmic alterations, I do not assume that Doueiry necessarily owes an allegiance or fidelity to the original piece. I acknowledge that each of these works functions as a representational entity that circulates in the public sphere and has particular effects and imperatives. Though based on Khadra's novel, Doueiry's work is after all an autonomous artistic piece to regard and evaluate as such. However, there is value in considering the effects of and reasons for certain choices and deviations, as Brian McFarlane recognises in his chapter 'Reading Film and Literature.'[15] Doueiry's deviations from the novel reveal significant qualities about the norms that allow the film to become a success. His own commitment to portraying a 'balanced' perspective also comes across more strikingly when compared to Khadra's novel. The commitment to balance in the traumatic context that Doueiry constructs proves troubling when plugged back into its larger field of power relations. The subtle ways in which Doueiry adapts Khadra's novel, then, are worth reflecting on next as they expose the film's polemic agenda in various ways.

15 Brian McFarlane, 'Reading Film and Literature,' in *Literature on Screen*, ed. Deborah Cartmell and Imelda Whelehan (Cambridge: Cambridge University Press, 2007).

Doueiry insists on portraying the unbreachable chasm between Palestinians and Israelis, an idea admittedly not all together false, but when advanced as the primary issue is somewhat problematic. In one instance, for example, in the second half of the film when Amin attempts to find explanations for his wife's actions in the West Bank, he hears a priest tells him,

> We could debate this for months and years but we'll never come to the same conclusion. You have your life we have ours. You have your views we have ours. We'll never agree on anything. This is how it is.[16]

In the novel, this conversation occurs during one of Amin's multiple encounters in the West Bank and while not inconsequential, the book gives it much less weight. The film portrays this scene as a kind of climax in Amin's understanding of the conflict. Right after the conversation, a reflective and distraught Amin looks upon the landscape of the West Bank in solitude. Placing this conversation with the priest at such a pivotal moment in the film bears significant implications for Doueiry's overall agenda. These kinds of representations emphasise the incompatibility of national narratives and the ever-growing gap between them, as well as the difficulty of choosing sides in a conflict in which each side experiences its own losses and own tragedies. While seemingly virtuous in its neutrality, such representation, however, obstructs any movement towards understanding and reconciliation in its insistence on the unbreachable nature of the conflict. More importantly, the binary takes as its assumption the relative equality of both sides and thus ignores the blatant power difference that characterises the asymmetrical struggle. By insisting on the difficulty of choosing sides, Doueiry once again refocuses the politics at the heart of the novel; instead of a narrative of oppression, the film becomes a narrative characterised by apolitical sentimentality. Such depoliticisation becomes even more evident when compared to the climactic speech in the novel. After Amin has been held captive for six days in a crowded cellar, a commander approaches him:

> I daresay you've learned how to hate. If not, this experiment has been useless. I shut you up in here so you could develop a taste for hatred and a desire to act on it. I haven't humiliated you as a matter of form. I don't like humiliating people. I've felt humiliation, and I know what it is. When a person has been scorned, when his self-esteem has been wounded, all tragedies become possible. Especially if he recognizes that he's impotent,

16 *The Attack*, directed by Ziad Doueiry (2012; Poperinge: 3B Productions, 2013), DVD.

> with no means of restoring his dignity. I believe that the best school for hatred is located in this very place. The instant when you really learn to hate is the one in which you become aware of your impotence. It's a tragic moment – the most appalling, the most abominable of all...I wanted you to understand why we've taken up arms, Dr. Jaafari, why our teenagers throw themselves on tanks as though they were candy boxes, why our cemeteries are filled to overflowing, why I want to die with my weapons in my hand, and why your wife went and blew herself up in a restaurant. There's no worse cataclysm than humiliation. It's an evil beyond measure, Doctor. It takes away your taste for life. And until you die, you have only one idea in your head: How can I come to a worthy end after having lived miserable, and blind, and naked?[17]

This speech greatly differs from what Doueiry selects as the climax of Amin's political understanding. For one thing, rather than focalising on unachievable understanding, the commander's address to Amin concentrates on the painful effects of structural violence. In this sense, the commander provides a more compelling contextualisation for Palestinian violence and fury. Doueiry's priest does acknowledge the struggles that Palestinians go through ("our cities are being buried by tanks, our children can't remember what the word school means") yet his final statements reveal a kind of renouncement – an insistence on no hope for mutual understanding. The commander's speech, however, does not leave room for this impartiality. His description of humiliation and account of hatred operate affectively as they conjure up an image of suffering and powerlessness. Doueiry does not represent this image of impotence. Instead, he offers a watered down image of Palestinian existence paralleled by a commitment to show the other side – to reveal the difficulty of choosing sides in such a conflict. And while Doueiry correctly acknowledges that the situation is not black and white, both Israeli and Palestinian traumas still need to be framed by the larger context of power relations in which they are situated. As Khadra's Adel tells Amin in relation to Sihem's motives, "It was as if you were firing up a barbecue in a burned-out yard. You saw only the barbecue; she saw the rest, the desolation all around, spoiling all delight."[18]

One of the major questions driving Doueiry's film forward, then, is the question *why* Sihem did what she did and, more than that, *how* she could, in fact, have committed such an atrocious act when she and her husband were so thoroughly assimilated into Israeli culture and treated so hospitably by their Jewish

17 Khadra, *The Attack*, 219.

18 Ibid., 227.

friends and peers. In the book, Amin is not driven forward by the question *why;* rather, he struggles to decipher a sign that would have indicated Sihem's intentions to him: "all I can think about is the sign I wasn't able to decipher at the time, the sign that remains a mystery today."[19] This distinction is a significant one as I will reveal shortly. The film provides various explanations to this question. Amin's friend and investigator of the attack says,

> Something snaps in their brain and they're off. It can happen to anyone. It can fall on you like a tile or grow inside you like a worm. They don't see the world the same way. You're just waiting for the moment to cross the threshold.[20]

His explanation seems favoured in the film as it parallels Amin's nephew's words towards the end of the film: 'The day she got to Jenin. Something snapped in her head. The massacre she saw was indescribable.... I think that's what pushed her over the edge.' Adel's event-driven description of Sihem's prelude to violence localises the impetus for her motives in one bound instance. Such explanations do not necessarily do justice to the type of accumulated trauma described in Khadra's account:

> Sihem must have been carrying that hatred inside her forever, long before she met me. She grew up among the oppressed, as an orphan and an Arab in a world that pardons neither. She must necessarily have had to bow very low, like me, except that she could never straighten up. The memory of certain compromises imposes a heavier burden than the weight of the passing years. To go so far as to pack herself with explosives and walk out to her death with such determination, she must have been carrying around a wound so awful, so hideous that she was too ashamed to show it to me; the only way for her to be rid of it was to destroy it and herself together, like a possessed man who jumps off a cliff in order to triumph over his demons and his weakness.[21]

In this instance, Amin reflects on the trauma that drove Sihem to her violent end. While Amin still finds what Sihem did inexcusable, the wound that he describes gives her intentions more weight. Sihem's wound resounds with Cathy Caruth's conception of trauma as 'the wounded psyche…the story of a wound

19 Ibid., 106.
20 *The Attack*, dir. Ziad Doueiry.
21 Khadra, *The Attack*, 229.

that cries out, that addresses us in the attempt to tell us of a reality or truth that is not otherwise available.'[22] Significantly Amin's description of Siham's trauma is not based on one particular event; rather, her wound results from years of oppressed existence and structural violence.[23] While Caruth roots her conceptualisation of trauma in the event, her idea of trauma as an 'enigma of survival' and not just an 'effect of destruction'[24] resonates with Sihem's struggle of existence in the world that she and Amin inhabited. This nuanced articulation of trauma in Khadra's account renders Doueiry's rationalisation of Sihem's motives questionable. Doueiry gives weight to Adel's explanation through his filmic techniques. As Adel says to Amin that the massacre in Jenin pushed Sihem over the edge, the camera shifts to a shot of Amin walking against a background of rubble, which we can assume stands for the remnants of Jenin. In one of the more effective and poignant frames of the film, the camera lingers on a spray painted block of concrete that reads *Ground Zero*. In these final scenes, Doueiry serves to offer some explanation or contextualisation for Sihem's actions. The effectiveness of the 'ground-zero' shot, however, has less to do with the insight it offers into Sihem's motives. Instead, the significance of the shot stems from the uncanniness that the spray-painted term affectively stirs up as it evokes another national trauma that preoccupied international attention and changed the landscape of world politics. Ultimately, the emphasis on Sihem's motives in the film is actually quite problematic as Talal Asad would argue in his famous book *On Suicide Bombing*. Asad critiques accounts from the left to the right that seek to offer explanations behind the motives of suicide bombers arguing that,

> Motives in general are more complicated than is popularly supposed and the assumptions that they are truths to be accessed is mistaken: the

22 Cathy Caruth, *Unclaimed Experience: Trauma, Narrative, and History* (Baltimore: John Hopkins University Press, 1995), 4.

23 For more on the ethics of reducing trauma to a singular event, see Gen' Ichiro Itakura's chapter, "Re-imagining Atomic Bombing and 9/11: Kamila Shamsie's *Burnt Shadows,*" in this volume. Itakura makes a similar claim to mine in reading Shamsie's *Burnt Shadows*. He argues that the ethical potential of the book lies in the ability to relate personal trauma to a broader context. Here he employs the evocative phrase, "mourning in a global dimension" to gesture towards the ethical possibilities of regarding personal suffering in terms of the suffering of an Other. While Doueiry perhaps intends to represent the relationality that Itakura discusses, he ends up reproducing a narrative of trauma that not only ignores entrenched power structures, but also insists upon the very distinctness and irreconcilability of Palestinian and Israeli traumas.

24 Ibid., 58.

> motives of suicide bombers in particular are inevitably fictions that justify our own responses but that we cannot verify.[25]

In his account, Asad generally seeks to point out the contradictory nature of viewing the violence perpetrated by suicide bombers as exceptional in light of other forms of violence that are regarded as more legitimate. He seeks to unpack the discourses surrounding terrorism, war, and suicide bombing, in order to shake Western assumptions that lead to the justification of some forms of violence over others. The point, however, that I want to draw from this is that by focusing so much on the question *why* in the film, the representation works to subtly instil a sense of ambivalent horror at the suicide bombing in order to showcase Israeli vulnerability, just as it later on, in its commitment towards a balanced portrayal, contextualises Palestinian violence. As Asad points out, however, 'the feeling of vulnerability among Israelis and their supporters is not equivalent to the objective gains (territorial, military, economic, cultural…) that the Jews have made in Palestine over a century.'[26] Asad claims, furthermore, that Israeli vulnerability is 'rooted not in an evaluation of contemporary Palestinian power but in a collective trauma resulting from genocide – perpetrated against Jews in Europe by European Christians.'[27] Asad, then, highlights the source of Israeli vulnerability in order to reveal the unequal nature of the conflict and the inherent asymmetry of power relations that characterises it. While Asad attributes feelings of Israeli vulnerability to the collective trauma of the Holocaust, he then questions the viability of the term collective trauma asking, 'Is there such a thing as collective trauma? Or is there really only the traumatised condition of several individuals represented down the generations as the experience of a unified nation?'[28] Interestingly enough, this perspective is echoed in Khadra's book: one of Amin's acquaintances, old Yehuda, an elderly Israeli man who lost many relatives and friends to the Holocaust asks, 'I occasionally wonder whether some of my memories aren't… the result of traumatic experiences I had well after the war, in dark theatres where they showed documentaries about Nazi atrocities.'[29] Here Yehuda suggests an idea often recounted in memory studies. This perspective 'leads us away from understanding memory as a purely "natural" or "automatic" activity…and the product of unmediated gaze, and hence away from accuracy as

25 Talal Asad, *On Suicide Bombing* (New York: Columbia University Press, 2010), 3.
26 Ibid., 24.
27 Ibid.
28 Ibid.
29 Khadra, *The Attack*, 78.

the only criterion by which to evaluate memory."[30] Instead, this conceptualisation of memory invites us to recognise how 'memory is always and inevitably culturally and socially mediated.'[31] There is obviously value in recognising how cultural and social processes mediate memory; however, I would not go as far as Asad in dismissing the viability of the term *collective trauma*. To dismiss the notion of collective trauma based on the idea that collective memory is mediated amounts to ignoring the various ways that individual memory is also culturally mediated as well as the creative and significant interplay between individuality and collectivity that ultimately produces memory.[32]

Earlier in this chapter I mentioned a qualitative distinction in the nature of the different traumas represented in the film, a difference often unaccounted for in canonical trauma theory. I wish now to elaborate on this point in order to conclude my remarks about the unethical nature of representation in Doueiry's *The Attack*. As I alluded earlier, conventional trauma theory more often than not focuses on event-driven traumas. These conceptualisations have often been accused of having a Western bias because they do not account for more embedded forms of traumatising violence, like for instance those associated with colonialism.[33] Efforts, then, to 'decolonise' trauma theory so to speak often recall Laura Brown's well known articulation of the term 'insidious trauma' which refers to the 'traumatogenic effects of oppression that are not necessarily overtly violent or threatening to bodily well-being at the given moment but that do violence to the soul and spirit.'[34] Similar to this strain of thought, theorists have also criticised the emphasis on individual psychology

---

30 Michael Lambek, "The Past Imperfect: Remembering as Moral Practice," in *Tense Past: Cultural Essays in Trauma and Memory*, ed. Paul Antze and Michael Lambek (London: Routledge, 1996), 239.

31 Ibid.

32 José van Dijck, 'Mediated Memories: Personal Cultural Memory as Object of Cultural Analysis,' *Continuum: Journal of Media and Cultural Studies* 18.2 (2004): 268. For an example of the interplay between collective/public and individual/private memory, see Mark Callaghan's "Reflections on the Wall: Artefacts and Valediction at the Vietnam Veterans' Memorial" in this volume. Callaghan recounts how the *Vietnam Veterans' Memorial*, a public monument aimed at collective commemoration, prompts personal memorialisation. His account reveals how the lines between public and private memory often converge in significant ways. This example resonates with my own articulation of how individual memory emerges within a fluctuating social network and in connection to a collective context.

33 Michael Rothberg, 'Decolonising Trauma Studies: A Response,' *Studies in the Novel* 40 (2008): 228.

34 Laura Brown, 'Not Outside the Range: One Feminist Perspective on Psychic Trauma' in *Trauma: Explorations in Memory*, ed. Cathy Caruth (Baltimore: John Hopkins University Press, 1995), 107.

in conventional trauma theory, which they argue does not do justice to more collective experiences of abuse like colonial trauma.[35] As Kai Eriksen has pointed out,

> In order to serve as a generally useful concept, "trauma" has to be understood as resulting from a *constellation of life experiences* as well as from a discrete happening, from a *persisting condition* as well as from an acute event.[36]

I draw attention to these alternatives to canonical trauma theory to shed light on the nature of Palestinian suffering as an embedded structure of everyday life. Doueiry's balanced representation of suffering does not do justice to this quality because by aiming to reveal both points of view, the film shifts attention away from the gross injustices and daily humiliation, pain, and suffering that structure Palestinian lives. The effect of this representation is of course achieved subtly with the frame only slightly shifted, yet it is this slight shift of focus that ultimately accounts for the unethical portrayal of trauma and suffering in the film. As Adrienne Rich has argued,

> If to "aestheticize" is to glide across brutality and cruelty, treat them merely as dramatic occasions for the artist rather than structures of power to be described and dismantled - much hangs on that word "merely."[37]

Bibliography

Albrecht-Crane, Christa and Dennis Cutchins ed., *Adaptation Studies: New Approaches.* Madison: Fairleigh Dickinson University, 2010.

Asad, Talal. *On Suicide Bombing.* New York: Columbia University Press, 2007.

Awad, Amal. 'Book Review: The Attack: A Novel.' Review of *The Attack by Yasmina Khadra. Electronic Intifada,* 18 December 2006. Viewed 13 January 2015. http://electronicintifada.net/content/book-review-attack-novel/3509.

35 Stef Craps and Bert Guelens, 'Introduction: Postcolonial Trauma Novels,' *Studies in the Novel* 40 (2008).

36 Kai Erikson, 'Notes on Trauma and Community' in *Trauma: Explorations in Memory,* ed. Cathy Caruth (Baltimore: John Hopkins University Press, 1995), 185.

37 Adrienne Rich, 'Legislators of the World,' *Community Development Journal* 42.4 (2007): 423.

Brown, Lara. 'Not Outside the Range: One Feminist Perspective on Psychic Trauma.' In *Trauma: Explorations in Memory*, edited by Cathy Caruth, 100–112. Baltimore: Johns Hopkins UP, 1995.

Caruth, Cathy. *Unclaimed Experience: Trauma, Narrative, and History*. Baltimore: John Hopkins University Press, 1995.

Craps, Stef and Gert Buelens. 'Introduction: Postcolonial Trauma Novels.' *Studies in the Novel* 40. (2008): 1–12.

Van Dijck, José. 'Mediated Memories: Personal Cultural Memory as Object of Cultural Analysis.' *Continuum: Journal of Media and Cultural Studies* 18.2 (2004): 261–277.

Erikson, Kai. 'Notes on Trauma and Community.' In *Trauma: Explorations in Memory*, edited by Cathy Caruth, 183–199. Baltimore: John Hopkins University Press, 1994.

Felman, Shoshana and Dori Laub. *Testimony: Crises of Witnessing in Literature, Psychoanalysis, and History*. New York: Routledge, 1992.

Khadra, Yasmina. *The Attack*. Translated by John Cullen. New York: Anchor Books, 2007.

LaCapra, Dominick. 'Traumatopisms: From Trauma via Witnessing to the Sublime?' In *History and its Limits: Human, animal, violence,* 59–89. Ithaca: Cornell University Press, 2009.

Lambek, Michael. "The Past Imperfect: Remembering as Moral Practice." In *Tense Past: Essays in Trauma and Memory*, edited by Paul Antze and Michael Lambek, 235–254. London: Routledge, 1996.

Maslin, Janet. 'In "The Attack," an Arab-Israeli learns too late of a terrorist stranger in the family.' Review of *The Attack,* by Yasmina Khadra, *New York Times*, 15 May 2006, Sunday Book Review. Viewed 13 January 2015. http://www.nytimes.com/2006/05/15/books/15masl.html?_r=0.

McFarlane, Brian. 'Reading Film and Literature.' In *Literature on Screen*, edited by Deborah Cartmell and Imelda Whelehan, 15–28. Cambridge: Cambridge University Press, 2007.

Monk, Katherine. 'Ziad Doueiry's The Attack Banned in the Arab World.' *Canada.com*, 8 August, 2013. Viewed 13 January 2015. http://www.canada.com/entertainment/Ziad+Doueiri+Attack+banned+Arab+world/8763477/story.html.

Rich, Adrienne. 'Legislators of the World.' *Community Development Journal* 42.4 (2007): 422–424.

Roth, Michael S. *Trauma, Memory, and History: Essays on Living with the Past*. New York: Columbia University Press, 2012.

Rothberg, Michael. 'Decolonising Trauma Studies: A Response.' *Studies in the Novel* 40. (2008): 224–234.

Schwab, Gabrielle. *Haunting Legacies*. New York: Columbia University Press, 2010.

The Attack. Directed by Ziad Doueiry. 2012. Poperinge: 3B Productions, 2013. DVD.

CHAPTER 3

Re-imagining Atomic Bombing and 9/11: Kamila Shamsie's *Burnt Shadows*

Gen'ichiro Itakura

> Once he is in the cell they unshackle him and instruct him to strip. He takes off the grey winter coat with brisk efficiency and then – as they watch, arms folded – his movements slow, fear turning his fingers clumsy on belt buckle, shirt buttons.
>
> They wait until he is completely naked before they gather up his clothes and leave. When he is dressed again, he suspects, he will be wearing an orange jumpsuit.[1]

Thus begins Kamila Shamsie's critically acclaimed 'post-9/11' novel, *Burnt Shadows*. This 'prologue' encapsulates the wide scope of the novel as well as its psychological and ethical depth. The unnamed male character's forced disrobing, as well as the orange jumpsuit, evokes the sexual humiliation undergone by prisoners of the Guantánamo Bay detention camp. Furthermore, the title of the novel, the reader soon learns, refers to the shadows burnt on Hiroko's back by the atomic bomb in Nagasaki on 9 August 1945.[2] These two elements anticipate the novel's 'global' approach to the events that took place on 11 September 2001. The 'global' outlook of this novel sharply contrasts leading British and American novelists' responses that express 'the mélange of anger and anxiety' within the white population and unwittingly reveal their inability to extricate themselves from 'a kind of imaginative paralysis.'[3] On the other hand, the prologue does not provide any spatial or temporal specificity except for the deictic. This apparent lack reframes immediate socio-political concerns into more abstract, hypothetical questions of human ethics and psychology.

---

1 Ibid., 1.

2 Needless to say, Shamsie is not the first writer to relate the atomic bomb attacks on Hiroshima and Nagasaki to the events commonly known as '9/11.' As the topos 'ground zero' was used to refer to the epicentres of the atomic bombs before 2001, the re-emergence of the term allegedly suggests the association of those two in America's popular imagination. See Gene Ray, *Terror and the Sublime in Art and Critical Theory: From Auschwitz to September 11 and Beyond* (London: Palgrave, 2005), 56.

3 Robert Eaglestone, 'The Age of Reason Is Over ... an Age of Fury Was Dawning,' *Wasafiri* 22.1 (2007), 19; Richard Gray, 'Open Doors, Closed Minds: American Prose Writing at a Time of Crisis,' *American Literary History* 21.1 (2009), 135.

 | DOI:10.1163/9789004385931_004

In this chapter, I would like to explore the ways Hiroko's struggles to work through the trauma are represented in relation to the novel's panoramic scope of modern history and geopolitics. Despite the novel's apparently 'postcolonial' or 'post-9/11' concerns – the residues of British colonialism, the rise of the mujahideen in Central Asia, the 'War on Terror'[4] – it is the trauma Hiroko experiences in the atomic bomb attack, especially at the loss of her German fiancé, Konrad Weiss, that has a lasting impact on her life. First, I will identify the nature of the trauma suffered by Hiroko through analysis of the first part of the novel entitled 'The Yet Unknown World – Nagasaki, 9 August 1945,'[5] as well as numerous flashbacks to that day throughout the book. Hiroko's experience is also complicated by her subsequent losses: her Pakistani husband Sajjad Ashraf is shot by mistake; and her son Raza is arrested and most likely detained indefinitely. Then, I would like to trace her struggles to work through the trauma and move away from narcissistic preoccupations with her own suffering towards a more sensible consideration of suffering of the others. Through this shift, I argue, the novel helps the reader learn not only to 'mourn in global dimensions' but also to realise the 'precariousness of life.'[6]

1 Hiroko's Trauma

Hiroko's traumatic experience of the atomic bomb in Nagasaki can be summed up as the experience of various forms of dehumanisation. Indeed, Shamsie's novel is founded on a certain kind of abstraction, or focus on such a concept, as opposed to the directness of the survivor narrative. It scarcely provides graphic details of victims, dead bodies and ruins after the attack. This lack sharply contrasts Japanese 'atomic-bomb' literature or the body of writing mainly by atomic bomb survivors, ranging from Tamiki Hara's frequently anthologised short story 'Natsu no Hana' ['Summer Flowers'] to Keiji Nakazawa's manga *Hadashi no Gen* [*Barefoot Gen*]. Hara's narrator is horrified at the sight of a 'herd of indescribably disfigured victims' ('gengo ni zessuru hitobito no mure') by the

4 For Shamsie's view of 'privileged' and 'unprevileged' migrancy, see Cara N. Cilano, *Contemporary Pakistani Fiction in English: Idea, Nation, State* (Abingdon, England: Routledge, 2013), 223–228. For the parallel between America's 'necropolitical logic' of the 'war on terror' and that of atomic warfare, see Stephen Morton, *States of Emergency: Colonialism, Literature and Law* (Liverpool: Liverpool University Press, 2013), 223. For an analysis of Shamsie's secularist-liberal political stance, see Ruvani Ranasinha, 'Resistance and Religion in the Work of Kamila Shamsie,' *Culture, Diaspora, and Modernity in Muslim Writing*, ed. Rehana Ahmed, Peter Morey and Amina Yaqin (Abingdon: Routledge, 2012), 210–213.

5 Shamsie, *Burnt Shadows*, 4–30.

6 Butler, *Precarious Life*, 12.

river, whilst Nakazawa's eight-year-old hero encounters a number of victims with heavy burns and melted skin.[7] Shamsie apparently chooses not to follow the tradition of this atomic-bomb literature to re-imagine the impact of this traumatic event.[8] Nor does she investigate the aftermaths of the bomb, notably the prevalence of acute radiation syndrome and radiation-related illnesses, the subsequent moral breakdown and the Atomic Bomb Casualty Commission's sheer disregard of the victims' human rights and dignity. By minimising the 'shock' factors, however, Shamsie foregrounds Hiroko's experience of trauma and its enduring impact. Nagasaki after the bomb is perceived as the landscape devoid of light or life, replete with debris, the 'sound of fire' and the 'smell of dead flesh.'[9] Later, Hiroko explains to Sajjad this dehumanising effect of the atomic bomb:

> Those nearest the epicentre of the blast were eradicated completely, only the fat from their bodies sticking to the walls and rocks around them like shadows.... I looked for Konrad's shadow. I found it. Or I found something that I believed was it. On a rock. Such a lanky shadow. I sent a message to Yoshi Watanabe and together we rolled that rock to the International Cemetery ... She pressed a hand against her spine at the memory. And buried it.[10]

The contrast is obvious. The atomic bomb here instantaneously annihilates human lives, making the bodies disintegrate and evaporate. Their bodies bear no resemblance to humans or indeed to any living organism. Shamsie carefully avoids lyricism to recount the reduction of human bodies to 'shadows' – an attempt reminiscent of Hara's typographical and/or orthographical experiments.[11] In the meantime, Hiroko tries to restore the human from the

7 Tamiki Hara, 'Natsu no Hana,' *Natsu no Hana, Shingan no Kuni* [*Summer Flowers, The Land of My Heart's Desire and Other Stories*] (Tokyo: Shinchō-sha, 2000), 148; Keiji Nakazawa, *Hadashi no Gen*, vol. 1 (Tokyo: Chōbun-sha, 1975), 253–271; Nakazawa, *Hadashi no Gen*, vol. 2 (Tokyo: Chōbun-sha, 1975), 2–7, 15–18, 19, 32–46, 65–66, 68–69, 73–77, 83–84, 101-1-2, 108, 118. All English translations from Japanese are mine.

8 In fact, many Japanese writers have made the same choice as Shamsie, partly because the atomic bomb has been widely considered, like the Holocaust, the 'primal experience' that denies all but the survivors. John Whitter Treat, *Writing Ground Zero: Japanese Literature and the Atomic Bomb* (Chicago, IL: University of Chicago Press, 1995), 27.

9 Shamsie, *Burnt Shadows*, 27.

10 Ibid., 76–77; first ellipsis added.

11 Hara uses katakana to describe the absence of the 'human' and the presence of the 'odd' and 'mechanical' into which the atomic bomb reduces human bodies. Hara, 'Natsu no Hana,' 159, 158. Katakana, a Japanese syllabary mainly used to transliterate foreign words,

dehumanised landscape. She finds a 'lanky' shadow on a rock and brings it to the cemetery to 'bury' it in place of Konrad's body. This contrast implicitly suggests Hiroko's horror is caused by this dehumanisation. This complete dematerialisation of human life recurs in a different context when Hiroko has a miscarriage two years later. Her daughter's presence has only been felt as 'a stirring within, a series of hiccups and kicks,' but nevertheless she is traumatised by the deprivation of life allegedly in an 'act of mercy.'[12]

Hiroko's horror at dehumanisation surfaces even after she becomes emotionally more mature. When her husband Sajjad Ashraf is shot dead, she is upset by his skin's 'coldness' and 'unyieldingness,' as well as the 'hardness' of his lifeless penis, and tries to find part of him that still feels 'alive.'[13] The 'hardness' of his dead body contrasts the 'softness' while he was alive. When Hiroko remembers Konrad, she unconsciously seeks solace in resting her fingers on Sajjad's mouth and moustache.[14] It is not merely lifelessness but transformation that horrifies her. In her effort not to traumatise children or to internalise her trauma, she makes up 'fairy tales' in place of more realistic accounts of her experience in Nagasaki. One of her 'fairy tales' unwittingly reveals the source of her horror:

> There was the one about the girl whose dying father slithers towards her in the shape of a lizard; she is so horrified by his grotesqueness it takes her years to understand that his final act was to come towards her, after a lifetime of walking away.[15]

Hiroko sees her father, severely injured and deformed, 'slither' towards her.[16] The iconicity of images of crawling human figures, commonly found in Japanese 'atomic bomb' literature and photographs, encapsulates the horror of dehumanisation. This iconicity appears precisely where an individual victim-writer's personal experience of trauma merges with certain 'ahistoricity' of some of masterpieces of atomic-bomb literature. As John Whitter Treat argues,

---

notably technical terms and scientific jargon, is rarely if at all used to express emotions, except for ones of non-humans such as ghosts and artificial intelligence.

12 Shamsie, *Burnt Shadows*, 205. Worthwhile noting, although totally different in reality, Hiroko feels this medical 'mercy killing' as traumatising as the atomic bomb, an industrialised genocide, considered less cruel in America's necropolitical discourse. Ray, *Terror and the Sublime in Art and Critical Theory*, 102.

13 Shamsie, *Burnt Shadows*, 240.

14 Ibid., 205.

15 Ibid., 177.

16 Ibid., 27.

the tragedy of the atomic bombings that has thrust the victims into 'unknown and meaningless suffering' can only be intelligible or recognised as a tragedy by making it knowable – in other words, ahistoricising it.[17] Hiroko's 'fairy tale' evokes the same kind of ahistoricity by inciting primeval horror as Gen's first reaction – 'Min'na obake daaa!' ['Oh no, everyone here's a monster!'] – to heavily disfigured victims in *Hadashi no Gen*.[18] Hiroko's 'fairy tale' is not merely predicated upon her real experience but also upon a more deep-seated, primeval horror of humans turning into something else or shape-shifting shared not only by the survivors of the atomic bombing but also by many people across cultures, given the prevalence of folktales of horrifying shape-shifters.

Significantly, the atomic bomb provides a threat to her autonomy as an individual, as a human. Indeed, the burns on the back can be read as trauma inscribed on her body. Hiroko's stigma invariably functions as a reminder of her experience of the atomic bomb and her horror at the sheer dehumanisation it brings to her hometown. However, her scars also represent death in life, the inanimate in the animate.

> She glides her hand over her shoulder, touches flesh where there should be silk. Moves her hand further down her back, touches what is neither flesh nor silk but both. She wonders if this has something to do with the burning she felt as she fell. Now there is no feeling. She taps the place that is neither flesh nor silk. There is no feeling at all.[19]

The burns here are perceived as 'neither flesh nor silk,' neither human nor artificial, neither animate nor inanimate. In fact, it is not usually the melting of the garments but the intense flash of the atomic bomb that causes burns on the skin covered by the dark portions of the garments. Furthermore, this ambiguous condition of burns does not typically haunt a victim in Japanese atomic-bomb literature. Keloidal scars stigmatise protagonists in reality and fiction, notably in Minoru Betsuyaku's famous play *Zō* [*The Elephant*], whereas

17 Treat, *Writing Ground Zero*, 64.

18 Nakazawa, *Hadashi no Gen*, vol. 1, 254. However, such description is often accompanied by the protagonist's sense of guilt or shame, rarely found in Western literature of atomic bombs. Kyōko Hayashi's short story 'Akikan' ('The Empty Tin') centres on this theme, whilst Fumiyo Kōno's manga *Yūnagi no Machi* [*The City of Evening Calm*] provides an excellent example of visualisation of the heroine's sense of guilt. See Kōno, *Yūnagi no Machi, Sakura no Kuni* [*The City of Evening Calm and The Country of Cherry Blossoms*] (Tokyo: Futaba-sha, 2004), 23–24.

19 Shamsie, *Burnt Shadows*, 26.

not only haemoptysis and diarrhoea but also alopecia or the loss of hair – which frequently appears in *Hadashi no Gen* – signals the onset of fatal radiation-related illnesses. Despite these oddities, however, Shamsie adds thematic depth to these literally skin-deep, stylised scars. Hiroko perceives her injury as the process that dehumanises – at least in part – her body, literally and symbolically.

> Her finger can feel her back but her back cannot feel her fingers. Charred silk, seared flesh. How is this possible? Urakami Valley has become her flesh. Her flesh has become Urakami Valley. She runs her thumb over what was once skin. It is bumped and raw, lifeless.[20]

Her burns are now linked to the modern history of the Urakami Valley area, as they continue to function as a reminder of the atomic bombing of Nagasaki. This symbolic meaning does not eclipse the importance of the lifelessness of her skin. She is eternally bound up with the Urakami Valley of August 1945 or what it stands for: devastation and dehumanisation by an atomic bomb. Given the immensity of this historical event, Hiroko fears being subordinated to this temporality and locality and thereby deprived of anything irrelevant to the atomic bomb.

This horror also accounts for Hiroko's resistance to the labelling of '*hibakusha*' or the atomic bomb victim,[21] not often explored explicitly in Japanese atomic-bomb literature but nevertheless offering insight into the victims' psychological trauma. Hiroko explains to Elizabeth:

> I don't want to hide these burns on my back, but I don't want people to judge me by them either. Hibakusha. I hate that word. It reduces you to the bomb. Every atom of you.[22]

Importantly, she does not describe the social exclusion or segregation of *hibakusha* in such words as 'prejudices' or 'discrimination' as many Japanese would do. Both Betsuyaku's *Zō* and Kyōko Hayashi's short story 'Matsuri no Ba' ['The Festive Place'] explore various forms of discrimination against *hibakusha*, especially the type of discrimination from which the victims suffer all the more intensely for the postwar government's legislation to 'save' *hibakusha* on an

---

20 Ibid., 27.

21 In Japanese, the word *hibakusha* literally means a person killed or wounded in a bomb attack, notably an atomic bomb attack. It is also used to describe a person exposed to hazardous radioactive substances after the bomb.

22 Shamsie, *Burnt Shadows*, 100.

admittedly superficial level. Instead, Hiroko draws our attention to the dehumanising aspect of this stigmatisation. She does not fear the exposure of her own 'deformity' or the grotesqueness of her back to the scrutinising gaze of the public. Rather, she is terrified of being 'reduced' to 'the bomb.' The use of the label *hibakusha* no longer defines her individuality and her identity but her having survived a bomb attack. Her decision to leave Japan stems not so much from her desire to escape from humiliation and persecution as her repulsion for such dehumanisation. Interestingly, her son Raza encounters prejudices against *hibakusha* and their children in India, but in a way different from Japanese narratives of *hibakusha* mostly set in Japan. Salma, Raza's then girlfriend, explains to him on the phone why her parents do not allow her to marry him – an episode reminiscent of Kiyomi Hotta's play *Shima* [*The Island*]:

> Nagasaki. The bomb. No one will give their daughter to you in marriage unless they're desperate, Raza. You could be deformed.... You might have something you can pass on to your children. I've seen the pictures. Of babies born in Nagasaki after the bomb.... This is how people think about you.[23]

It is not so much visible signs of *hibakusha* like keloids or alopecia as being born to a *hibakusha*'s family that arouses or intensifies fear and prejudices against them. Salma's choice of imprecise words ('deformed' and 'something') reveals her own – and her parents' – lack of knowledge or first-hand experience of witnessing the victims' suffering. In other words, this ignorance reduces Raza to the name of his mother's birthplace or what it stands for: the atomic bomb. Looked at with this hindsight, Hotta's *Shima* examines a similar kind of dehumanisation through the labelling. Like Raza, Hotta's hero Manabu Kurihara is forced to give up his beloved, Reiko Kido, who loves him more faithfully and passionately than Salma loves Raza. Although a *hibakusha* with burns on the back and with a birthplace – Hiroshima, in his case – whose name does not incite an acute fear among the Kido family, Manabu is 'reduced to the atomic bomb' in a highly similar way: he is banished into the realm of the living dead, all those people deprived of their individuality, let alone free will. His last words, '*Kuso, ikite miseruzo*' ['I must survive by all means'], are often interpreted as his will to challenge his own tragic fate, but it can also read as his resistance to this particular type of dehumanisation.[24] In this – perhaps

23 Ibid., 189; ellipses added.

24 Kiyomi Hotta, *Shima*, *Nihon no Genbaku Bungaku* [*Japanese Atomic-Bomb Literature*], vol. 12, ed. Kenzaburo Oe et al., (Tokyo: Horupu, 1983), 83.

unconventional – way, Hiroko's resistance sheds light on a hitherto unexplored aspect of *hibakusha*'s suffering or psychological trauma.

2 Hiroko's Mourning

Burnt Shadows does not merely provide a psychological study of its protagonist's personal trauma; rather, it adds an ethical dimension to this trauma. This ethical theme develops in two stages. First, Shamsie traces the ways Hiroko comes to terms with her personal trauma and manages to move on to a higher ethical stage. At the outset, she consciously tries to repress the trauma and negate her past, even though she belongs to positive thinkers or, to use her own words, 'those who could step out from loss.'[25] Then, she goes through a series of ordeals to attain a certain level of moral maturity. Secondly, Shamsie implicitly suggests that the readers should recapitulate Hiroko's moral development until they finally acquire the ability to mourn in global dimensions, rather than remain mired in the melancholia. This development can compare with Freud's analysis of 'melancholia' in relation to 'mourning.' According to Freud, melancholia is accompanied by an 'extraordinary diminution in [one's] self-regard, an impoverishment of [one's] ego on a grand scale' that makes the patient to expect to be punished, whilst mourning is a self-controlled action.[26] By showing that Hiroko clearly steps out of this melancholia, Shamsie invites the reader to participate in a more meaningful act of mourning.

Indeed, Hiroko translates her personal sorrow into a more universal ethical theme. Fifty-six years after the attack, she tries to relativise her experience by reading books and manages to suppress her personal sorrow and anger at the atomic bomb. She confesses her doubt about the importance of the event to Kim.

> My stories seemed so small, so tiny a fragment in the big picture. Even Nagasaki – seventy-five thousand dead; it's just a fraction of the seventy-two million who died in the war. A tiny fraction. Just over .001 per cent. Why all this fuss about .001 per cent?[27]

25 Shamsie, *Burnt Shadows*, 146.

26 Sigmund Freud, 'Mourning and Melancholia,' *On the History of the Psychoanalytic Movement, Papers and Metapsychology and Other Works*, ed. and tr. James Strachey (London: Vintage, 2001), 245–246.

27 Shamsie, *Burnt Shadows*, 293. 75,000 is a strangely underestimated number. According to Nagasaki City's official record, 162,083 people died because of the atomic bomb attack and radiation-related illnesses.

By this questioning, she clearly does not endorse – or expect Kim to endorse – an American myth of Hiroshima and Nagasaki according to which the annihilation of the two cities and 330,000 lives was a 'necessary' action. Nor does she expect such a personal comment as Kim's, a comment that no matter how small the number may be, the bombing of Nagasaki is important for her because she experienced it. Rather, Hiroko strenuously strives to consider her personal loss, her personal tragedy in a broader context, making it into an ethical question. She becomes less and less personal towards the end.

> You just have to put them in a little corner of the big picture. In the big picture of the Second World War, what was seventy-five thousand more Japanese dead? Acceptable, that's what it was. In the big picture of threats to America, what is one Afghan? Expendable. Maybe he's guilty, maybe not. Why risk it? … But right now, because of you, I understand for the first time how nations can applaud when their government drop a second nuclear bomb.[28]

Interestingly, Hiroko somehow channels her personal sorrow and anger at various events culminating in her son's arrest into a more extensive consideration of moral justice and acceptability of disregarding suffering in the others. She discovers the same structure of feelings in the American myth of Hiroshima and Nagasaki and in the popular narrative of the War on Terror: Japanese or Muslim lives are not conceived of as lives in the 'big picture' that always puts US citizens at the centre. Like Judith Butler, Hiroko condemns that which has 'foreclosed' our 'ability to mourn in global dimensions.'[29]

Hiroko does not so much predicate her indictment of Americans upon her political position as her sense of morality. After her remark, Hiroko and Kim lapse into an awkward silence.

> The silence that followed was the silence of intimates who find themselves strangers. The dark birds were between them, their burnt feathers everywhere.[30]

The bird-shaped burns on her back used to act as a mere reminder of her past trauma; but they now function as a guarantor of difference – the difference between those who can understand other people's suffering and mourn their lives and those who cannot. Like these burns, her trauma is inscribed in

28 Ibid., 362; ellipsis added.
29 Butler, *Precarious Life*, 12.
30 Shamsie, *Burnt Shadows*, 362.

her body. Now the burns begin to connote her ability to suffer and mourn for other people, as if their suffering were felt like her own burns. According to Emmanuel Levinas, such a realisation of other people's sufferings opens an ethical perspective.[31]

> Dans cette perspective se fait une différence radicale entre la *souffrance en autrui* où elle est, pour *moi* impardonnable et me sollicite et m'appelle, et la souffrance *en moi*, ma propre aventure de la souffrance dont l'inutilité constitutionnelle et congénitale peut prendre un sens, le seul dont la souffrance soit susceptible, en devenant une souffrance pour la souffrance, fût-elle inexorable, de quelqu'un d'autre.[32]

> In this perspective there is a radical difference between *the suffering in the other*, where it is unforgivable to *me*, solicits me and calls me, and suffering *in me*, my own experience of suffering, whose constitutional or congenital uselessness can take on a meaning, the only one of which suffering is capable, in becoming a suffering for the suffering (inexorable though it may be) of someone else.[33]

Suffering in the Other (*souffrance en autrui*) is quintessentially meaningless. So is suffering in oneself (*souffrance en moi*), as long as only experienced as unbearable pain it inflicts upon an individual. Suffering in oneself makes sense and opens up a new ethical perspective on interpersonal relationship only when it becomes suffering for suffering in the Other (*souffrance pour la souffrance de quelqu'un d'autre*) – that is the only ethical sense that, according to Levinas, suffering in oneself can make. This ethical turn appears in Hiroko's 'dark birds' or 'burnt shadows.' They do not have any ethical meaning as long as they remain her personal trauma, suffering in oneself. They open up a new ethical horizon only when they appear as suffering in the Other. Her final remark thus represents not merely her righteous indignation against America's neo-imperialism but also her move towards a higher, more advanced stage of interpersonal ethics.

This ethical turn affects our reading of this novel, especially its prologue. The unnamed guards 'instruct' Raza to take off his clothes and 'wait.' They do

31 Emmanuel Levinas, *Entre Nous: Essais sur le penser-à-l'autre* (Paris: Grasset, 1991): 110–111; *Entre Nous: Thinking-of-the-Other*, tr. Michael B. Smith and Barbara Harshav (New York: Continuum, 2006): 80–81.

32 Levinas, *Entre Nous: Essais sur le penser-à-l'autre*, 111.

33 Levinas, *Entre Nous: Thinking-of-the-Other*, 81.

'watch' him, but just to check if he finishes undressing himself, proving totally devoid of compassion or interest in what he is thinking of or how he must be feeling.[34] They are not only 'faceless' but also indifferent to other people's faces. In Levinas' interpersonal ethics, the irreducible otherness of the face engenders our moral imperative, 'thou shall not kill,' which has ethical implications far beyond its Judeo-Christian theological roots.[35]

> Le lien avec autrui ne se noue que comme responsabilité, que celle-ci, d'ailleurs, soit acceptée ou refusée, que l'on sache ou non comment l'assumer, que l'on puisse ou non faire quelque chose de concret pour autrui. Dire : me voici. Faire quelque chose pour un autre. Donner. Être esprit humain, c'est cela. L'incarnation de la subjectivité humaine garantit sa spiritualité ... Dia-conie avant tout dialogue : j'analyse la relation inter-humaine comme si, dans la proximité avec autrui ... son visage, expressif en autrui (en tout le corps humain est, en ce sens, plus ou moins, le visage), était ce qui m'*ordonne* de le servir.[36]

> The tie with the Other is knotted only as responsibility, this moreover, whether accepted or refused, whether knowing or not knowing how to assume it, whether able or unable to do something concrete for the Other. To say: here I am [*me voici*]. To do something for the Other. To give. To be human spirit, that's it.... Dia-chrony [sic.] before all dialogue: I analyze the inter-human relationship as if, in proximity with the Other ... his face, the expressive in the Other (and the whole human body is in this sense more or less face), were what *ordains* me to serve him.[37]

All ethically meaningful interpersonal relationships are founded upon the sense of responsibility, with dialogue preceded by 'dia-conia' (*dia-conie*), read here as the act of serving or the readiness to serve the Other as apparent in the biblical phrase '*me voici*.'[38] Such interpersonal relationships cannot be

---

34 Shamsie, *Burnt Shadows*, 1.

35 Emmanuel Levinas, *Étique et infini: Dialogues avec Philippe Nemo* (Paris: Fayard, 1982): 81; *Ethics and Infinity: Conversation with Philippe Nemo*, tr. Richard A. Cohen (Pittsburgh, PA: Duquesne University Press, 1985), 87.

36 Levinas, *Étique et infini*, 93–94; ellipses added.

37 Levinas, *Ethics and Infinity*, 97; ellipses added. The word 'dia-chrony' in Richard A. Cohen's English translation should read 'dia-conia.'

38 '*Me voici*,' translated as 'Here I am' or 'Here am I,' is the words that appear frequently in the Old Testament, most notably in Genesis 22:1 where Abraham uses the phrase to show God his readiness to serve Him.

established without recognition of the 'face' or irreducible individuality. Neither 'dia-conia' nor 'dialogue' takes place in the prologue of the novel, where the unnamed guards order the unnamed prisoner to take off his clothes and see him do it. The absence of interpersonal relationship between them is confirmed by the guards' indifference to the unnamed prisoner's – most likely Raza's – face. Nothing in him arouses any sympathy, let alone '*ordains*' them 'to serve him.' Suffering in him remains truly inutile in the commonest meaning of the word. This paradoxically contrasts the difference between their total apathy and the reader's ability to see the 'face,' understand its signification, and translate it into their own action.

3 The Atomic Bomb and 9/11

Hiroko's mourning in *Burnt Shadows* links the atomic bombing of Nagasaki to 9/11 in a way that makes it possible to restore the ability to 'mourn in global dimensions,' to borrow Judith Butler's words.[39] Butler uses this phrase to illuminate – and then criticise – the *de facto* prohibition of mourning for people of certain ethnic origins or religious backgrounds or excessive emphasis on narcissistic melancholia in post-9/11 America and, by extension, its allies in 'War on Terror.' Considering our act of grieving and its political uses, she proposes a possibility of channelling grieving in better directions:

> But this can be a point of departure for a new understanding if the narcissistic preoccupation of melancholia can be moved into a consideration of the vulnerability of others. Then we might critically evaluate and oppose the conditions under which certain human lives are more vulnerable than the others, and thus certain human lives are more grievable than others. From where might a principle emerge by which we vow to protect others from the kinds of violence we have suffered, if not from an apprehension of a common human vulnerability?[40]

According to Butler, our ethical sense of responsibility is founded upon our consideration of 'the vulnerability of others,' which includes Levinas' suffering for suffering in the Other (*souffrance pour la souffrance quelqu'un d'autre*). She translates this ethical consideration into a debate on the politics or political implications of our grieving and mourning. *Burnt Shadows* also opens a new

39 Butler, *Precarious Life*, 12.
40 Ibid., 30.

perspective on mourning in the post-9/11 globalised world or introduces a new context in which to discuss this issue.

Unlike Jonathan Safran Foer's *Extremely Loud and Incredibly Close*, *Burnt Shadows* explores the themes of loss from people marginalised in the dominant discourse of the West. In Foer's novel, 'Mohammed Atta' is cited as an 'evil,' abhorrent figure who Oskar Schell believes stands in stark contrast to his 'good' father, though no Muslim characters appear in this book.[41] Oskar plays a recorded interview of Tomoyasu, a survivor of the atomic bombing of Hiroshima, on his portable cassette player.[42] Foer chooses not to explore this subject further or give as much importance to Tomoyasu's story as he does to those of victims of the Dresden bombing and the 9/11 terrorist attacks. Underprivileged and/or underrepresented ethnic minorities such as young American Muslims and non-Japanese victims of the atomic bomb are naturally excluded from the landscape of *Extremely Loud and Incredibly Close*.[43] This absence, according to Butler, has foreclosed our ability to 'mourn in global dimensions.' Also, it is precisely this void that *Burnt Shadows* tries to fill by shedding light on and familiarising hitherto underrepresented groups of people. The novel requests from the reader to extend their sympathy by encouraging a better understanding of sufferings and concerns affecting people from diverse backgrounds at different times in history.

Significantly, Hiroko's view of two 'grounds zero' forges a link between the two events rarely if at all discussed together and thereby provides a new perspective for contemporary readers in English-speaking countries, a large majority of whom allegedly reluctant to extend their sympathy to victims of one of the incidents. Hiroko compares the ground zero of New York to that of Nagasaki as if the latter were more familiar than the former. Needless to say, the atomic bombing of Nagasaki took place earlier in history and opens the first chapter of *Burnt Shadows*, which helps increase the reader's familiarity to the event. Nevertheless, Anglophone readers, a majority of whom are from former Allies of World War II, are more likely exposed to an American myth of the atomic bombings as necessary actions, arguably rooted in and endorsed by the 'long tradition of American moral exceptionalism' and the 'promise of the Enlightenment tradition.'[44] According to this myth, the United States is qualified

41 Jonathan Safran Foer, *Extremely Loud and Incredibly Close* (London: Hamilton, 2005), 159.

42 Ibid., 187–189.

43 That may not apply to Japanese atomic-bomb literature, as it often provides an appropriately multiethnic, multicultural landscape with Koreans and Western prisoners-of-war. Even manga like *Hadashi no Gen* has episodes of an American victim and a Korean family. Nakazawa, *Hadashi no Gen*, vol. 2, 36–37, 177–192.

44 Ray, *Terror and the Sublime in Art and Critical Theory*, 102.

to employ 'mass terror' such as nuclear bombings to what its nation considers 'just causes' and thereby 'enlighten' a non-European nation. Needless to say, there has been a well-founded counter-argument: the nuclear means may well be 'judged disproportionate and counterproductive to the end of a free and perpetual peace;' furthermore, it 'globalizes the threat of instantaneous extermination.'[45] According to some, an 'institutionalized racism' can be detected behind the decision of the Truman administration to execute mass killings.[46] When Hiroko sees a photo of a young New Yorker with the words '*MISSING SINCE 9/11*' and '*IF ANY INFORMATION ABOUT LUIS RIVERA PLEASE CALL* … ,' the memory of Nagasaki temporarily overwhelms her:

> Hiroko thought of the train station at Nagasaki, the day Yoshi had taken her to Tokyo. The walls plastered with signs asking for news of missing people. She stepped closer to take in the smile of Luis Rivera, its unfettered optimism. In moments such as these it seemed entirely wrong to feel oneself living in a different history to the people of this city.[47]

Pictures with notes pasted on the wall constitute one of the iconic images of 9/11 circulated in the globalised Western news media, but the image of Luis Rivera here does not simply refer the reader to this already familiar narrative of post-9/11 melancholia. It also helps the reader reimagine the bombing of Nagasaki so that they can fully understand the suffering of victims as well as the terror effect of the atomic bomb on Nagasaki on Japanese people – the number of casualties during the bombing of Nagasaki alone rises 50 times above the total casualties of the 9/11 multiple attacks – and a strong reaction or hatred it might have incited. By de-familiarising 9/11, Shamsie provides a context in which to understand the two events in global dimensions.

Interestingly, Hiroko suddenly recalls Nagasaki when seeing a beautiful photograph of Afghanistan, one of the countries most frequently demonised or at least dismissed as creatures 'outside the "human"' in the Western media.[48] Abdullah shows her a photo of Kandahar before the wars and points out to her that since it was taken the trees have been cut down, landmines have been planted and cluster bombs have been scattered.[49] That somehow brings back memories to her:

45 Ibid., 102.
46 Ibid., 102.
47 Shamsie, *Burnt Shadows*, 274.
48 Butler, *Precarious Life*, 32.
49 Shamsie, *Burnt Shadows*, 309–310.

> Hiroko nodded, touching the page as reverently as Abdullah had. It was difficult to find photographs of Nagasaki that preceded the bomb, but Kim had presented her with what remained in the Burton family of George Burton's old pictures – Azalea Manor, the bund, Megane-Bashi when the river was high – and when she looked at them she was surprised by how strong a grip childhood had on her ageing mind.[50]

Not even 'a ground zero,' Kandahar has taken an apparently different course of history. The reader cannot decipher whether Hiroko fully sympathises with Abdullah or understands his frustration and rage. Despite these, however, the above quotation calls to mind the possibility that the gap between the two – two individuals, two cities, two histories – can be filled by such respectfulness to the others as Hiroko's 'reverence,' accompanied by an effort to find a link between oneself and the Other, not by complete identification with the Other.

Such reverence helps develop the ethical question of the novel: channelling trauma to an ethical action. Indeed, the scope of the novel goes far beyond a simple act of accommodating people formerly excluded in the Western media. Hiroko does not efface herself – or rather strip herself of her memories and cultural baggage – to identify fully with Abdullah, who ends up drawn to an Islamist ideology. She does not simply indulge in her reminiscences about her past, either. She remains respectful of Abdullah. Their coexistence can read as a critique of the post-9/11 intellectual climate that understands everything in a clear-cut dichotomy of good and evil, just and unjust and that bans critical discourse, as shown in Rodolph Giuliani's response to Alwaleed bin Talal's remark.[51] Shamsie does not duplicate this black-and-white worldview, nor does she turn it upside down. Instead, Hiroko's respectfulness can read as a critique of intolerance, as it allows those considered non-existent to assume a certain level of reality.[52] Her willingness to participate or 'serve' opens a meaningful interaction.

> Abdullah continued to turn the pages of the book, stopping briefly on some pictures, lingering over others. Occasionally he'd point out a detail to Hiroko – a goat rearing on its hind legs in the corner of one photograph with the poise of a dancer, a kite flying high above a dome painted an identical green which made the kite appear an escaping roof tile.

50 Ibid., 311.

51 Butler, *Precarious Life*, 12.

52 Butler argues that an inclusion of the excluded does not constitute a valid critique; rather, ontological questioning of reality does. Ibid., 33.

> Sometimes he'd point to an object and identify it in Pashto – she'd repeat the word, pleased when she found any overlap with Urdu and delighted when she found resemblance to the Hindko words she had learnt while in Abbottabad.[53]

The image of a man and a woman reading the same book here implies a certain level of intimacy – almost sexual, despite Hiroko's age in this part of the novel – an interpretation endorsed by the references to the pleasure she feels. Despite their difference, they manage to forge a rapport, albeit temporary, to the extent where they feel comfortable with each other's presence. Hiroko's sitting with Abdullah can be compared to Levinas' conception of the interpersonal relationship or 'true togetherness,' the first step towards the escape from a solitary being, as a 'togetherness of face-to-face' ('ensemble de face à face'), not a 'togetherness of synthesis' ('ensemble de synthèse').[54] Hiroko treats Abdullah with due respect as a human being. In this sense, Hiroko manages to find a way to deal with the Other – which can be seen as an ethical action on her part.

4 Conclusion

In *Burnt Shadows*, Shamsie translates the protagonist's trauma into a more ethically meaningful act, a personal experience of horror into a responsible action. Like many literary works on the atomic bombs, it indicts dehumanising aspects of the bomb, though in a less graphic manner. Konrad's transformation into a shadow on a rock, as well as her father's metamorphosis into a lizard, encapsulates the kind of dehumanisation the novel condemns. It conjures a primordial horror of shape-shifting and the blurring of boundaries between the animate and the inanimate – or life and death – and the total annihilation of life. The experience of trauma such as Hiroko's also appears in post-9/11 literature. In Foer's *Extremely Loud and Incredibly Close*, the empty coffin of the young protagonist's father signifies this sort of annihilation and therefore produces a traumatic effect on the son.[55] Interestingly, Hiroko does not merely channel her trauma into an ethical question – how she should 'mourn' the loss in the 'big picture' of world history – but suggests that this ethical question deserves lifelong pursuit.

---

53 Shamsie, *Burnt Shadows*, 311.
54 Levinas, *Éthique et infini*, 72; *Ethics and Infinity*, 77.
55 Foer, *Extremely Loud and Incredibly Close*, 36, cf. 172–173.

Indeed, Shamsie manages to add a new dimension to atomic bomb literature as well as post-9/11 literature by turning the trauma into an ethical theme. Towards the end of the novel, Hiroko's burns take on another meaning – the one other than her personal trauma – namely her own suffering experienced as suffering in the Other. This ethical turn can read as an attempt to reintegrate the traumatised self rather than recapitulate the melancholia or 'acting out.'[56] In this respect, not only does the novel interrogate the widely-held narratives of Hiroshima/Nagasaki and 9/11 but with this ethical turn it also helps broaden the scope of literary representation of trauma.

Bibliography

Butler, Judith. *Precarious Life: The Powers of Mourning and Violence*. London: Verso, 2004.

Cilano, Cara N. *Contemporary Pakistani Fiction in English: Idea, Nation, State*. Abingdon, England: Routledge, 2013.

Eaglestone, Robert. 'The Age of Reason Is Over … an Age of Fury Was Dawning.' *Wasafiri* 22.2 (2007): 19–22.

Foer, Jonathan Safran. *Extremely Loud and Incredibly Close*. London: Hamilton, 2005.

Freud, Sigmund. 'Mourning and Melancholia.' In *On the History of the Psychoanalytic Movement, Papers and Metapsychology and Other Works*. Edited by James Strachey, 237–260. Translated by James Strachey. London: Vintage, 2001.

Gray, Richard. 'Open Doors, Closed Minds: American Prose Writing at a Time of Crisis.' *American Literary History* 21.1 (2009): 128–251.

Hara, Tamiki. 'Natsu no Hana.' ['Summer Flowers.'] *Natsu no Hana, Shingan no Kuni.* [*Summer Flowers, The Land of My Heart's Desire and Other Stories.*] Tokyo: Shinchō-sha, 2000. 140–162.

Hayashi, Kyōko. 'Akikan.' ['The Empty Tin.'] *Giyaman Biidro*. [*Cut Glass.*] Tokyo: Kōdan-sha, 1978. 7–26.

Hotta, Kiyomi. *Shima*. [*The Island.*] In *Nihon no Genbaku Bungaku*. [*Japanese 'Atomic-Bomb' Literature.*] Edited by Kenzaburo Oe et al., 9–83. Tokyo: Horupu, 1983.

Kōno, Fumiyo. *Yūnagi no Machi, Sakura no Kuni*. [*The City of Evening Calm and The Country of Cherry Blossoms.*] Tokyo: Futaba-sha, 2004.

Levinas, Emmanuel. *Entre Nous: Essais sur le penser-à-l'autre*. Paris: Grasset, 1991.

56 For Levinas' discussion of psychosis and ethics or a sense of responsibility, see Emmanuel Levinas, *Otherwise than Being or Beyond Essence*, tr. Alphonso Lingis (Pittsburgh, PA: Duquesne University Press, 2011): 142.

Levinas, Emmanuel. *Entre Nous: Thinking-of-the-Other*. Translated by Michael B. Smith and Barbara Harshav. New York: Continuum, 2006.

Levinas, Emmanuel. *Ethics and Infinity: Conversations with Philippe Nemo*. Translated by Richard A. Cohen. Pittsburgh, PA: Duquesne University Press, 1985.

Levinas, Emmanuel. *Éthique and infini: Dialogues avec Philippe Nemo*. Paris: Fayard, 1982.

Levinas, Emmanuel. *Otherwise than Being or Beyond Essence*. Translated by Alphonso Lingis. Pittsburgh, PA: Duquesne University Press, 2011.

Morton, Stephen. *States of Emergency: Colonialism, Literature and Law*. Liverpool: Liverpool University Press, 2013.

Nakazawa, Keiji. *Hadashi no Gen*. [*Barefoot Gen.*] Vol. 1. Tokyo: Chōbun-sha, 1975a.

Nakazawa, Keiji. *Hadashi no Gen*. [*Barefoot Gen.*] Vol. 2. Tokyo: Chōbun-sha, 1975b.

Ranasinha, Ruvani. 'Resistance and Religion in the Work of Kamila Shamsie.' In *Culture, Diaspora, and Modernity in Muslim Writing*. Edited by Rehana Ahmed, Peter Morey and Amina Yaqin. Abingdon, England: Routledge, 2012. 200–214.

Ray, Gene. *Terror and the Sublime in Art and Critical Theory: From Auschwitz to Hiroshima to September 11 and Beyond*. London: Palgrave, 2005.

Shamsie, Kamila. *Burnt Shadows*. London: Bloomsbury, 2009.

Treat, John Whitter. *Writing Ground Zero: Japanese Literature and the Atomic Bomb*. Chicago, IL: University of Chicago Press, 1995.

CHAPTER 4

Filming Trauma: Bodiless Voice and Voiceless Body in Beckett's *Eh Joe*

Svetlana Antropova

1 Introduction

The television play, *Eh Joe*, first recorded in 1966, was first broadcast by BBC2 with Jack MacGowran as Joe, and Sian Phillips as Voice. At least thirteen versions of this play have been preserved on tape making it Beckett's most reproduced teleplay.

Eh Joe is practically staged in the dark cellar of Joe's mind. MacGrowan defines this play as 'the most gruelling twenty-two minutes I have ever had in my life', and later he writes that 'It's really photographing the mind. It's the nearest perfect play for television that you could come across, because the television camera photographs the mind better than anything else'.[1] The camera performs the role of an all-seeing eye zooming in between the Voice's speeches throughout the film, and at the end, the camera slowly dollies in to a close-up of Joe's face. Jeanette Malkin writes that 'this short film sets up a context and frame for the study of obsessive introspection of unwilled memory'.[2] Samuel Beckett manages to scan the mind through unusual television devices: complete separation of camera and voice, limitation of the versatility of the camera, invisibility of the voice owner, partial inaudibility of words towards the end, and the photogenicity of an intensely listening face.[3] Based on the principle of silent movies with a soundtrack of a woman's voice added, *Eh Joe* records Joe's silence and achieves complete vocacentricity. The screening, though simple in nature, reveals a very complex relation between the three presumably autonomous objects: gaze/camera, the voice and the body/Joe. As a result, a shift from the signifier to the signified causes the character/body to become a sheer recipient for the flow of memory: Joe is transformed into a mere listener to a disembodied voice. Consequently, traumatic memory becomes the protagonist of

1 Ibid., 538.

2 Jeannette R. Malkin, *Memory-Theatre and Postmodern Drama* (Ann Harbour: University of Michigan Press, 1999), 37.

3 Ruby Cohn, *A Beckett Canon* (Ann Arbor: University of Michigan Press, 2001), 293.

 | DOI:10.1163/9789004385931_005

the play. While focusing on the artistic representation of trauma on television, this chapter addresses the use of disembodied voice and its relation to PTSD in the screening of trauma. The Voice in *Eh Joe* embodies trauma, becoming form and content of this play.

2 Disembodied Voices

Disembodied voices and voiceless characters become frequent entities/characters in Beckett's plays, such as in *Not I, Ohio Impromptu, That Time* and so on. Although counterparts, they hint at the possibility of a unity, as the body normally houses a voice, and the audience always want to identify a disembodied voice and attach it to a certain body. But Samuel Beckett never fully grants this wish since no 'host' body appears on stage or in the film, voices function as autonomous entities. Obviously, a distinction emerges between a disembodied voice in the theatre and a disembodied voice in the cinema. One-directional, a bodiless voice in the theatre comes from a loudspeaker, that is, from one place, whereas in a film a disembodied voice tends to occupy all sonic space onscreen as well as off-screen: 'Cinema has a frame, whose edges are visible, we can see where the frame leaves off and off-screen space starts'.[4] A voice, therefore, belongs to both spaces while an image always stays in a frame, which certainly creates dramatic tension, as no trace exists of the initial relation that links the voice to the image.

> Being in the screen and not, wandering the surface of the screen without entering it, the acoustmêtre brings disequilibrium and tension. He invites the spectator to *go see*, and he can be an invitation to the loss of self, to desire and fascination.[5]

In her analysis of the film *The Attack*, Tarraf gives a very interesting example of acoustmêtre – the phone call from Sihem before committing suicide bombing. The call also replayed at the end of the film serves not only as a trauma trigger, but as a framing device as well. The ghost voice of a person no longer alive haunts Amin as he is trying to work through traumatic loss. Sihem's voice though acoustmêtre still has a body through the images of her projected in the movie. The voice in *Eh Joe*, on the other hand, functions as a complete acoustmêtre, namely a voice acting as an acoustic presence, not connected to

4 Michael Chion, *The Voice in Cinema* (New York: Columbia University Press, 1999), 22.
5 Ibid., 24.

an image.[6] Therefore it may be analysed from several perspectives: the voice as a material presence (speech), the voice as a being or a shade of an image, the voice as power and the voice as a theatrical object. This disembodied voice possesses all of the specific characteristics of the acoustmêtre: ubiquity, panopticism, omniscience, and omnipotence.

Presumably, the voice of the woman heard in this play belongs to a dead person and resurrects Joe's worst memories, the memories so intimate that only Joe can know. Hence, it establishes a victim-perpetrator relation. The Voice's knowledge of Joe's past gives it complete power over him and to make matters worse the bodiless Voice possesses the ability to see, that is, panopticism. 'Look up, Joe, look up, we're watching you',[7] says the Voice. As the omnipresent Voice comes from everywhere, Joe has no place to hide from it. Consequently, Joe develops an obsession with the Voice. According to Michel Chion, bodiless voices in the cinema take the audience back to an archaic stage, the first months after birth and the months of gestation, during which the voice was 'everything and everywhere'.[8] From this perspective, Joe's room may read as a womb/tomb and the Voice as an umbilical cord that nurtures/tortures Joe with his memories, while trapping him in the complicated web of his past. Undoubtedly the first acoustmêtre in life is the mother, and the greatest acoustmêtre of all is God, which bears relevance to this discourse, since the Voice in the film alludes to God and his ensuing punishment to Joe. Furthermore, the Voice guides the action and sets the pace for the film, and for the process of remembering. Joe, who remains obstinately silent, only mimes out his reaction to what the Voice is saying. Rodriguez-Gago states that these disembodied voices in Beckett's oeuvre serve as 'the aural traces of memory',[9] especially traumatic memories, since one of the major symptoms of trauma is the loss of an authoritative voice. Malkin even goes further and refers to Beckett's voices as time-conflators: 'his voices, remembering or remembered voices, develop in, cut through, and often conflate time'.[10] The immaterial quality of the voice

6 Michael Chion provides the definition of a complete acoustmêtre as voice acting as an acoustic presence, not connected to an image. Michael Chion, *The Voice in Cinema* (New York: Columbia University Press, 1999), 20.

7 Samuel Beckett, *The Complete Dramatic Works* (London: Faber & Faber, 1986), 363.

8 Chion, *The Voice in Cinema*, 27.

9 Antonia Rodriguez-Gago, 'The Embodiment of Memory (and Forgetting) in Beckett's Late Women's Plays', in *Drawing in Beckett: Portraits, Performances and Cultural Contexts*, ed. Linda Ben-Zvi (Tel Aviv: Assaph Books Series, 2003), 114.

10 Jeanette Malkin, *Memory Theatre and Postmodern Drama* (Ann Arbor: University of Michigan Press, 1999), 38.

and its ability to travel through time parallels the materiality of a body trapped in the present moment.

The disembodied voices in Beckett's plays not only distort time or narrate characters' memories but they become uprooted-from-the-body memories and gain a theatrical life of their own, and as a consequence the first personal pronoun singular of the discourse is lost and the character stripped of his past. The dissociation of a character from his own memories points to an identity disruption, the past self shattered to pieces and distorted by an outside narrator. The bodiless voice *per se* becomes a cinematographic device to represent dissociation, as a traumatic memory acoustically lives outside the body. In *Eh Joe* the Voice takes on the role of Joe's troubled conscience as well as his traumatic memory, narrated from a perspective of an outsider who once formed part of Joe's life. The Voice belongs to his ex-lover, rendering the neutrality of narration unacceptable: the Voice blames Joe for his merciless acts and makes him responsible for causing pain to other women.

In the analysis of a disembodied voice from psychoanalytical perspective, Sigmund Freud's theory proves relevant. In *Beyond the Pleasure Principle*, Chapter 3, Freud describes the occurrence of traumatic memories in relation to hearing voices in one's head, totally outside the control of the victim.[11] Freud points out the importance of outside voices that may invade the head of a traumatised person. If we remember the Tasso's legend Freud refers to in the abovementioned book, we may single out the importance of the outside voices, which can invade the head of a traumatised person and intensify the traumatic recall. These voices may vary, but they share a feature: they normally try to remember the episode or a part of the person's life when the traumatic event occurred. As a traumatic event is not processed into an autobiographic memory, it belongs to the subconscious and the voice/s manifest these non-processed memories – the memories yet-to-be-told, leaking into the conscious present. Therefore, hearing voices characterises trauma and, in this play, the Voice of a dead woman assaults Joe's privacy every night – harassing him with the fragments of his own painful memories. Perhaps a figment of Joe's guilty conscience, the Voice questions its own existence: 'You know that penny farthing hell you call your mind ... That's where you think this is coming from, don't you?'[12] Furthermore, these voices may represent different personalities entombed in a person's mind (multiple personalities theory), as Jung argues.

11 Sigmund Freud, *Beyond the Pleasure Principle*. Trans. James Strachey (London, New York: W.W. Norton, 1961).

12 Samuel Beckett, *The Complete Dramatic Works*, 364.

> Aspects of consciousness, according to Jung, can become almost independent personalities and might even 'become visible or audible. They appear as visions, they speak in voices which are like the voices of definite people' (Jung, 80).[13]

According to Jung's theory, the voiceless body and the bodiless voice in *Eh Joe* form part of one obscure entity. The voice describes itself as a 'whisper' in Joe's mind. Therefore it functions as the product of Joe's imagination, which he wants to throttle at all costs, for he does not want to remember. Alienation results from the shift of the pronouns from 'I' to 'you', the personal pronoun 'I' wiped out from the narration. The accusatory 'you' presupposes a dialogue that never occurs in the play. Tormented by inner devils, Joe cannot pathologically face up to his own past and accept the voice as his own. Deep at heart, he craves for peaceful silence and oblivion. Moreover, the impossibility to narrate those memories in the first person singular also points to their rejection, and, obviously, contributes to their cyclic nature.

Recent studies on PTSD may offer an explanation to Joe's silence:

> During the provocation of traumatic memories, there is a decrease in activation of Broca's area – the part of the brain most centrally involved in the transformation of subjective experience into speech. [...] Simultaneously, the areas in the right hemisphere that are thought to process intense emotions and visual images show significantly increased activation.[14]

As the Voice mercilessly weaves the narrative of Joe's painful memories, recreating past images, it reactivates Joe's traumas and renders him speechless. While a camera dollies up on a close-up of his face, the audience become aware of Joe's painful listening. Face muscles quivering, lips pressed together, as though blocking the words from coming out, face frowning in pain, dreamy eyes, dazed expression: Joe remembers and re-experiences the long-forgotten emotions.

---

13 Stanley E. Gontarski, *A Companion to Samuel Beckett* (Oxford: Blackwell Publishing Ltd, 2010), 155.

14 Bessel A. van der Kolk, 'Trauma and Memory', in *Traumatic Stress: the Effects of Overwhelming Experience on Mind, Body, and Society*, ed. Bessel A. van der Kolk, Alexander C. McFarlane and Lars Weisaeth (New York, London: the Guildford Press, 1996), 287.

3 *'The Passion of Our Joe'*

In an interview with the German critic Siegfried Melchinger, Samuel Beckett refers to the main theme of the play as 'one striving to see one striving not to be seen, [...] It is his passion to kill the voices which he cannot kill'.[15] The impossibility to kill the voices might be of an existential matter: if we understand these voices as memories, should they disappear, memory-less Joe would turn into a shallow carcass without any identity. Hence, these voices sustain him, although they envenom his existence.

The only character of this play, Joe feels paranoid about being alone and displays all the symptoms of anxiety as though he is facing a potential threat to his life. He imprisons himself in a scarcely furnished room and his only link with the outer world is a slut who occasionally comes to perform services for him. The room itself looks more like a ward than a real home; and as the film is shot in black-and-white, it adds shabbiness and a nightmarish quality to the setting. Joe, wearing an old dressing-gown and slippers, sits on the edge of his bed. Both words 'bed' and 'edge' deserve our attention in the analysis of the film.

The only piece of furniture, the bed, is evoked several times during the play, thus it acquires other levels of meaning. The film starts when Joe is getting ready to sleep. His cyclical 'going-to-bed' routine consists of his sitting on the bed, then going to the window, then to the door, then to the cupboard, and finally his sitting on the edge of the bed. The Voice also makes reference to the bed in her very first speech: 'Why don't you go to bed? ... What's wrong with that bed, Joe? ... You changed it, didn't you? ... Made no difference?'[16] The reference deserves our attention, since Joe is already sitting on the edge of his bed; in the stage direction Beckett specifies: 'Joe seen from front sitting on edge of bed, relaxed, eyes closed'.[17] So, which bed does the Voice refer to? Taking into consideration the English proverb 'you made your bed; now lie in it', the Voice may actually refer to his present situation, when Joe has to bear the negative consequences of his wrongdoings. Feeling remorse, Joe fears to go to sleep because of possible nightmares. Furthermore, if we take Joe's room for a womb, the bed may read as a 'cradle', the only place of comfort for Joe. The bed is both alpha and omega of our lives and in old age, a bed stands not only for comfort, but also for confinement. As a textual symbol, a bed relates to the vulnerability and the innocence of sleep as well as representing the sexual. Since Joe used to be a seducer with many falling in love with him and many abandoned by him,

15 Jonathan Kalb, *Beckett in Performance* (Cambridge: Cambridge University Press, 1966), 103.

16 Samuel Beckett, *The Complete Dramatic Works*, 362.

17 Ibid., 361.

when the Voice accuses Joe of changing beds she may actually refer to Joe's capacity for changing women. Incapable of forming a stable relationship, Joe normally left them without any explanation, vanishing into thin air.

Besides the word 'bed', the prominence of the word 'edge' throughout the play signals that it attracts more attention in the Voice's narration. On the edge of his life, Joe sits on the edge of the bed listening to the Voice. At the same time this word is used in relation to the girl's sacrifice. She, together with Joe, was 'sitting on the edge of her bed in her lavender slip',[18] and later she 'goes on down to the edge and lies down with her face in the wash…'.[19] Three times she goes 'down the garden and under the viaduct',[20] three times Joe goes to the door, window, cupboard, and later both Joe in the present and she, in the past, return 'home': Joe to the comfort of his bed, and the girl to the 'comfort' of forgetting, death. I claim that Joe unconsciously re-enacts her suicide, though unable to reach its finality, which justifies the prominent use of the word 'edge'. The word means 'on the point of', presupposing a last step to reach something, but Joe proves incapable of doing it, which speaks of his cowardice. His cowardice, together with a probable re-enacting of trauma only makes him withdraw more and more into the cocoon of his subconscious, voluntarily locking himself in his shabby room.

At the beginning of the play the camera shoots Joe from behind, as though he averts the camera gaze. With his back rigid and fully alert, Joe frantically inspects his surroundings in search of possible intruders, like a small child afraid to go to sleep. He even kneels down and looks under his bed. This extreme paranoia together with total isolation from the world only points to Joe's ontological insecurity. Finding nothing, Joe closes his eyes and relaxes, when suddenly the Voice starts to speak: 'No one can see you now … No one can get at you now',[21] no one except the Voice:

> You might turn around to surprise him [the disembodied voice], since he can always be behind you. This is the paranoid and often obsessional panoptic fantasy, which is the fantasy of total mastery of space of vision.[22]

Thus the first time the camera focuses on Joe he looks defenceless; already two intruders have invaded his private world – the voice and the camera's eye. The room, his private cocoon of security, is not voice/camera-proof.

18 Ibid., 365.
19 Ibid., 366.
20 Ibid., 365–366.
21 Ibid., 362.
22 Michael Chion, *The Voice in Cinema*, 24.

Internal rather than external, the danger that terrifies Joe comes from within his head. The internal intruder/s emanate from the voices of his disturbed memory which started one June night and went on and off for years. The moment of the voices' appearance coincides with the suicide of a girl seduced and abandoned by him. Joe learns about her death from an article in *The Independent.* The suicide of his loved one affects Joe. And the merciless Voice brings to life their last meeting: '...Bundling her into her Avoca sack... Her fingers fumbling with her big horn buttons...Ticket in your pocket for the first morning flight...'.[23] This scene reminds the spectators of Joe already putting her inside a coffin, or of a burial ceremony; hence, her suicide may read as a consequence of their separation. Joe already decided to run away and to forget, betraying her and their love. Broken-hearted, the girl committed suicide, effecting Joe's seclusion and total withdrawal into 'that penny farthing hell you call your mind'.[24] The mind in turn becomes the container of the accusatory voices that haunt his memory, which though imaginative, become his private torturers for past sins.

The tension of listening mounts and reaches its climax, when the Voice blames him for the girl's death. Does the sense of guilt and further remorse make Joe reject his memories? What frightens him? 'The passion of our Joe', as the Voice mockingly says, brings to mind 'the passion of our Lord' and parallels the text of the film with the Bible. Voices of memories accompany Joe on his personal Way of the Cross. The burden of his past sins becomes more and more unbearable, some unpardonable in the eyes of God, such as suicide. Therefore, Joe's desire to kill the voice stands for the act of forgetting and, subsequently, absolution. Joe suffers remorse, Joe remembers, his heart '...crumbles when you lie down in the dark...'.[25] From the very beginning the Voice condemns Joe to hell for the greatest sin of all: betrayal of Love.

> Not all biblical quotations are doom-laden. The threatening voice in *Eh Joe* summons up images of faithful as well as faithless love. "Great love", she says, apropos the dead girl: we may hear in the background saying, "Greater love hath no man than this, that a man lay down his life for his friends..." John 15:13.[26]

23 Ibid.

24 Samuel Beckett, *The Complete Dramatic Works,* 362.

25 Ibid.

26 Katherine Worth, *Samuel Beckett's Theatre: Life Journeys* (Oxford: Clarendon Press, 1999), 124.

Although a womaniser, Joe felt for this girl, this 'spirit made light'.[27] Consequently, Joe feverishly wants to protect 'light' in his life. Obsessively afraid of darkness in all of its symbolic meanings, he keeps the lamp always on in his room, and fears extinction of light, or death. Joe even uses euphemisms to avoid the word 'to die', substituting it with 'to expire' or 'to still', for example when he says: 'Isn't that what you told me? ... Before we expire ... The odd word...'.[28] Therefore, Joe feels indirectly responsible for extinguishing this 'spiritlight',[29] foreseeing his punishment in hell, which inevitably leads to his crisis of faith. Loss of faith goes hand-in-hand with hopelessness. With paradise lost, Joe has to accept the finality of death and the state of non-existence.

Paradoxically, the Voice, which condemns Joe to hell, does not belong to the girl in a lavender slip but to one of his ex-lovers. And the camera witnesses Joe's sins; private becomes public and adds to Joe's sense of shame. While Joe wants to kill the voices and wade off the traumatic memories, the camera gets closer and closer to his face until it freezes on a close-up of his eyes and nose, as though penetrating deep into his mind.

4 The Voice from Hell

The Voice in *Eh Joe* can stand for the voice of Joe's memory, analysed in terms of its acoustic characteristics, gender and narration. The Voice has a hallucinatory quality: Beckett insists on it being 'low, distinct, remote, little colour, absolutely steady rhythm, slightly slower than normal'.[30] Traumatic memories mostly remain on the subconscious level and have a ghost quality, appearing and disappearing, making the world lived in seem unreal. Here the Voice creates an impression of coming from the grave, just as other voices torturing Joe: the voices of his parents and other voices of the dead who loved him. Love acts as the clue to the voices' audibility, love which Joe could not reciprocate. The Voice pictures Joe as a parasite used to live and nurture on the love of others and now 'throttling the dead in his head'.[31] Surprisingly, the voices of all these dead people eventually cease to exist in Joe's head and their succession is linear, possibly because the voices die out as Joe has assimilated the memories

27 Samuel Beckett, *The Complete Dramatic Works*, 365–366.
28 Ibid., 362.
29 Ibid., 366.
30 Ibid., 359.
31 Ibid., 363.

narrated by them. It stands to reason that a traumatic experience, once understood, starts to form part of a person's present personality.

The Voice has a characteristic rhythm with pauses of one second between phrases and seven seconds long between paragraphs. Beckett writes to Schneider on 7 April 1996: 'Voice should be whispered. A dead voice in his head. Minimum of colour. Attacking. Each sentence a knife going in, pause for withdrawal, then in again'.[32] Joe's face reflects his internal torment, while his listening becomes more and more intense: 'face: practically motionless throughout, eyes unblinking during paragraphs, impassive except in so far as it reflects mounting tension of listening'.[33]

Regarding gender and origin, the Voice belongs to one of Joe's lovers. The information given about the Voice's past 'idyll' with Joe is rather scarce: 'Like those summer evenings in the Green ... In the early days ... Of our idyll ... When we sat watching the ducks ... Holding hands exchanging vows...'.[34] Joe loved listening to her voice 'like flint glass',[35] which he 'could have listened to ... for ever'.[36] The last remark sounds rather sarcastic as Joe would indeed listen to the haunting voice forever; the voice transforms into his present perpetrator. Once in love with Joe, the Voice cannot forget their brief romance. It makes hateful comparisons between Joe and her other affair: '...But I found a better ... As I hope you heard ... Preferable in all aspects...'.[37] The Voice hankers after Joe. It uses an accusatory tone and spits poison, constantly calling for Joe's attention: the name 'Joe' pronounced thirty-one times during the whole play suggests that the Voice dreads not to be heard. The first speech in the play contains ten questions that the Voice asks Joe in a feeble attempt to establish communication.

The ten speeches and nine camera movements during the play bear resemblance with Dante's *Divine Comedy*. The number 'nine' may connect to Dante's nine circles of Hell, and, therefore, to the descent into hell or to the passion of 'our Joe' as the Voice says. The latter rejects Joe's possibility of gaining 'that old paradise you were always harping on...'.[38] Furthermore, the Voice does not function as a Saint, a feature in common with Joe. Speaking about paradise

32 Phillip B. Zarrilli, 'Acting at "the nerve ends": Beckett, Blau, and the Necessary', *Theatre Topics* 7 (1997), Baltimore: the John Hopkins University Press), 113.
33 Beckett, *Complete Dramatic Works*, 359.
34 Ibid., 363.
35 Ibid.
36 Ibid.
37 Ibid., 364.
38 Ibid., 363.

it says that it 'is not for the likes of us',[39] thus hinting that it comes from hell. The whispering Voice creates verbal images from Joe's past, interrupted by the camera movements: the voice and the camera never coincide. Therefore, we may view nine camera movements in the light of mnemonics,[40] although only one *locus* is present: Joe's mind. The zooming-in effect allows the spectator to penetrate deeper into Joe's memory. As such, the ten speeches interrupted by nine camera movements may read as 'memory' images created by the Voice. The nine camera movements also do not constitute a mere coincidence in this play; Beckett was familiar with Dante's *The Divine Comedy*, itself based on mnemonics,[41] and consequently on hermetic memory. So the number of camera movements acquires significance, Joe taking an allegorical journey into his sinful past with the Voice as his guide.

---

39 Ibid.

40 According to mnemonics, memories are stored in our brain in both forms: as unforgettable images against the background of places (*memoria rerum*) and in words (*memoria verborum*). Frances A. Yates in his book *The Art of Memory* (1966, El Segundo, CA: Redwood Press, Ltd.) presents the development of the mnemonics method from *Ad Herennium* to the Renaissance Fludd's theatre. Although mnemonics has to do with artificial memory, it bears many common features with the memories of trauma; both artificial and traumatic memories belong to long-term memory. Therefore, the storage of striking violent images in the memory of a traumatised person very much calls to mind mnemonics, since the rules for conjuring images look similar: 1) novelty, 2) bizarre, striking quality; 3) comic or violent nature. The major difference lies in the voluntary method to remember with mnemotecnics, and in the case of trauma, the storage in the subconscious, thus the memory is involuntary. Traumatic images stored on the subconscious level prove more difficult to forget or to erase and tend to penetrate into the conscious level. Paradoxically, we try to repress our traumas, but we are doomed to relive them. Furthermore, emotions and sensations always accompany the storage of images in trauma. Without any doubt, these stable memories recur in time.

41 Frances A. Yates' *The Art of Memory* (1966) dwells upon the problems of artificial memory from the perspective of mnemonics. In classical rhetoric, images and text mapped onto virtual places aid the memory of orators. Memory mattered to orators because they had to deliver long speeches with total accuracy. In fact, memory was of such value that an art of memory designed to strengthen natural memory developed. Frances A. Yates explains that this artificial memory depended upon the recollection of images. Artificial memory functioned as "inner writing" the orator reviewed while presenting a speech, observing the places and their contents, the images, and recovering the memories for things (the subject matter) that those images represented. Yates presents the development of the mnemonics method from *Ad Herennium* to the Renaissance Fludd's theatre. Significantly, psychologists still use mnemonics nowadays in reference to memory storage, which only proves its validity. Nowadays psychologists make a distinction between the encoding mnemonic (the images that one creates in our brains) and the organisational mnemonic (*loci*) construction that encodes the images in a specific order.

In mnemonics the fifth locus contains crucial information for the one remembering. Likewise, the fifth camera movement marks something essential for Joe – his faith:

> How's your Lord these days? ... Still worth having? ... Still lapping it up? ... The passion of our Joe ... Wait till He starts talking to you ... When you're done with yourself ... All your dead dead ... Sitting there in your foul old wrapper ... [...] Silence of the grave without the maggots ...[42]

The verbal images created by the Voice in this speech have a Dantesque feel in their nature. The language becomes more and more aggressive, the Voice actually spitting the words out, accusing Joe of his sins and threatening him with God's punishment. This obsession with punishment may result from the Voice's frustration at its inability to inflict any physical harm on Joe. Unable to be his executor, she calls for someone above who can execute the punishment, someone Joe respects and fears. 'Wait till He starts talking to you', it says. Ruby Cohn points out that 'the text witnesses to a crisis of faith'.[43] Joe's present situation may read as the Day of his Final Judgment, with the Voice as his public prosecutor. Joe, on the other hand, deprived of voice, cannot defend himself and with no lawyer present he has already been sentenced to hell.

The most crucial memory of Joe's appears in the narration of the girl's suicide, which belongs to the ninth camera movement of the teleplay. The whole speech describes the girl's three attempts to commit suicide: by drowning, wrist-slitting and taking sleeping pills. In form, the whole speech resembles a director's stage instructions, with the voice trying to re-enact the girl's suicide. Past and present collide in this memory fragment, since the Voice only uses the present simple in her narration. The sentences simultaneously become more fragmented and precise as her life comes to its closure. The opening directions 'Warm summer night ... All sleeping ... Sitting on the edge of her bed in her lavender slip ...'[44] set the action in time and place. The only description of the girl is 'her lavender slip'. And the Voice masterfully plays with different meanings of this word:

42 Beckett, *Complete Dramatic Works*, 364.
43 Ruby Cohn, *A Beckett Canon*, 294.
44 Beckett, *Complete Dramatic Works*, 365.

> Gets out in the end and slips out as she is...[45]
> Tears a strip from the slip and ties it round the scratch...[46]
> Slip clinging the way the wet silk will...[47]

Beckett uses the polysemic[48] word 'slip' to create several layers of meaning, making the text multilevel in associations. Used as a trigger of Joe's memory, as well as an instrument of torture, the 'slip', as an intimate item of clothing, reminds Joe of their love-making. But this slip is brutally torn apart in order to bandage her wrist wounds. 'Slip' as a verb means that her life is actually slipping away. In addition, 'slip' with the meaning of 'slickness' has sexual connotations, while the characteristic of 'wetness' places the story close to the water: 'Faint lap of the sea through the open window...'[49] and bears the association of slicker blood trickling from the girl's hands. Furthermore, 'slip' visually contributes to the evasion of this girl from a life of suffering.

The Voice also plays with the word 'cut' in significant ways:

> Cut a long story short doesn't work...[50]

Its figurative meaning applies to the narration literally: the girl was attempting to cut her veins to end her life. In comparison with the word 'slip', the meaning of 'cut' falls flat and narrows the understanding of the text. From time to time the speech is coloured by Voice's vehement remarks, as though she tries to take revenge for both of them. Her remark about the Gillette blade has an excruciatingly cruel meaning: 'Gets out the Gillette ... The make you recommended for her body hair...'.[51] The Voice indirectly makes Joe an active participant of this act, attributing him the role of a murderer.

At the end of the play the Voice starts to lose its strength and gets fainter, but on purpose. Above the inaudible whisper, Joe can make out only a few words, highlighted by Beckett:

45 Ibid.
46 Ibid., 366.
47 Ibid.
48 Possible meanings of the word 'slip' include 'the act of avoiding capture', 'a young slim person', 'a minor mistake due to lapses of memory', 'a socially awkward act', 'a woman's undergarment', 'an artefact consisting of a narrow flat piece of material', 'slickness', 'pass out of one's memory', etc. if these definitions come from a dictionary you should document them.
49 Beckett, *Complete Dramatic Works*, 365.
50 Ibid., 366.
51 Ibid.

> ...All right ... You've had the best ... Now *imagine* ... Before she goes ... Face in the cup ... Lips on a *stone* ... Taking Joe with her ... Light gone ... "*Joe Joe*" ... No sound ... To the *stones* ... Say it now, no one'll hear you ... Say "Joe" it parts the *lips* ... *Imagine* the hands ... The *solitaire* ... Against a *stone* ... Imagine the *eyes* ... Spiritlight ... Month of June ... What year of your Lord? ... *Breasts* in the stone ... And the *hands* ... Before they go ... *Imagine* the hands ... What are they at? ... In the *stones* ...[52] (italics in the original)

The sequence of the words pronounced louder includes: *Imagine, stone, 'Joe Joe', stones, lips, Imagine, solitaire, stone, eyes, Breasts, hands, Imagine, stones.* On the one hand, the Voice tries to reconstruct the girl's body in Joe's memory, making her body alive again but only for the briefest of moments. Lips, breasts and hands, that used to caress Joe, end up gone forever. The fragile line between life and death is represented by 'light gone'. But on the other hand, the Voice recreates the moment of her death when the breathing body transforms into a corpse – a stone. The Voice appeals to Joe's imagination to feel the grief and solitude of a person already doomed, by using the word 'imagine' three times in this short speech.

The use of stones has several interpretations. Stones are used instead of flowers in Jewish burials, for example. In the Bible, an altar – the holy place where one makes offers to God – is no more than a pile of stones. When Abraham binds his son Isaac for sacrifice, he does this on a stone. And the most sacred shrine in Judaism, after all, is a pile of stones – the wall of the second Temple burial ceremony. In the play, the Voice may be recreating the girl's burial ceremony, ancient in its nature, as well representing her as a human sacrifice for love. Besides, people who committed suicide were never buried in cemeteries, so the girl practically becomes part of nature separated from the rest of the world. Other aspects of the symbolic use of stone should include first that a stone acts as a 'male' substance in many cultures, whereas earth symbolises femaleness because of the plant life it nurtures and supports.[53] As a counterpart to earth's more fragile produce, hard stone was perceived as a male phenomenon. The hardness of stone and its deep penetration into the earth obviously add to its significance as a male symbol. Furthermore, the girl dying among the stones may read as her final act of union with Joe, her fusion with him and his

52 Ibid., 366–367.

53 Otto Rank, *El Trauma del Nacimiento*. Trans. H.F. de Saltzmann, (Buenos Aires: Editorial Paidos, 1961).

memory, or as the Voice says 'taking Joe with her'. The girl's final words, parting her lips on the stone, are 'Joe, Joe'. And silence is the answer.

Finally, worth mentioning linguistically the Voice expresses itself through the language of torture. The verbs of mental thuggee appear throughout the play: 'throttle, muzzle, spike, squeeze, tighten, silence, garrotte, mum, strangle, stamp out, exterminate, kill, choke'. They may refer to Joe's constant struggle with the voices or his attempt to kill his own unpleasant memories. Beckett writes in *The Expelled*:

> Memories are killing. So you must not think of certain things, or those that are dear to you, or rather you must think of them, for if you don't there is the danger of finding them, in your mind, little by little. That is to say, you must think of them for a while, every day several times a day, until they sink forever in mud. That's an order.[54]

We will never know whether Joe will be able to kill those voices or if eventually they will drive him mad. The last direction – 'image fades but the voice continues whispering'[55] – only hints at the possibility that voices will endure.

5 Conclusion

Filming trauma involves a complex process: the event itself belongs to the past, but it affects the present. Thus, the explicit representation of a traumatic event in a film or visual arts will fail to depict its heterogeneous nature. Callaghan writes that '…as trauma cannot be represented by "normal", accessible means and must be instead depicted in such a way that the viewer can approach the work autonomously'. Vivian also discusses the question of an 'autonomous' gaze to observe trauma in reference to collage, and both, Callaghan and Vivian agree on a minimalistic abstraction as trauma representation. As such, the surface simplicity of *Eh Joe* may read as abstraction, trauma not explicitly filmed, but with a life of its own in the movie through varied filming devices.

In *Eh Joe* Samuel Beckett manages to portray this tangled relation between past and present through innovative television techniques: a body without a voice, invisibility of the owner of the voice or a voice without a body, partial inaudibility of the words towards the end, and the photogenicity of an intensely listening face, all of which have been analysed in this chapter. Based

54 Samuel Beckett, *The Unnamable. The Three Novels* (New York: Grove, 1958), 33.
55 Beckett, *Complete Dramatic Works*, 367.

on the principle of silent movies shot in black and white, the soundtrack of a whispering voice takes the spectator into the realm of the unreal and the unrepresentational, the very domain of trauma. A silent body in pain and a voice without a body, although intentionally separated, are intrinsically linked: one cannot survive without the other. The analysis of the disembodied voice, discussed as an acoustmêtre, has highlighted several of its functions. Theatrically, it becomes uprooted-from-the-body memory and Joe's painful consciousness. At the same time, the Voice acts as Joe's guide on his private path to hell. In form, it is used as a cinematographic device to represent dissociation. Lacking a body, the voice can travel between the two realms: past and present, creating a hallucinatory atmosphere in this play and bridging past and present.

Bibliography

Beckett, Samuel. *The Complete Dramatic Works*. London: Faber & Faber, 1986.

Beckett, Samuel, *The Unnamable. The Three Novels*. New York: Grove, 1958.

Caruth, Cathy. *Unclaimed Experience: Trauma, Narrative and History.* Baltimore and London: Johns Hopkins University Press, 1996.

Cohn, Ruby. *A Beckett Canon.* Ann Harbour: the University of Michigan Press, 2001.

Dante, Alighieri. *The Divine Comedy*. (vol. 20). Trans. Henry F. Cary New York: P.F. Collier and Son Corporation, 1965.

Freud, Sigmund. *Beyond The Pleasure Principle.* Trans. Stratchey, James. New York and London: W.W. Norton, 1961.

Gontarski, Stanley E. *A Companion to Samuel Beckett.* Oxford: Blackwell Publishing, 2010.

Knowlson, James. *Damned to Fame: The Life of Samuel Beckett.* London: Bloomsbury, 1997.

Malkin, Jeannette. *Memory-Theatre and Postmodern Drama.* Ann Harbour: the University of Michigan Press, 1999.

Rank, Otto. *El Trauma del Nacimiento*. Trans. H.F. de Saltzmann. Buenos Aires: Editorial Paidos, 1961.

Rodriguez-Gago, Antonia. 'The Embodiment of Memory (and Forgetting) in Beckett's Late Women's Plays'. In *Drawing in Beckett: Portraits, Performances and Cultural Contexts*, edited by Linda Ben-Zvi, 113–127. Tel Aviv: Assaph Books Series, 2003.

Yates, Frances, A. *The Art of Memory.* El Segundo, CA: Redwood Press, 1966.

Zarrilli, Philip B. 'Acting at "Nerve Ends": Beckett, Blau and the Necessary'. In *Theatre Topics* 7. Baltimore: the John Hopkins University, 1997.

CHAPTER 5

The Disturbance of Images

Paul Vivian

This study explores the appropriation of images, their fracture and unmaking in relation to the practice of collage. It attempts to identify a means of articulating the relationship of trauma occurring within an image, a trauma that results from the 'collage act', and concurrently its relation to forms of dramatic change via a corporeal reading of the image and intervention. 'Images are animated beings with desires, appetites. Demands and drives of their own', W.T.J. Mitchell asserts, adding that an image is internally operative, a totality demanding our attention, an assembly of persistence, a representation or record containing sense data that is animated within memory beyond the purely visual.[1] Vilëm Flusser, the philosopher, interprets the photographic image as signifying 'something "out there" in space and time that they have to make comprehensible to us as abstractions'.[2] We identify images in this way by acknowledging signification. In advertising for instance, meaning is established a priori, emphatically directed to establish communication as quickly as possible. Of course semiotics offers a long established form of reading an image. Ferdinand de Saussure (1857–1913) defines it as follows 'A science that studies the life of signs within society is conceivable. It would be part of social psychology and consequently of general psychology. I shall call it semiology (from Greek semeion "sign"). Semiology would show what constitutes signs, what laws govern them'.[3]

Slavoj Žižek makes the observation that a reassessment of Adorno's much quoted dictum that there can be no poetry after Auschwitz should now read as 'no prose after Auschwitz'. The problem of a post-holocaust world perhaps is that we must at all costs avoid attempts at realism. He proceeds to discuss the role of poetry in accurately abstracting this post-condition. The application of an 'explanation', Žižek believes, will never clarify the inexplicable. Instead in his words, the role of poetry itself is the most accurate means of articulating

1 Norman Bryson, *Artforum International Magazine,* November (2005): 408.
2 Vilém Flusser, *Towards a Philosophy of Photography* (London: Reaktion Books Ltd, 2012), 8.
3 Robert Stam, ed., *New Vocabularies in Film Semiotics* (London: Routledge, 1992), 4.

 | DOI:10.1163/9789004385931_006

an impossibility that Adorno views as barbarism. Again, to further this, Žižek draws on an old saying, 'that music comes in when words fail'. Further, he identifies the words of American poet Wallace Stevens, whose personal philosophy was firmly entrenched in the view that poetry's role is to be 'description without place'.[4] This description does not search for some illustrative rationalisation, a false account; it only functions as a means to create a form of abstraction, a poetic exploration.

A post-modernist outlook provides the most adequate means to deliberately and furtively seek a means by which not to illustrate or articulate the present or recent situation but actually to reveal its confusion and abhorrent logic. This key admittance, particularly for the arts, suggests that the role of any artist's practice is to present the inexplicable, not a simplistic answer to a problem. The emergence of DADA in 1916 illustrates the destabilising of the expressionist abstract representation of their present crisis i.e. the First World War. All this perhaps advances that one cannot convincingly actually represent, illustrate or confirm experiences of horror through realism. Following this approach one can discount forms of realism representing the world in a romantic context and alternatively perhaps the artist must submit to ideas such as 'atemporality', William Gibson's assessment of the nature of time and the subsequent multiplicities of history within the body of the Internet.[5]

Antonio Negri's assertion that philosophy has no function without action can be interpreted as our ability or requirement within the real world to process and enact conceptual ideas, an a priori that realises meaning. For Negri this belief is supported by an enthusiasm for art, though only at the moment it emerges as abstraction. Whilst exiled in France during the 1980s as a result of his alleged involvement in the kidnapping and murder of politician Aldo Moro, Negri wrote on the subject of Art. Through a series of letters Negri explores the nature of material and artistic production within a post-modern, post-Fordist context and re-examines the purpose of art in its present context. In his critique of modernism, Negri views the modern as an era that '...does not realise itself as a process but as an essence, it offers itself as result. The people of Papua, or Dersu Uzala enter the future of history, as of now. The pain is huge, the damage is incalculable. But this is the way it is. The modern is effectual, including the places where modernisation is not and it is this inverse relation between the time of the process and the effectuality of the result'. What Negri means when he says 'The modern is effectual' is that for the modernist the end result is primary, that it does not suffice. The discursive and

4 Slavoj Žižek, *Violence* (London: Profile Books, 2009), 5.

5 Bryant Griffiths, *Shifting Strands* (London: Sense Publishers, 2012), 42.

developmental, the potential for change, all aspects that become subsumed within the 'end result', have, during the post-modernist era provided possibilities for more open-ended artworks, an art perhaps more responsive and more sympathetic to the changing nature of society, sites, spaces and cultures and less about monument, masterpiece or icon, an art that is more philosophical.[6] In Negri's view the 'modern' removes all 'romantic possibility of understanding life as a seeking and truth as a product of a constructive dialectic'.[7] As a result of these views Negri sees abstraction as revealing a new quality of being. He goes on to explain that this revelation highlights an always present quality. In this context, he refers to the singularities of labour in creating a whole. As Negri states, this in itself is essentially abstract.

To return to Wallace Steven's view that poetry or fiction should serve the practice of 'description without place', Jacques Rancière in 'The Distribution of the Sensible: Politics and Aesthetics' returns to Plato, highlighting the Platonic view that the question of fiction amounts primarily to a question regarding the distribution of places. This 'atonal' process of art functions as a means of confronting an uncertain world. Perhaps never a means of feigning comprehension, the indeterminate nature of being or truth is perhaps central to the practice of art. In Stanislaw Lem's 'Solaris' and the well-known cinematic version by the great Russian director Andrei Tarkovsky, the planet and the focus of scientific investigation exists as a metaphor for our delusion of assumed understanding. Astronaut scientists locate a planet covered with a vast ocean; they consider the planet a living, conscious being. In order to attempt to control the planet they bombard the ocean with X-rays. However, they slowly realise the ocean actually irradiates the astronaut scientists themselves, manifesting before them memories of their past. These phantom images are so real that each in turn begins to distrust anything they see or believe. As one of the characters explains, "man has gone to other worlds and other civilizations without having explored his own labyrinth of dark passages and secret chambers, and without finding what lies behind doorways that he himself has sealed".[8] Furthermore, there is the understanding, a realisation, 'We have no need of other worlds. We need mirrors'.[9]

Whilst we have so far begun to introduce the idea of an art appropriate to reflecting the inexplicable, so far we have hinted at this as an intention of art, arts

6 Antonio Negri, *Art and Multitude* (London: Polity Press, 2011), 4.

7 Antonio Negri, *Art and Multitude* (London: Polity Press, 2011), 4.

8 Peter Swirski, *The Art and Science of Stanislaw Lem* (London: McGill-Queen's University Press), 163.

9 Lem Stanislaw, *Solaris* (London: Faber and Faber, 2003), 125.

methodology viewed or presented here as both poetic and necessary. This necessity in the field of collage comes from a desire to present an urgent response to the world of images or importantly 'appearances'. A tacit form of collage, the focus of this study, enables actions that perhaps controversially cannot be placed beneath a surface, as with a painting, print, image on a screen, photograph or photoshopped composition. However crude an observation, these approaches cannot, as processes, imitate or replace the perverse imposition, and pleasure of the hand interacting with the physical material of paper.

However, it is worth pausing and remembering that this essential concept of art has also been applied as a contemporary tool of political propaganda. In certain instances, it has served to maintain the autocratic Vladimir Putin, or as an indeterminate political system across Europe that has seen the distinctions of left and right blurred, resulting in the rise of extremist political ideologies. In itself this conceptual process has its origins in arts' own acceptance of the 'indeterminate' as a strategy for regarding the making and thinking around images and objects. Putin's appointment of Vladislav Surkov, the principal ideologist within the Kremlin, clearly illustrates this, with Russia's political situation often seen as a managed form of democracy.[10]

Surkov adopted a strategy of 'confusion' enacted by the Kremlin. He encouraged and provided support to both extremist left and extremist right elements of the political spectrum, becoming central to the recent ambiguities in Ukraine, a conflict that was or wasn't. However, all the time he proved extremely open about the enactment of this indeterminacy, or confusion. Surkov himself was influenced by the 'No Wave' conceptual art scene of the 1980s, based on a rejection of the orthodoxies propounded by the unsurprisingly named, more historically lauded 'New Wave' movement. Across music, visual art, film, fiction and theatre, No Wave proved more underground than widely popularist. In the visual arts, the movement put the emphasis upon indeterminacy, with no guiding stylistic framework, in short rejection for its own sake. Applied in the political field, Surkov could engineer a highly seductive strategy arguably currently imported in western politics and the media. Documentarian and commentator Adam Curtis calls this approach to News media, 'oh dearism'.[11]

This means the deliberate inference of confusion to nullify critique, and ultimately to maintain power. For instance, one could say that this methodology was actively applied during the Bosnian Serbian conflict and the second invasion of Iraq to ensure that political and military ideology was sustained by public opinion. With reference to these ideas one could argue that he Balkans

10 Al Campbell, dir. *Newswipe episode #1.3* (London: BBC, 2009) 8th April.

11 Ibid.

conflict was presented as a conflict of religious positions originating from the darkest medieval era. Viewed as a highly complex disagreement, this disinformation sought to both confuse and, eventually through public perception, justify a non-interventionist strategy by the rest of Europe. To the public this would play out as a conflict where one could not conveniently identify a villain, as there was no simple narrative. Meanwhile, mass genocide was occurring. Again with regards to Iraq, the narrative was presented in much more palatable terms. There was an aggressor, a central figure – Hussein – and a solution, the liberating western coalition, the Christian West as the heroic salvation of the Iraqi people. This narrative was played out even when the internal complexities of Iraq were equally as alienating to the popular imagination as those of the Balkans. A form of Wallace Steven's 'description without place' served to confuse the public and thereby pacify the need, or the call for intervention, in the Serbian-Bosnian conflict. So this chapter illustrates this model of abstraction applied externally from its origins within the arts, and specifically from forms of collage by presenting a distrustful model of trauma enacted for political ends. In the 1990s the Anglo-American attempts at re-westernising Afghanistan included expected capitalist models of self-interest and strangely, to encourage cultural appreciation, the educating of young Afghans on the complexities conceptual art.[12]

We should also focus upon this notion of indeterminacy. Rancière further explains that, within the context of what he terms the 'regime of politics', as a result of the 'structure-giving' forms emerging from art, a practice of artistic production reflects the indeterminacy of both the identities, and de-legitimation of speech and, finally, the deregulating partitions of space and time. In other words, this becomes for Rancière a platform for fantasy, a space to refuse any limit on possibility, enacting Plato's dramatic space. This refusal, the means for this indeterminacy, and by default trauma, is perhaps best illustrated by Dostoevsky's hero and narrator in *Notes from the Underground.* Ill and suffering with numerous ailments, the narrator denies help, stating,' I know very well I'm harming myself and no one else. But still, it's out of spite that I refuse to ask for the doctor's help. So my liver hurts? Good let it hurt even more'.[13]

---

12 In relation to her persuasive criticism of Ziad Doueiry's film adaptation of *The Attack*, Tarraf justifiably points out that in ignoring the complexities of Jewish and Arab ideological tensions, the film becomes a form of political sanitisation. This also appears in the US foreign policy context, with the 9/11 narratives of Bush and the later Cold War initiatives of Reagan, both fulfilling agendas that deliberately discounted the intricacies of the ethnic, religious and political in order to progress policy using 'fantasy' as leverage.

13 Cathy Caruth, ed., *Trauma: Explorations in Memory* (London and New Jersey: The John Hopkins University Press, 1995), 20–21.

The abstraction of an image deliberately forces indeterminacy as opposed to affording a forced or accidental by-product of artistic intervention. In contrast to the subjects in Susan Hiller's 2000 work 'Witness', All the participants or sampled voices experienced phenomena outside of their everyday experience. Within the work, subjects recall seeing UFOs or angels when confronted by inexplicable phenomena. They cannot help but rationalise these experiences with clichéd forms of the irrational. What art, and in the case the modus of collage, can achieve, is a form of stasis, a revelation and acknowledgement of impossibility, a space of indeterminacy that becomes a form of perceptual and emotional paralysis.

In approaching the space applicable to these ideas, my own research and practice began to locate the found image as a space already full, not to discount that a blank page, piece of paper or canvas cannot be full as Cégeste in Cocteau's *Orphée* with his blank book Poetry demonstrates.[14] At the outset, the photograph becomes an opposition to indeterminacy as it fixes the world in many ways. Hans Belting explains that a photograph is either 'a kind of replica of the world' or else 'an expression of the medium that created it'.[15] In itself a primary means of interpreting the world, photography informs memory and imagination, and Susan Sontag sees it as a grammar, informing an ethics of seeing. Vilem Flusser makes an important observation that photographs interpose themselves between the world and us. Instead of representing the world, they block it in order to make us a function of the images we create. In other words not a truth, they serves as a form of rationale that in effect perverts what we actually experience. Maurice Blanchot identifies the essence of a photograph as something consisting of a hidden yet manifest absence as presence.,[16] the absence suppressed by the 'image'. Belting also points out that photographic images symbolise our perception of the world and our remembrance of it.

Lacan's critiquing the practice of 'archive' is also worth remembering.[17] Élizabeth Roudinesco explains that Lacan viewed this as a limiting agent – the archive becomes something that places boundaries around knowledge and ignores the potential of indeterminacy, an indeterminacy in both knowledge itself and experience. History, in his view, is simply not fixed. An archive is overly certain of retaining all information required or that might be necessary to retain and store about a particular subject. The changing nature of photography,

---

14 Jean Cocteau, dir. *Orphee* (France: The Criterion Collection, 2008).

15 Hans Belting, *An Anthropology of Images* (New Jersey: Princeton University Press, 2011), 144.

16 Michael Bracewell et al., ed., *John Stezaker* (London:Whitechapel Gallery/Ridinghouse, 2011), 17.

17 Élizabeth Roundinesco, *In Spite of Everything: Lacan* (New York: Verso, 2014) 51.

as modernity confronted by an ever-more uncertain world, meant that as a means of capturing an external reality or truth photography became suspect and irrelevant. If anything, perhaps it could be said that photography serves as a token of the real, or perhaps a trace.

Visual art of course has sought to emulate the imprecise nature of memory; it could be argued that more recent explorations in theories, such as hauntology or retromania (the recycling of past histories in art and popular culture), contribute to revealing an alternative to the simplistic stories we tell ourselves, stories that previously presented a black-and-white narrative regarding ideas encompassing conflict, the social, ethnicity and religious paradigms. These theories only go to illustrate the creation of false narratives masquerading as prose. As Hito Steyerl puts it in her book *In Free Fall: A Thought Experiment on Vertical Perspective* we are effectively without horizon, without a stable paradigm of orientation.[18] A distinction however exists between the photograph and recollection, the popular misconception being that an image itself is functions as a manifestation of memory. A photograph may act as a means to activate memory, but is not itself memory. The lens, a filtering apparatus sees a totality, a whole, whereas memory is itself fragmented, surrounded and pock marked with blacked out areas, zones of resistance.

The practice of collage has become a means of addressing the illusionary and problematic role of photography. Artists have utilised the apparatus of iconoclasm, a mechanism of fundamentalist belief, as a means of returning the image to the 'real'. The surrealists responded to the image and collage as perversions; prosthesis or apparitions works were modelled upon forms of delirium, or plays on fantasy. Opposed to an emancipation of life, many artists have utilised collage to reconnect the image to the indeterminacies of the real. Hito Steyral asserts that 'discipline is a form of conflict', referring here to artistic practice.[19]

A reading of German artist Hannah Hoch's practice, for instance, could be framed in the sense that it made no point to retreat to pure aestheticism. Art was for her an allegorical mechanism to disturb the surface of an image, to distribute the elements of the photographic image. The manipulation of images, their transformation via haptic processes contrasts the editing of images via digital media or through an interface. The essential difference in these two approaches lies in the role of the body. Physical actions, together with that of the

18 Hito Steyerl, *In Free Fall: A thought experiment on vertical perspective* (London: E-Flux press, 2012), 1.

19 Florian Dombois, et al., *Intellectual Birdhouse: Artistic Practice as Research* (London: Koenig Books, 2012), 55–62.

intellect, assume or create an affirmation of authorship, an imposition. This approach results in an actual tacit association connected with critical intent.

In this, the artist aims at a manipulation classifiable as a form of trauma so that the viewers' gaze observes the trauma of the image. As the recent survey at Tate Britain 'Art under Attack', curated by Tanitha Barber and Stacy Boldrick demonstrated, the practice of iconoclasm underscores many of the motivations and developments within the history of art.[20] Surrounded by images, we engage in a relationship of immersion. The image by its very nature is not an inanimate representation, but a charged surface, in both the content and natural association. Whether imposed, or embedded, image is a form of appearance that requires analysis. It requires us to look and engage.

The specific manipulation of images for media/press purposes is well known. Images can become constructed to play on our concern, empathy and ethical guilt. In actuality (the real) this disassembling of appearances, like Surkov's application of 'No Wave' conceptual practices within the Kremlin, has consequences, as we have already established. In 1993 during the Bosnian-Serbian conflict the destruction of the Stari Most Bridge in Mostar held a particular place in the social and historical culture of the city – not a military strategic target but a symbol and hub for this once cosmopolitan city. Couples met, courted and married on this bridge. Such an action effected an undoing of memory, not simply the destruction of a way into and from the city, but an assault on collective memory.

The collage act, the breaking of images in relation to this context, focuses on refashioning the communication of memory encompassed within the body of an image or images. This differs from a simple act of decorative aesthetic modification or enhancement; it functions as a deliberate critical act of undoing. By way of explanation we can return to Rancière's assertion of an affect resulting in mirroring the indeterminacy of identities, the de-legitimation of speech and the deregulation of partitions of space and time.[21] The production upon, and affecting of, images can primarily disturbs collective or personal memory. The photograph, and what it portrays, can be resisted through the altering of an image in what appears to be an act of transgression itself. In any conflict, the abuse of monuments, images and cultural property act as a by-product of protest and resistance.

Central to its primary thesis, 'Art under Attack' demonstrates the persistence of methods that emphasise the destruction of the inanimate as a means

---

20 Tabitha Barker, et al., *Art Under Attack: Histories of British Iconoclasm* (London: Tate Publishing, 2014), 9.

21 Jacques Rancière, *The Politics of Aesthetics* (London: Bloomsbury Revelations, 2013), 9.

to save the living. The exhibition itself provided numerous examples of these actions whether motivated by political or religious intention. The disassembling of an icon or image exemplified transcend a simple act of vandalism; in some cases, particularly in the twentieth century, they are contextualised as the only means of protest to fight oppression.

The practice of collage lies at the heart of historical and contemporary artistic forms of iconoclasm. Collage functions as a peripheral activity in the practice of the artist. Like drawing, it can occasionally be seen less as an apparatus of critique and more as a form of contingent image making, a cheerful recycling of materials sourced from some form of residue and/or excess. Yet the practice itself has been a form of visual and critical response to major conflicts since the First World War. It has played a significant role in providing a voice for dissent. One could also argue that the work of the great German artist John Heartfield evidences the role collage played in providing an altruistic and disobedient voice. Nearly seventy years later with manipulated photographs and magazine fashion spreads Martha Rosler's 'Bringing the War Home' made visual, the distance in perception and awareness of the conflict in Iraq, a perception and awareness not bridged by extensive ideologically driven media coverage. As Lacan states 'truth shows itself in a fictional structure'.[22] This could be argued to be collage's starting point.

When we come to examine the transformation of images, the role of collage is bound to any consideration with its origins founded upon the disassembling of the pictorial surface. Not concerned with utopian ideals of progress, collage presents a chaotic vision of the present, a complexity drawn from the insistence of an overbearing visual world, like the rejection of civilisation witnessed by Norman Lewis in Naples after its liberation in 1944, documented in his book *Naples '44*.[23] The traumatising of the image allows us to respond to an excess and to a residual tide of visual information. Collage can disrupt the passivity of our gaze, formed by coercion, or compliance, by means of an images code. As Žižek explains 'Fantasy is a screen that protects us from the real'.[24]

Collage, in a very real sense, is a means of 'making sense', a means of understanding trauma itself, like JG Ballard's collection of short stories – 'The Atrocity Exhibition'. As Ballard explains, the application of an erroneous association to the death of John F Kennedy, a motor race, is not so much a slur, or an act of

22 Jacques Lacan, *Ecrits* (New York: W.W. Norton & Company, 2007), 742.

23 John Gray, *The Silence of Animals* (London: Penguin, 2014), 17.

24 Mathew Flisfeder, et al., *Zizek and Media Studies: A reader* (London: Palgrave Macmillan, 2014), 133.

vandalism, but as Ballard explains 'it was an attempt for me to make sense of that tragic event.'[25]

Freud theorised that an aggressive instinct keeps threatening civilised society. Freud himself acknowledged that the external world prompts these acts of violence, that it 'can rage against us with the most powerful and pitiless forces of destruction'. Potentially a mimesis of conditions, collage acts from the external world and contextualises these conditions through the manipulation of images. Collage also provides an apparatus to respond to the play of appearances within a source image.[26]

It is worth noting that the advent of 'collage', in its original translations, innocently means 'to glue', and coincides with the First World War arriving as it did in the early 1910s. This perfectly illustrates Freud's Death Drive theory, and, with a newly established European Avant Garde, becomes the epitome of an artist's response to the chaos of that conflict and its follow-up in 1938. The First World War promoted a means of divergence, instigating the death drive, leading artists to attack images with the apparatus of social iconoclasm. An important aspect of this lies in the agitation from outside, an external pressure that instigates the dismantling and disassembling of an image, as Freud suggests. One can easily consider that memory and images themselves intertwine and that this symbiotic relationship is only agitated when one discusses photography in the context of memory. Memory and images promote a form of solipsism, a preoccupation with our own emotional state, as we mostly view images from an egocentric point of view.

As a fixing of time and place, Roland Barthes describes the photographic image as violent in that 'it fills the sight by force' nothing being 'refused or transformed'.[27] In other words photography in itself acts as an antagonist of memory.[28] It resists the inconsistency and flow of recollected images. Barthes importantly questions a photograph's ability to record actuality, the impossibility of representing a present moment. An image, for instance, can of course itself be a record of suffering, such as Donald McCullin or Franke Eigen's images of war crimes in Kosovo. It can perhaps present an image that may defy

---

25 J.G. Ballard, *The Atrocity Exhibition* (New York: Flamingo Modern Classics, 2006).

26 Sigmund Freud, *Civilisation and its Discontents* (Chrysoma Associates Ltd ebook, 2000–2005), 8.

27 Elizabeth A. Castelli, et al., *Interventions: Activists and Academics respond to Violence* (London; Palgrave Macmillan, 2004), 39.

28 In Antropova's chapter regarding Beckett's *Eh Joe*, the voice is read accurately as an acoustmêtre, a presence without location or body. In this sense, photography's illusory substance, an image resting within a paper surface or existing on screen mirrors the disembodied voice acting as Joe's 'provocateur of memory'.

intervention, such as a lynching in a Southern American state, Abu Ghraib humiliations, or the scratch marks lining the walls of a gas chamber in Auschwitz. In such instances the photograph perhaps presents a reality stripped of appearances. In the first instance, though, these intolerable images offer a disruption of illusion, an objection to representation, shock in their authenticity.[29] Yet the nature of photography both reveals its power, and its powerlessness. Concurrently, artist Richard Prince, whose work engages 'found' images, identifies the potential for the image or the photograph to be the 'virtuoso real', an image that in some way may contain the possibility of truth.[30] This truth is in a sense the potential for not simply a veil of appearances; it does not exclude images of moral horror but includes the potential for commercially produced images to have some semblance of 'truth', as with images that function within ideological frameworks of consumerism.

Returning to images of horror, whether those of Abu Ghraib or Auschwitz, this impenetrable 'truth' perhaps has found itself wounded by adaptation and repetition. Paul Virilio, recalling his friend Jacqueline Lichtenstein viewing 'piles of suitcases, ... mounds of dentures and eyeglasses' at Auschwitz, expressed surprised at how unmoved she was. He could not understand how Lichtenstein failed to be overwhelmed. She exclaimed that to her these remnants of lives appeared as if in a contemporary art museum.

The Internet, contributes to a saturation of visual media unprecedented in our lifetime. However a question remains as to whether this emancipation in images through a more improved dispersion actually enables us to become closer to the real, through their horror intensified by revealing more, or whether this dispersion ends up creating a distance and passivity.

In the 2000 exhibition, 'Without Sanctuary', a collection of snapshots and postcards from the late 1800s through to 1968, provided an exhibition that spanned America's legacy of racist vigilante fuelled murder. These visual documents evidently become more horrific and more present when the image is transposed to the throwaway context of a postcard. In essence, the postcard 'translation' cemented the nature of evil, intensifying their casual recording. In a sense these adaptations of the image functioned in essence as a form of collage.[31]

29 In Mark Callaghan's chapter, a penetrating examination of Maya Lin's Vietnam War memorial he cites Dori Laub's theory that any significant trauma causes a temporal cessation of comprehensible representation.

30 David Evans, *Appropriation* (London: Whitechapel Press, 2009), 85.

31 As 'Without Sanctuary' testifies, following a lynching's aftermath the role of an image as souvenir further dehumanised each victim. Itakura's chapter 'Re–imagining Atomic

The essential element of any critique or consideration of photography is in its range of illusion. Photography acts as a simulation, particularly when one considers the predominance of digital manipulation and the transformation of images within news and entertainment media. A popular example of this illusion occurs within the Ridley Scott film adaptation of the Phillip K Dick novel 'Do Androids dream of Electric Sleep'.[32] In Bladerunner, replicants, human-like cyborgs, are provided with false memories and false images. For instance, each replicant receives snapshots of a family to consolidate and confirm a memory that never existed, a construction validating a life never lived. Rheims Cathedral could be seen as a totality of medieval architecture destroyed in the First World War, becoming terrifyingly fragmented – its frame, ornament and function, a metaphor for the aesthetic unity of an image and in violence, its parts, its code, widely dispersed. As Mao states, 'There must be destruction in order for there to be construction'.[33]

Massimiliano Gioni, a curator of New Museum New York's 'The Un-monumental Picture' addresses the intention of collage well 'When real bodies explode in the streets of Baghdad and the acts of submission and torture we thought only possible in the fantasy of the Marquis de Sade are carried out in military prisons and transmitted by TV around the world, a new strange space of representation seems to emerge where the distinction between hyper-reality and surrealism is completely blurred ... there are artists who try to contrast these visions by using collage to make sense of the insanity'[34] Gioni goes on to describe collage as a 'Dirty medium, infected as it is by waste, it appropriates residues and leftovers, trafficking with what is deemed to be valueless'.[35]

The very first collages produced during Picasso and Braque's radical development of Cubism presented fractured surfaces and forms that depicted generally squalid still lives. These evoked spaces at the periphery of the everyday. Occasionally inset into these combined visual elements of paint and contingent materials, newspaper fragments referenced reports of the First World War. The nature of collage very much resembles that of a Trojan horse activity enabling the secreting of messages and information. Its presence as a medium is an essential critical tool; it mirrors the fractured and fragmented nature of the external world. Cubist collage was essentially of and from the world, with

Bomb and 9/11' highlights the pejorative term 'Hibakusha' a dialectical means of devaluing the individual from, the social to semiotic sign, in this case identified as 'a survivor'.

32 Ridley Scott, dir. *Bladerunner* (U.S.: Warner Brothers, 1981).

33 Mao Zedong, *The Red Book* (San Francisco: China Books & Periodicals Inc.,1910).

34 Richard Flood, Massimiliano Gioni and Laura J. Hoptman, *Collage: The Unmonumental Picture* (New York: New Museum, 2007) 13.

35 Ibid., 11.

its representational forms constructed from everyday materials, a frame bordering an image, itself imitating the window like presentation of images, constructed from wallpaper.

Throughout his conversations with Sylvère Lotringer published as 'The Accident of Art', Paul Virilio explains that art provides a stripping of appearances, an embracing of uncertainty. His views acknowledge that what we perceive as absolute is unbelievable unless it is brought to our attention. In order to do this, the artist must essentially traumatise the image and thereby confront the viewer. The breaking or editing of an image acknowledges the fact that memory, supposedly fixed by an image, can, by the intervention and imposition of collage, serve as a metaphor for traumatic experiences encountered by the body or the unknowing of the self and its body. Collage's traumatising act thus becomes an art of, and for, our time. If we take the example of Hamlet's father's ghost's arrival, this becomes in a sense a moment where, for Hamlet, time is unhinged. This unhinging is essentially caused by the 'critical', namely the spectre that actively disturbs the unsuspecting mortal subject such as Hamlet and us. For Hamlet this is a seismic rupture. Hamlet begins to question, and for the first time, he therefore begins to doubt.

In considering collage and Derrida's thesis, I feel it must be reversed. The image is out of time, half dead, zombie-like, unreal. The intervention or addition functions as the living element. This action unhinges or activates the image, making it present. Trauma becomes a form of awakening, necessary to enact a critical artistic response, one that Virilio states is our current inability to think beyond a future violence or catastrophe. We are all perhaps in a state of mistrust; simple stories and fables have no useful function in the context of the indeterminate mosaic-like complexities activating our current political, environmental and social circumstance. Addressing the image via physical intervention this acts, if anything, as a metaphor for external disorder beneath, what is, and was previously, presented as certain.

Bibliography

Allen, James, John Lewis, Leon F. Litwack, Hilton Als. *Without Sanctury: Lynching Photography in America.* New Mexico: Twin Palms Publishers, 1999.

Barthes, Roland. *CameraLucida*. London: Vintage, 2000.

Barthes, Roland. *The Pleasure of the Text.* New York: Hill and Wang, 1975.

Belting, Hans. *An Anthropology of Images: Picture, Medium, Body*. Princeton NJ: Princeton University Press, 2011.

Brockelman, Thomas. *The Frame and the Mirror: On Collage and Postmodernism.* Illinois: Northwestern University Press, 2001.

Caruth, Cathy, ed. *Trauma: Explorations in Memory.* London and New Jersey: The John Hopkins University Press, 1995.

Curtis, Adam. *Oh Dearism and the Non Linear War.* UK: BBC, 2009.

Derrida, Jacques. *The Specters of Marx: The State of the Debt, the Work of Mourning and the New International.* London: Routledge, 2006.

Dillon, Brian. *Ruins.* London: Whitechapel Gallery, 2011.

Dombois, Florian, Ute Meta Bauer, Claudia Mareis and Michael Schwab. *Intellectual Birdhouse: Artistic Practice as Research.* London: Koenig Books, 2012.

Douglas, Caroline and Kate Brindley. *Transmitter Receiver: The Persistence of Collage.* London: Hayward Gallery Publishing, 2011.

Elden, Stuart. *The Birth of Territory.* Chicago and London: University of Chicago Press, 2013.

Evans, David, ed. *Appropriation.* London: Whitechapel Gallery, 2009.

Gray, John. The Silence of Animals. London: Penguin, 2014.

Flood, Richard, Massimiliano Gioni and Laura J. Hoptman. *Collage: The Unmonumental Picture.* New York: New Museum, 2007.

Flusser, Vilëm, *Towards a Philosophy of Photography.* London: Reaktion Books, 2000.

Gamboni, Dario. *The Destruction of Art: Iconoclasm and Vandalism since the French Revolution.* London: Reaktion Books, 1997.

Klanten, Robert, Hendrik Hellige and James Gallagher, eds. *Cutting Edges: Contemporary Collage.* Berlin: Die Gestalten Verlag, 2011.

Lem, Stanislaw. *Solaris.* London: Faber and Faber, 2003.

Lotringer, Sylvere. *The Accident of Art.* Los Angeles: Semiotext, 2005.

Lütticken, Sven. *Idols of the Market: Modern Iconoclasm and the Fundamentalist Spectacle.* Berlin: Sternberg Press, 2009.

Mitchell, W.T.J. *What do Pictures Want? The Lives And Loves Of Images.* Chicago and London: University of Chicago Press, 2005.

Rancière, Jacques. *The Future of the Image.* Translated by Gregory Elliott. London: Verso Books, 2009.

Rancière, Jacques. *The Emancipated Spectator.* London: Verso, 2009.

Rancière, Jacques. *The Politics of Aesthetics.* London: Verso, 2004.

Stezaker, John, Dawn Ades and Michael Bracewell. *John Stezaker.* London: Whitechapel Gallery, 2011.

Sontag, Susan. *Regarding the Pain of Others.* London: Penguin, 2004.

Taylor, Brandon. *Collage: The Making of Modern Art.* London: Thames and Hudson, 2006.

Žižek, Slavoj. *Violence.* London: Profile Books, 2009.

PART 2

Creativity and Trauma Recovery

CHAPTER 6

Shaping Personality through Suffering: The Transformative Writing of Pat MacEnulty

Kate Burton

Life, believe, is not a dream
So dark as sages say;
Oft a little morning rain
Foretells a pleasant day.

Sometimes there are clouds of gloom,
But these are transient all;
If the shower will make the roses bloom,
O why lament its fall?

CHARLOTTE BRONTË, *'Life'*[1]

∵

Brontë's quasi-romantic poem written in 1839 when Charlotte was twenty-three provides an apt entry point from which to begin this chapter. 'Life' exudes a sense of spiritual yearning, of our individual journeys as an unavoidable, yet beautiful, struggle. Pat MacEnulty's novels and short stories document this paradox. She openly and frequently references her writing as a form of therapy, and keenly acknowledges its transformative potential and spiritual significance:

> Transformative writing is writing that seeks to connect, understand, and illuminate. Although transformative writing is therapeutic, it's not *just* that. Transformative writing strives for a level of artistry that, to borrow from Faulkner, uplifts our souls. Transformative writing may inform, it

1 Charlotte Brontë, 'Life' in *The Poems of Charlotte Brontë* (*Currer Bell*) (London: Forgotten Books, 2012), 81.

 | DOI:10.1163/9789004385931_007

> may entertain, and it may heal, but it also does something more. It connects to and transmits something of our human/divine nature.[2]

From trauma, to self-destructive behaviour, and beyond, MacEnulty uses the literary to navigate territories of suffering in her quest towards self-awareness. Hers is a journey pervaded by the 'dark clouds' and 'gloom' of which Brontë speaks, while her writing seeks to articulate the chaos of life as she works towards accepting its flows.

MacEnulty's early writing predominantly depicts the radical and progressive era of 1970s America. She situates drug addiction at the centre of her response to social concerns regarding the (re)construction and practice of self in the face of traumatic experience. Her emergence onto the literary scene in 2002 saw critics describe her work as attention grabbing due to the powerful representation of her overriding themes of 'corruption,' 'depravity,' 'abuse' and 'violence.'[3] Despite positive, but often brief and biographically-oriented, reviews of her early publications, no extended scholarly research on MacEnulty's writing exists: interviews with the author, and book reviews serve as the only consideration of her work. Some, though, have an incisive character. Without expressly giving her debut novel, *Sweet Fire,* a generic category, reviews frequently refer to it as a novel with both dark and gritty content. The *Sun Sentinel* suggests that '*Sweet Fire* is part novelist memoir, part crime fiction, part coming of age novel.'[4] Whilst the *Guardian Unlimited* acknowledges that 'MacEnulty can write and if *Sweet Fire* smacks of art as therapy, her lean, easy prose propels her story beyond the personal, making for more than convincing fiction.'[5] *The Language of Sharks* was also favourably received by critics: *The Observer* labelled the book as having a 'disciplined prose that no one will be

2 Pat MacEnulty, 'Sunday Sermon: Writing as Spiritual Practice,' *Open Salon*, 11 March 2012, viewed 30 March 2013, http://open.salon.com/blog/pat_macenulty/2012/03/11/sunday_sermon_writing_as_spiritual_practice. MacEnulty's insistence that her writing is a spiritual practice that serves as a catalyst to overcome trauma, calls to mind Hinton's chapter on resiliency. Hinton similarly highlights that spirituality can be a successful strategy to overcome and transform traumatic experience; it helps to foster resilience in the face of adversity.

3 John Sears, 'Crawling from the Wreckage: *The Language of Sharks* by Pat MacEnulty' (book review), *Pop Matters*, 11 May 2004, viewed 20 January 2010, <http://www.popmatters.com/review/language-of-sharks/>.

4 Oline Cogdill, Book Review of *Sweet Fire*, *South Florida Sun-Sentinel*, 8 June 2003, viewed 20 January 2010, <http://patmac.webs.com/sweetfirehtm>.

5 Hephzibah Anderson, 'A Junkie Comes of Age' (book review), *Guardian Unlimited*, 1 February 2003, viewed 20 January 2010, <http://patmac.webs.com/sweetfirehtm>.

able to read without thinking of Hemingway'[6] while *Kirkus Reviews* described the short stories as a series of emotive 'short, sharp jabs.'[7]

Although both *The Language of Sharks* and *Sweet Fire* defy simple genre categorisation, these texts can be considered complex trauma narratives. Trauma is detectable not only as acts wilfully inflicted by others, such as Trish's abduction by her estranged alcoholic father in *Sweet Fire,* but also in the tormented psyche of bright but disillusioned female characters who experience social isolation and alienation; or what could more appropriately be termed a 'traumatology of loneliness.' This isolation results from an unusual level of self-perception, of being Other, a state which frequently occurs in individuals with high levels of giftedness and creativity. MacEnulty's characters haunt the fringes of society and repetitively lament their lack of a real sense of belonging. Traumatised female protagonists use drugs as an archetypal defence mechanism to escape the suffering of an existence built on the foundations of a dysfunctional childhood, disturbing adolescent encounters, and an over-arching and painful sense of difference.

Following trauma, whether this is abuse, abandonment, or the pain of social difference and marginalisation, and irrespective of its perceived level of severity, MacEnulty's sensitive and intense protagonists undertake a nomadic journeying of the self in an attempt to find their soul, or to retrieve their inner child; a journey not unlike MacEnulty's scriptotherapeutic process. MacEnulty's writing is a space for working through her trauma; each text is a site of healing.

1 The Voice of the Wounded

As Laurie Vickroy states, 'Testifying to the past has been an urgent task for many fiction writers as they attempt to preserve personal and collective memories from assimilation, repression or misrepresentation.'[8] Furthermore, trauma fiction 'reflects a growing awareness of the effects of catastrophe and oppression on the individual psyche.'[9] For MacEnulty, Trish in *Sweet Fire,* like many of her characters, functions as a conduit to explore such memories. In interviews, MacEnulty candidly reveals her childhood and personal experiences of

6 David Mattin, Book Review of *The Language of Sharks, The Observer*, 21 March 2004, viewed 20 January 2010, <http://www.theguardian.com/books/2004/mar/21/features.review4>.

7 Book Review of *The Language of Sharks, Kirkus Reviews*, 15 March 2004, viewed 20 January 2010, <https://www.kirkusreviews.com/book-reviews/pat-macenulty/the-language-of-sharks/>.

8 Laurie Vickroy, *Trauma and Survival in Contemporary Fiction* (Charlottesville: University of Virginia Press, 2002), 1.

9 Ibid.

trauma. Whilst the material she writes for *Salon*, an online news and entertainment website, provides insight into the themes that insistently and repetitively resurface in her writing. Caruth classically asserts that 'a rethinking of reference is aimed not at eliminating history but at resituating it in our understanding, that is, at precisely permitting *history* to arise where *immediate understanding* may not.'[10] This statement holds not only when examining *Sweet Fire* but facilitates an understanding of the development of MacEnulty's oeuvre.

The collected stories in *The Language of Sharks* provide episodic glimpses into the trauma that MacEnulty openly discusses in interviews, and later references explicitly in her memoir *Wait Until Tomorrow* (2011). However, MacEnulty's novels and short stories juxtapose self-disclosed instances of trauma, like the rape of her mother, against material that she has not openly referenced, such as protagonists who work as call girls, lured by the easy access to drugs afforded by their pimps and clients. Regardless of what is autobiography and what is fictional embellishment, echoes of trauma haunt MacEnulty's fiction. Even in the fast paced thriller, *Time to Say Goodbye* (2005), whose protagonist, Patsy Palmer, MacEnulty states is nothing like her,[11] memories of abandonment resurface in a fragmented fashion throughout the narrative, as Patsy attempts to process the effects of her isolation. Thus MacEnulty's writing serves as a process of transformation and 'working through' for the author. Novels such as *Time to Say Goodbye* (2005), *From May to December* (2007) and *Picara* (2009) are comparatively more plot focussed than driven by the sense of authorial voice that prevails in MacEnulty's earlier work, yet parallels with the author's life clearly appear. As Caruth asserts, narratives of trauma offer

> a literary dimension that cannot be reduced to the thematic content of the text or to what the theory encodes, and that, beyond what we can know or theorize about ... [they] stubbornly persist in bearing witness to some forgotten wound.[12]

MacEnulty's writing builds on this premise: her 'literary dimension' encompasses her entire career trajectory. She insistently returns to the site of trauma, creating a bricolage of narratives that attest to the referential force of such events on her life.

---

10 Cathy Caruth, *Unclaimed Experience: Trauma, Narrative and History* (Baltimore and London: The Johns Hopkins University Press, 1996), 11.

11 See MacEnulty's Amazon profile page: <http://www.amazon.com/Pat-MacEnulty/e/B001K8ERXC/ref=dp_byline_cont_pop_book_1> (viewed 17 June 2010).

12 Caruth, *Unclaimed Experience*, 5.

Heavily influenced by Caruth, Anne Whitehead notes the conceptualisation of trauma in fiction:

> Novelists have frequently found that the impact of trauma can now adequately be represented by mimicking its forms and symptoms, so that temporality and chronology collapse, and narratives are characterised by repetition and indirection. Trauma fiction overlaps with and borrows from both postmodern and postcolonial fiction in its self-conscious deployment of stylistic devices as modes of reflection or critique.[13]

Trauma fiction mimics the symptomatology of trauma at a formal level, and for MacEnulty this mimicking spans not only individual texts, but is recognisable when considering a broader overview of her publications. Her career development documents the scriptotherapeutic process at work. A crisis of personal history appears: texts ricochet between acknowledging traumatic experience and hiatuses of repression; narratives are disjointed and lack an obvious linear flow. This model of a non-relational temporal relationship to the past resembles Freud's *Nachträglichkeit.* A form of possession or haunting, a ghost of remembering is detectable throughout MacEnulty's texts; and her writing uncovers, and subsequently exorcises, these traumatic memories.

The short stories in *The Language of Sharks* offer a series of disconnected and fragmented memories woven together with recurrent themes of abuse, self-destruction, addiction, and finally, redemption. Pieced together, these fragments constitute a whole of sorts, albeit a whole shattered both in temporal representation and structure. *The Language of Sharks* repeatedly attempts to tell what appears to be the same story. As Richard Rhodes attests, 'Repetition is the mute language of the abused child'[14] and whilst MacEnulty's versions may differ in protagonist and setting, they repeatedly attempt to grapple with an intimate and personal awareness of trauma. Her characters exist in a dimension where states of dissociation are frequently experienced: a dimension born from the chaos of traumatic experience. *Sweet Fire* may offer these chaotic and fragmented narratives with a greater sense of structure than MacEnulty's short story collection, yet repetition and absence of linearity still

---

13 Anne Whitehead, *Trauma Fiction* (Edinburgh: Edinburgh University Press, 2004), 3.

14 Richard Rhodes in Judith Herman, *Trauma and Recovery: The Aftermath of Violence from Domestic Abuse to Political Terror* (New York: Basic Books, 1997), 110–111. Similarly, this manifestation of trauma as part of the creative process is echoed in France Forcier's chapter. France Forcier acknowledges the compulsion to repetitively re-enact the trauma and the repeated emergence of dissociative states in her work as both professional dancer and choreographer.

characterise the novel. Structured around the memories of traumatised protagonist, Trish, the narrative reflects the disordered inner turmoil of a life built around a central core of abandonment, repeated traumatic experience and a drug-addled existence.

To return to *The Language Sharks*, 'Blue Abstraction,' the first story in the collection is powerfully effective in spite of, or perhaps because of, its brevity. If only slightly in excess of one page, MacEnulty paints a tremendously compelling and savage picture of a dysfunctional marriage. Using art as a metaphor for life, the story examines the traumatic instability of the relationship between a philandering musician and his wife, whom he abandons during her pregnancy, from the perspective of their unborn child. After returning home 'forehead gashed and bloody' because his student and lover has 'thrown a metronome at him,' the narrator's mother is left 'wondering whether life was worth the effort.'[15] This story not only evokes MacEnulty's own childhood abandonment but calls to mind the pain she later suffers when abandoned by her own partner whilst pregnant with their daughter. Concluding with the conception of MacEnulty's narrator, 'Blue Abstraction' ends as if it has only just begun:

> They had not kissed in months. He followed her to the room at the back of the apartment, fell with her into the bed and brushed his hand against her skin, swirled his fingers over her fine dark hair. While de Kooning worked late, creating a bright colossus of colors, letting ropes of oil paint drip from stiff brushes, one of my father's sperm permeated a seed, leaving the rest to drip along the white canvas of her thigh. Ah, but his pupil returned, and he left for good a few weeks later.[16]

MacEnulty's reference to de Kooning, an artist with a similarly distressing childhood, and an area subsequently explored in his art,[17] further highlights her acknowledging the necessity of creation as a response to the pain and destruction of traumatic experience. 'Blue Abstraction' serves as a prelude to the stories that follow, as the narrative explores the space that remains following the desertion of 'daddy.'

Abandonment is the first of a series of traumas represented in *The Language of Sharks*. The other stories in the collection, in turn, continue the traumatic paradigm by exploring the emotions and behaviour that result from the trauma

15 Pat MacEnulty, *The Language of Sharks* (London: Serpent's Tail, 2004), 1.

16 Ibid., 2.

17 John Elderfield, *De Kooning: A Retrospective; [published in conjunction with the Exhibition de Kooning: a Retrospective, at The Museum of Modern Art, New York (September 18, 2011–January 9, 2012)]* (New York: Museum of Modern Art, 2011), 50.

of infantile abandonment and neglect. The second story in *The Language of Sharks*, 'Floating on the Darkness,' continues the theme of paternal desertion. Yet, Lillian reflects on not only the loss of her father but her resulting fear that she will be abandoned again. Following an argument regarding Lillian's academic future and her mother storming out of the house in frustration, Lillian lays bare her deep-seated fear that anyone she is close to could desert her at any time,

> Maybe she wouldn't come back. People had disappeared – my father when I was six, my step-father ten years later. Just like *Star Trek* characters dissolving into molecular patterns on the transport pad.[18]

Such scenes of vulnerability and angst pervade MacEnulty's texts, anticipating the coping mechanisms later employed by protagonists in their struggle to survive.

'Floating on the Darkness' provides an example of MacEnulty's repetitive and insistent exploration of the concept of vicarious trauma. Unable to contain the psychological ramifications of the brutality she experiences at the hands of her partner, Lillian's mother forces her to bear witness to her traumatised and impoverished emotional state, 'He tried to kill me. Sometimes I wish he had,'[19] her mother laments. Grappling with the legacy of her mother's trauma burdens Lillian with a sense of enormous responsibility. The assimilation of the pain of the mother is integrated into Lillian's identity, marking her desire to ameliorate and exorcise it. Importantly, Lillian idolises and revers the mother figure; the mother-daughter bond is powerful and enmeshed, with a strong sense of shared personal history, as Lillian attests:

> It seemed as if she had always been with me even when I was by myself, like that long cord that keeps the astronauts from floating off into oblivion when they leave the space ship.[20]

Their relationship provides a mutually dependent source of love and protection, in spite, or perhaps increasingly because of, the idea that the violence of the father figure may sever their relationship at any time: 'He had wanted to take my mother away from me, to leave me all alone.'[21]

---

18 MacEnulty, *The Language of Sharks*, 6.
19 Ibid., 11.
20 Ibid.,13.
21 Ibid.

Inspired by witnessing the rape of her mother at the age of nine, 'Some Place to Live' constructs a further space in which MacEnulty explores the effects of bearing witness to the trauma of the mother. The story centres on Joey, a young boy forced to run for help after a man breaks into the family home and violently rapes his mother. The narrative is constructed from a series of flashbacks that Joey experiences in the aftermath of the trauma. Joey's memory of his mother's assault continues to intrude into his consciousness; violent eruptions of the past force their way into the present triggered by the free association of everyday objects:

> In the car, Aileen has her baby doll. She has undressed it and laid it on the back seat between them. Joey thinks back to that night again, running through the house ahead of Mr Watson, the quiet emptiness of the living room, the book face down on the floor, the dishes still piled in the kitchen sink, and the back door broken inwards, splintered at the hinges, open the wrong way. And the sounds from outside rustling and panting like wild dogs and his mother crying…
>
> He takes Aileen's blanket and covers the doll.[22]

Joey's intrusive re-experiencing of his mother's rape functions like the replaying of a short fragment of movie; a movie that hisses a haunting and distressing soundtrack that refuses language. Such flashbacks can be viewed as a 'prenarrative,'[23] a space in which Joey cannot yet fully interpret or integrate the series of events that haunt him. Joey's covering of the doll begins the defensive disavowal of the painful memories stemming from that night.

Dissociating these memories affords Joey the temporary ability to forestall the overwhelming psychic pain of the traumatic experience. However, undigested fragments of the traumatic experience function like Charcot's 'parasites of the mind,' and despite the brevity of the story Joey soon begins to recover a narrative that enables him to reconstruct the shattered inner schemata of his psyche:

> Aileen says the purple marker is the princess. Joey builds the boundaries of a castle for the princess out of pencils.
>
> Here is the living room, he says. He makes an opening for the front door.

22 Ibid., 170.

23 Judith Herman, *Trauma and Recovery: The Aftermath of Violence from Domestic Abuse to Political Terror* (New York: Basic Books, 1997), 175.

> Aileen pulls out the green shooter marble and says it is the dragon. She is wearing a pink Barbie nightgown and she rests her round cheek on one hand.
>
> The dragon wants to get in the castle, Joey says, pushing the green shooter through the pencils.
>
> Wait, Aileen says. Why doesn't the princess run away?
>
> She can't, Joey says. He doesn't know how he knows this, but he knows he is right.
>
> Why not? Aileen asks.
>
> The dragon will eat her children if she does, he says, and now he remembers how the door was already standing open when they came out of their bedroom. She would have had time to run. She heard the back door cave in. She had plenty of time to get out, but she had kept screaming, get out, get out, and her eyes were waiting, waiting for them before she stopped fighting, before she stopped screaming. The breeze coming in the window sends goose bumps on his arms. His head is light. Aileen's voice faraway. Then everything around him sharpens into focus and becomes solid and real once again.[24]

Joey's reliving of the event through marble play seemingly offers a cross between a semi-dissociated form of hypnotic re-enactment and self-imposed play therapy.[25] Janet's observations relating to the difference of processing between ordinary and traumatic memory led him to articulate how automatic behaviour and traumatic memory, or *restitution ad integrum* can be triggered if the trauma subject is reminded of the original trauma scene.[26] The text offers a short staccato representation of the children's playing, paralleling Joey's fragmented recollection of the traumatic event. Not until the toy dragon triggers the memory that the front door was already open can Joey fill in the gaps of his memory so that the details of that night return, deluging his psyche with a flood of events as if he were reliving them in the present. He is consequently afforded a more comprehensive recollection of the series of events surrounding

---

24 MacEnulty, *The Language of Sharks*, 176.

25 Like Janet's hysterics, children who have experienced trauma frequently re-enact the traumatic event through post-traumatic repetitive play. For examples, see Lenore Terr, *Too Scared to Cry: Psychic Trauma in Childhood* (New York: Harper Collins, 1990), 238, 239, 247.

26 See Bessel van Der Kolk and Onno van Der Hart, 'The Intrusive Past: the Flexibility of Memory and the Engraving of Trauma' *Trauma: Explorations in Memory*, ed., Cathy Caruth (Baltimore: The Johns Hopkins University Press, 1995), 158–182.

his mother's rape, finally providing the cohesive audio soundtrack to accompany his visual recollection of the trauma.

For Joey, such re-enactment also amounts to an attempt to gain mastery, as per Freud. 'Joey picks up the purple marble and bashes the dragon. The princess kills the dragon, he says.'[27] Although Joey's attempts to rewrite the events of that fateful night are seemingly futile, the killing of the dragon not only re-enacts his physical wish to destroy the rapist, it simultaneously awakens the memory of his mother opening the front door. He becomes aware of a pervasive sense of strength and protection in his mother: she orchestrated the children's escape, and consequently her own survival. Mastery may not be achieved, however, a measure of control is in some way restored.

The remaining stories in *The Language of Sharks* explore further incidences of violation and rape, and reflections on dysfunctional families and abusive relationships. Like much of MacEnulty's fiction, these themes entwined play their part in shaping the narrative.

2 A Traumatology of Loneliness

Initially, my focus on MacEnulty's literary representation of the traumatic concentrated on violence, rape, and mental abuse as wilfully inflicted by others. However, as my research into her work progressed, it became apparent that a more nuanced and complex form of trauma framed these more 'traditional' traumatic experiences. I began to recognise a preoccupation with the experience of otherness woven throughout MacEnulty's texts, specifically the experience of growing up as a highly gifted and creative female. Discussion of giftedness is more typically restricted to the fields of education and psychology. However, MacEnulty's representation of traumatic experience is inseparable from the emergence of the asynchronous developmental states of the gifted child and adolescent. In line with the research of gifted education specialist, Miraca Gross, and Polish psychologist and psychiatrist, Kazimierz Dąbrowski,[28] I suggest that for MacEnulty, the isolating qualities of growing up as a highly gifted and creative female function as a secondary form of trauma

27 MacEnulty, *The Language of Sharks*, 176.

28 A colleague of Abraham Maslow, Dąbrowski openly praised his research in the area of identity development. However, Dąbrowski's theory of personality development is not well known. Whilst his work is not solely a theory of giftedness, it has, in more recent years, found its home in the field of gifted education, widely recognised as providing an excellent framework for understanding the innate characteristics of many gifted and creative individuals.

detectable at the narrative level. This increasing fascination began the process of redefining MacEnulty's representation of trauma through the lens of the highly gifted female, an area that necessitated further attention in this context.

Trauma is spectral in nature and highly subjective in relation to intensity of personal experience. Like the indifference to suffering displayed towards Icarus' falling in 'Musée des Beaux Arts,' humankind frequently turns away from that suffering which we cannot understand. Moreover, all trauma has one universal effect: the emotional devastation of the individual. MacEnulty's characters manifest such emotional devastation, their fragile egos battered by the insensitivity of life. Bruised and scarred not only from traumatic experiences such as witnessing rape and domestic violence, they also suffer from isolation due to their inherent sense of difference, a result of their precocious development. The consequences of such isolation have much in common with the 'symptoms' that may develop as a result of emotional deprivation as it relates to attachment theory, which often includes an impairment in affective, cognitive, biological, and relational self-regulation. Connections can be identified between MacEnulty's experience of growing up gifted and creative in an education system and other social structures in which she was both underserved and misunderstood, and Herman's work on Complex PTSD,[29] and the diagnostic construct of DESNOS, or Disorders of Extreme Stress Not Otherwise Specified.

Miraca Gross' research on the identity development of gifted children builds on Erik Erikson's (1968) and Laurence Steinberg's (1985) theories of identity formation. Steinberg structures his theory of identity development around five key concerns, which Gross lists as:

> The development of identity – the quest for a personal sense of self and an acceptance of one's individuality; the growth of autonomy – the process of establishing oneself as an independent, self-determining individual; the search for intimacy and the establishment of peer relationships based on trust, openness, and a similarity of values; the management of one's developing sexuality; and the need to achieve, and be recognized for one's achievements.[30]

For gifted children and adolescents, particularly the highly gifted, however, such identity formation can be problematic. If successful identity development

29 See Judith Lewis Herman, *Trauma and Recovery: The Aftermath of Violence from Domestic Abuse to Political Terror* (New York: Basic Books, 1992).

30 Miraca U.M. Gross, 'The "Me" Behind the Mask: Intellectually Gifted Students and the Search for Identity,' *Roeper Review* 20. 3 (1998): 168.

depends on a child selecting 'from the smorgasbord of possible identities which are presented to her, those that best fit her current perceptions of who she is and what she might become'[31] and 'the search for intimacy and the establishment of peer relationships [is] based on trust, openness, and a similarity of values'[32] as Erikson and Sternberg assert, the asynchronous gifted child is quite possibly going to run into difficulties. Notably, Ann Klein and Debra Zehms' longitudinal study of the childhood and adolescence of gifted and non-gifted girls reported the self-concept of non-gifted girls increased between third and eighth grade, but conversely the self-concept of gifted girls decreased significantly.[33] Similarly, MacEnulty's gifted protagonists are not afforded the academic or social conditions in which they can develop optimally, and this leads to the traumatology of loneliness that pervades her writing.

In the short story 'Like Someone in a Coma,' from the collection *The Language of Sharks*, Liz describes how she 'has often felt that if you could open her up from her breastbone down you would see an emptiness as wide as the universe inside.'[34] Like many of MacEnulty's protagonists, Liz's educational trajectory is rendered problematic as a result of her obvious giftedness. That she works as a prostitute in order to finance her studies further complicates Liz's relationship to educational institutions. Her giftedness prevents authentic connection at school, whilst her interest in furthering her education precludes her from developing a relationship with the other sex workers: 'So far she has managed two semesters of junior college and gotten on the Dean's list both times';[35] however, 'She hasn't made any friends there, and it's not like she has a career plan.'[36] Nor does she identify with the girls she works with at the brothel who consider her 'weird.'[37] For an individual who thrives on learning, Liz is apathetic towards school. She laments how 'Her auntie teaches high school English and that is much worse than turning tricks as far as [she] can tell.'[38] In spite of desperately wanting to learn, Liz is still 'not sure why she bothers going to classes.'[39]

---

31 See Erik Erikson, *Identity: Youth and Crisis* (New York: Norton, 1968).

32 See Laurence Steinberg, *Adolescence* (New York: Knopf, 1985).

33 Ann G. Klein and Debra Zehms, 'Self-Concept in Gifted Girls: A Cross Sectional Study of Intellectually Gifted Females in Grades 3, 5, 8,' *Roeper Review* 19. 2 (1996): 30-33.

34 Pat MacEnulty, 'Like Someone in a Coma,' in *The Language of Sharks* (London: Serpent's Tail, 2004): 21.

35 Ibid.

36 Ibid.

37 Ibid., 16.

38 Ibid.

39 Ibid., 21.

In MacEnulty's novel *Sweet Fire*, Trish's childhood and adolescence follow a similar pattern. Isolation, books and learning feature constantly in her young life. At seven her life revolves around reading:

> [She] spent hours in the library. Inside it was cool; the beams of the high ceilings were carved in a rococo design. I would follow a small narrow staircase down to the children's section – The Black Stallion, The Black Stallion Returns, all the novels of Walter Farley that I read and believed in, a kid on an island with no one to love but a black horse.[40]

A couple of years later Trish is 'engrossed in *D'Aulaire's Mythology*'[41] and by twelve has moved on to Dickens' *Great Expectations*.[42] Such precocious literary interests provide little that would help a child to connect with her classmates and develop a sense of identity in relation to other children.

Unable to connect at college or in the workplace, characters like Trish and Liz, bear a deep sense of confusion relating to their identity and their place in the world. Their concept of self is so destabilised that they are left wondering if it is pathological:

> In [Liz's] introduction to Psychology class, she learned that schizophrenics do not really have split personalities. Which is a good thing because it means that even if she does feel like two completely different people, she is not a schizophrenic.[43]

Liz cannot find her 'place' in the world and this sees her effectively fashion two selves in order to cope with a sense of isolation so profound that she cannot fit in either of the worlds she inhabits. The split that occurs in Liz's psyche, as she attempts to exist in both of these worlds, resembles the split in consciousness that occurs in trauma victims who dissociate traumatic experiences from memory in order to survive in the present. This fashioning of separate selves is akin to survival mode for Liz, who 'doesn't understand why it feels as if the world is a shattered plate glass window no matter who she is.'[44] The shattered subjectivities of victims who suffer from more clinically accepted forms of trauma are paralleled in MacEnulty's characters as they grope to survive in

40 Pat MacEnulty, *Sweet Fire* (London: Serpent's Tail, 2003), 50.
41 Ibid., 51.
42 Ibid., 86.
43 MacEnulty, *The Language of Sharks*, 21-22.
44 Ibid., 22.

a world from which they feel so alienated that this isolation and subsequent social marginalisation both adds to the original traumatic experience and can also be deemed as traumatic in its own right.

3 Archetypal Defence Mechanisms and Machinic Assemblages

Sweet Fire and *The Language of Sharks* explore the relationship between innocence lost and an individual's subsequent focus on survival by means of the creation of an alternative and distorted sense of reality. The impact of traumatic experience on characters in these texts causes an apparent shattering of identity, leaving behind a fragmented and disrupted sense of self. MacEnulty creates spaces which portray protagonists as they grope for survival in a world saturated with suffering, cruelty and abuse as they attempt to reassimilate and reconstruct a sense of self and identity following psychical trauma. Both the novel and short stories offer detailed accounts of drug addiction as a response to harrowing childhood and adolescent encounters. References to domestic abuse, alcoholic father figures, familial breakdown and rape are woven through the text, whilst female protagonists with shattered psyches struggle to remain attached to life.

In *The Language of Sharks*, trauma strikes at Trish's developing psyche throughout childhood and adolescence, causing emotional disturbance. Following Janet and others, Jung's views on dissociation suggest that when trauma punctures the developing psyche of a child, overwhelming its capacity to synthesise and assimilate the traumatic experience, it fragments consciousness, resulting in what he calls 'splinter-psyches.'[45] Most significantly, he asserts that the ego is split as it attempts to create a self-care system. This self-care system, which Jung refers to as 'dyadic' in nature, involves the development of split-selves that involve both progression and regression. To elucidate, one part of the ego *progresses*, essentially growing up too fast, developing a precocious and false sense of self readily adapted to survival in the adult world and all of the trauma that this may involve, whilst the other *regresses* to the infantile stage of development and therefore has the potential for exposure to all of its associated vulnerabilities. The progressed part of the self then takes responsibility for the regressed splinter-psyche. Jung's self-care system, or dyadic self, consistently appears in MacEnulty's literature. Trish's story ricochets between the representation of an ego part tyrannical caretaker and part vulnerable child.

45 Jung in Andrew Samuels, Bani Shorter and Fred Plaut. *A Critical Dictionary of Jungian Analysis* (New York: Routledge, 1986), 33-35.

The novel begins with eighteen year-old Trish watching her husband sentenced to imprisonment for drug-related crime. Significantly, the text then directs the reader's attention to Trish's recollection of childhood experiences of trauma, narrated in the present tense. 'Prelude,' the third chapter of *Sweet Fire,* documents Trish's childhood as one marred by the damaging effects growing up in a family marred by alcoholism:

> When I am three years old, I live in a house where there is a green rug, a yellow dog, and a big boy who keeps snakes. Sometimes the boy rages like a lunatic, but I know he is not mad at me. I can sit beside him and feel the anger blow off him in waves. But he never raises his voice to me. My mother plays the violin, her face gets sad, and she flies away from us. The bow in her hand slices the air. I watch her hands a lot. They are gentle and soft and smell like food. The doors of the house are made of a reddish wood. The kitchen floor is covered in large black tiles. We have a long wooden table, and underneath it is a good place to be. Sometimes at night a man comes into this house. Everything gets loud then. I don't know what I've done. I hide when he comes. I hide under my crib, in my closet, anywhere I can. But I cannot get away from that yelling, booming, angry voice. As long as he doesn't find me, he will not hurt me. Did I see my mother fall like a tall pine tree? Or did I dream it as a picture-book illustration to the yelling, booming, angry voice?[46]

The voice of Trish as a child, with its excruciating sense of vulnerability and fear, is juxtaposed against the voice of the teenage drug addict who is both wise and hardened beyond her years. The novel repeatedly presents instances where the caretaking aspect of Trish's psyche steps in to protect her inner child. Such self-protection is triggered not only when she is actually endangered but at any intimation of vulnerability or developing a sense of dependence on others. Trish's drug use serves as a substitute for the authentic relationships that she has grown to fear. At twelve Trish laments how she can 'feel valves closing off inside [her] heart'[47] and by her late teens she yearns for a physical manifestation of her self-care system, one built from bricks and stone. Such yearning for a sacred space away from the traumas of existence somewhat recalls Jung's tower at Bollingen, a place built for solitary retreat and rejuvenation, and a craving Trish recognises as stemming from early childhood:

46 MacEnulty, *Sweet Fire*, 12.

47 Ibid., 89.

> When I was growing up, Jacksonville had an airport with a green control tower … I had been absurdly attached to the green control tower … I remembered another tower. An old square tower that looked like a piece of a castle, a ruin … I would wander around those sand-colored walls and pretend I was its lost princess. If I had been Rapunzel I would never have let down my hair. I would have stayed up in the protection of my tower forever. That is what I most desired, a stone tower impervious to the world's brusque cuffs.[48]

As a child, Trish's retreat into the realms of her imagination may have served as a disavowal of traumas past in her attempt to numb and dissociate as a response to distressing emotions. As an adolescent when such defences fail to protect her vulnerable ego she willingly resorts to anything to protect her fragile inner self, or what may be thought of as her 'inner child.' Most emphatically, Trish resorting to drugs amounts to a call to arms, even if such a call to arms is beyond her conscious control and may result in an accidental path to slow suicide. Academic and analyst, Donald Kalsched, outlines this process:

> Trauma doesn't end with the cessation of outer violation, but continues unabated in the inner world of the trauma victim, whose dreams are often haunted by persecutory inner figures … the perverse fact that *the victim of the psychological trauma continually finds himself or herself where he or she is re-traumatized.* As much as he or she wants to change, as hard as he or she tries to improve life or relationships, something more powerful than the ego continually undermines progress and destroys hope. It is as though the persecutory inner world somehow finds its outer mirror in repeated self-defeating "re-enactments" – almost as if the individual were *possessed* by some diabolical power or malignant fate.[49]

One must overcome methods of resistance prior to confronting one's trauma, and whilst Trish's self-care system is in overdrive, any such attempt would mean to admit the necessity of vulnerability and authentic connection, a state eschewed by many victims of trauma. For trauma victims,

> violation of the inner core of the personality is *unthinkable*. When other defences fail, archetypal defences will go to any lengths to protect the

48 Ibid., 101.

49 Donald Kalsched, *The Inner World of Trauma: Archetypal Defences of the Personal Spirit* (London: Routledge, 1996), 6.

> Self – even to the point of killing the host personality in which this personal spirit is housed (suicide).[50]

Consequently, Trish wonders if 'enough of this life' will even silence the voice that asserts such a resolute determination to survive.[51] Trish may exhibit a plethora of 'self-defeating re-enactments' as a response to trauma, yet the novel references glimpses of a significant and enduring spirit bent on survival. Trish's impenetrable inner self, or for Jung simply the *Self*, periodically raises its fragile yet resolute voice, belying the previously denied existence of a greater reservoir of internal strength:

> In spite of everything, I wanted to live. Even though there was an animal inside me that wanted to get out, even though I felt whacko sometimes and barely resisted the urge to slice open my blood tunnels, even though a raw pain that came from some unidentifiable source dogged me like giant horseflies, even though all these things, I had another voice in my head – one that told me to hang on no matter what.[52]

Kalsched explains how this 'remainder' of the self, as evidenced by Trish's desire to live 'represent[s] a core of the individual's imperishable personal spirit … This spirit has always been a mystery – an essence of selfhood never to be fully comprehended.'[53] Subsequently, a self-destructive existence emerges only temporarily in MacEnulty's texts. It appears as a spatiotemporal dimension characters inhabit until they can acknowledge the transformative potential of trauma. MacEnulty's characters are frequently heroin addicts who, somewhat paradoxically, utilise the drug as a form of self-imposed dissociation, as per Khantzian's self-medication hypothesis,[54] and to simultaneously 'work through' traumatic experience. Such behaviour, as it relates to the

---

50 Ibid.

51 MacEnulty, *Sweet Fire*, 37.

52 Ibid.

53 Kalsched, *The Inner World of Trauma*, 3. Kalsched's ruminations on the 'essence of selfhood never to be fully comprehended' calls to mind Bray's chapter where he recounts his experience of Holotropic Breathwork as a means to explore such a mystery. Like MacEnulty's attempts to exorcise traumatic memories stored in the body and hidden from consciousness through transformative writing, Bray explains how controlled breathing can serve a similar process. Both rely on a transcendence of the ego and attempt to achieve 'peak experience' or to reach 'creative flow' in the journey towards post-traumatic growth and psycho-spiritual transformation.

54 Edward J. Khantzian, 'The Self-Medication Hypothesis of Addictive Disorders: Focus on Heroin and Cocaine Dependence,' *American Journal of Psychiatry* 145.11 (1985): 1259–64.

isolation and subsequent trauma associated with high levels of creativity and intellectual giftedness, occurs, in part, as a result of social marginalisation and a lack of true peer relationships as well as a complex and volatile intrapsychic milieu.

Previous longitudinal studies have suggested that high levels of intelligence positively correlate with excess alcohol consumption and alcoholism. In 2011, the results of a study that examined the link between illegal drug use, drug addiction and gifted individuals, concluded that 'High childhood IQ may increase the risk of illegal drug use in adolescence and adulthood.'[55] Furthermore, Dąbrowski's extensive research led him to assert that certain individuals, due to high levels of existential anxiety and a complex and morally driven intrapsychic world, can be predisposed to a chaotic mental state that may lead to psychoneuroses, depression, anxiety, eating disorders, and other self-destructive behaviour.[56]

MacEnulty's works, however, suggest that, for some gifted and creative people, such acts of self-destruction function as a form of deterritorialization: a sacrificial destruction of the self necessary to create new possibilities for growth and transformation. Self-destructive behaviour contradictorily provides psychological stasis and the possibility of forming new connections. Like Deleuze and Guattari's 'schizophrenic,' MacEnulty's characters use of drugs enables them to take a 'body' already shattered by traumatic experience and dissolve any coherence it might retain whilst simultaneously propelling it forward in its process of becoming. Drug use provides characters with the ability to dissociate from their past in such a way that it enables a renewed sense of reengagement with their present. MacEnulty's characters' relationships with other 'users' repeatedly teach them much about life, and even serve as a form of therapy. Trish's relationship with the gifted and traumatised Carrie exemplifies this process. Although the relationship ends with Carrie's death, Trish finally has someone with whom she can discuss poetry and who is similarly sensitive to the rawness of life. Moreover, this formation of relationships between addicts is portrayed as a magical process:

> When you get off with someone, it means something. You are entering a pact, sealing your friendship or your love like children who prick their fingers and become blood brothers or blood sisters. You perform the

55 James White and G. David Batty, 'Intelligence across Childhood in Relation to Illegal Drug Use in Adulthood: 1970 British Cohort Study,' *Journal of Epidemiology and Community Health* 66 (2012): 767–774.

56 Kazimierz Dąbrowski, *Personality Shaping through Positive Disintegration* (Boston, MA: Little, Brown and Company, 1967).

> secret rituals together, mixing water and drug, administering the fire. You raise the needle like a chalice. You are witches, sorcerers, priests.[57]

In this way, MacEnulty's drug use, as fictionalised in the lives of her characters, and its literary representation serve as dynamisms toward mental and psychic disintegration for the creation of new social connections. Dąbrowski contends that human suffering can be a purifying process; it has the potential for transmutation, for 'giv[ing] birth to higher values.'[58] And whilst developing a dependency on drugs is considered a maladaptive response to trauma, for MacEnulty heroin appears to serve a similar purifying process. Massumi, writing on Deleuze and Guattari, asks:

> The question is not, Is it true? But, Does it work? What new thoughts does it make possible to think? What new emotions does it make possible to feel? What new sensations and perceptions does it open in the body?[59]

These questions serve equally well as a basis for considering the function of drug use in MacEnulty's writing. From the position of drug user, MacEnulty and her fictionalised autobiography can bring into existence a new space, and new lines of flight from which to continue in the process of becoming. Through their drug centred becomings, characters, and consequently MacEnulty, can find their tribe: groups of disaffected youths, often bright and troubled. These new social structures, created as a result of a shared foundation rooted in drug use, provide a level of connection that characters, like Trish in *Sweet Fire*, have not experienced previously. Their drugged bodies enter into new machinic assemblages with other drugged bodies and this nomadic journeying affects their relationship with social systems. Indeed, MacEnulty's protagonists depend on self-destructive behaviour and the relationships they form with other drug-users to facilitate a new and evolving identity position.

4 Mapping Chaos through Metaphor

MacEnulty's literary career addresses her trauma and addiction. She openly refers to her writing as a process of becoming and her literary spaces operate

---

57 MacEnulty, *Sweet Fire*, 119.

58 Dąbrowski, *Personality Shaping through Positive Disintegration*, 31.

59 Brian Massumi, *A User's Guide to Capitalism and Schizophrenia: Deviations from Deleuze and Guattari* (Cambridge, MA: MIT Press, 1992): 8. This calls to mind Hinton's chapter on resiliency and her suggestion that maladaptive behaviour such as drug use may in fact be viewed as a 'detour towards resiliency.'

through a series of translations and transformations. If past experiences of trauma need conscious acknowledgement in order to reassimilate and reconstitute psychic health, as many believe, then MacEnulty's repeated return to the literary serves as a scriptotherapeutic process. Trauma fiction mimics the symptomology of trauma at a formal level, and for MacEnulty this mimicking spans not only individual texts but also her publications at large. From her early short stories to the more recent memoir detailing the death of her mother, MacEnulty's writing exposes, and subsequently exorcises, traumatic memory, bringing it to the forefront of consciousness in a process of making sense of the disequilibrium produced in her psyche by trauma. Each short story and novel amounts to a transformative process, the text functioning, paradoxically, as both protective shield and analytic surface. Together, they form a framework of repetition upon which each subsequent recall and narration of the traumatic event serves to promote the surfacing of repressed memories into MacEnulty's consciousness:

> When we investigate the raw materials of our art through the lens of a character, we see it differently. Even when we are writing memoir or personal essays or in our journal, we take the substance of life and hold it up to the light. We learn something. We explore, we discover. We may simply have a greater understanding about ourselves or our situations, or we may change at some very deep level within ourselves.[60]

MacEnulty's narrative reflections serve both as dissociated object, analyst, and finally as an attempt at emancipating herself from the previously imposed bondage of traumatic experience. Her fictionalised autobiography serves as both autopsychotherapy and schizoanalysis, supporting her journey from egocentrism to altruism as she attempts to understand what it means to be truly human. She uses self-destructive behaviour and, subsequently, her fiction, to explore and remap identity: deterritorializing and reterritorializing in an ongoing process of maladjustment, positive disintegration and subsequent reintegration; forming new connections, territories, and becomings as she traverses

---

60 Pat MacEnulty 'What's so Transformative about Transformative Writing Anyway' (blog), *Alice Osborn: Write from the Inside Out*, 2 April 2012, viewed 2 January 2014, http://aliceosborn.com/writing/whats-so-transformative-about-transformative-writing-anyway/. MacEnulty's assertion that exploring one's trauma through the lens of the creative process functions as a coping strategy that can lead to transformation and self-understanding is mirrored in Schaub's chapter. Schaub explains how her photopoetry serves as a form of personal therapy which illustrates how she 'coped with traumas' and 'understood patterns' that she adopted to successfully 'disconnect from the traumatic sources.'

her emotional, psychological and literary landscapes. MacEnulty refers to this alchemical process as 'the art of spinning the leaden, painful moments of our lives (and the lives of others) into gold.'[61]

Bibliography

Anderson, Hephzibah. 'A Junkie Comes of Age.' *Guardian Unlimited.* 1 February 2003, viewed 20 January 2010. http://patmac.webs.com/sweetfirehtm.

Brontë, Charlotte. *The Poems of Charlotte Brontë (Currer Bell).* London: Forgotten Books, 2012.

Caruth, Cathy. *Unclaimed Experience: Trauma, Narrative and History*. Baltimore: JHU Press, 1996.

Cogdill, Oline. 'A Junkie Comes of Age.' *South Florida Sun-Sentinel.* June 8, 2003, viewed 20 January, 2010. http://patmac.webs.com/sweetfirehtm.

Dąbrowski, Kazimierz. *Personality Shaping through Positive Disintegration.* Boston: Little, Brown, and Company, 1967.

Deleuze, Gilles and Felix Guattari. *Anti-Oedipus: Capitalism and Schizophrenia.* Translated by Robert Hurley, Mark Seem and Helen Lane. London: Continuum, 1983.

Elderfield, John. *De Kooning: A Retrospective;* [published in conjunction with the Exhibition de Kooning: a Retrospective, at The Museum of Modern Art, New York (September 18, 2011–January 9, 2012)]. New York: Museum of Modern Art, 2011

Erikson, Erik. *Identity: Youth and Crisis.* New York: Norton, 1968.

Gross, Miraca. 'The "Me" behind the Mask: Intellectually Gifted Students and the Search for Identity.' *Roeper Review* 20. 3 (1998): 167–174.

Herman, Judith Lewis. *Trauma and Recovery: The Aftermath of Violence from Domestic Abuse to Political Terror.* New York: Basic Books, 1992.

Kalsched, Donald E. *The Inner World of Trauma: Archetypal Defenses of the Personal Spirit.* London: Routledge, 1996.

Khantzian, Edward J. 'The Self-Medication Hypothesis of Addictive Disorders: Focus on Heroin and Cocaine Dependence.' *American Journal of Psychiatry* 145.11 (1985): 1259–1264.

Klein, Ann G. and Debra Zehms. 'Self-Concept in Gifted Girls: A Cross Sectional Study of Intellectually Gifted Females in Grades 3, 5, 8.' *Roeper Review* 19.2 (1996): 30–33.

MacEnulty, Pat. *Sweet Fire.* London: Serpent's Tail, 2003.

MacEnulty, Pat. *The Language of Sharks.* London: Serpent's Tail, 2004.

61 Pat MacEnulty, 'Writing Retreat for Alchemists,' *Open Salon*, 23 September 2011, viewed 2 January 2014, http://open.salon.com/blog/pat_macenulty/2011/09/23/writing_retreat_for_alchemists.

MacEnulty, Pat. *Wait Until Tomorrow: A Daughter's Memoir.* New York: The Feminist Press at CUNY, 2011a.

MacEnulty, Pat. 'Writing Retreat for Alchemists.' *Open Salon,* 23 September 2011b, viewed 2 January 2014. http://open.salon.com/blog/pat_macenulty/2011/09/23/writing_retreat_for_alchemists.

MacEnulty, Pat. 'Writing, Exploring.' *Open Salon,* 30 January 2012a, viewed 2 January 2014. http://open.salon.com/blog/pat_macenulty/2012/01/30/writing_exploring.

MacEnulty, Pat. 'What's so Transformative about Transformative Writing Anyway' (blog). *Alice Osborn: Write from the Inside Out.* 2 April 2012b, viewed 2 January 2014. http://aliceosborn.com/writing/whats-so-transformative-about-transformative-writing-anyway/.

Massumi, Brian. *A User's Guide to Capitalism and Schizophrenia: Deviations from Deleuze and Guattari.* Cambridge, MA: MIT Press, 1992.

Mattin, David. 'Book Review of *The Language of Sharks.*' *The Observer.* March 21, 2004, viewed 20 January, 2010. http://www.theguardian.com/books/2004/mar/21/features.review4.

Samuels, Andrew, Bani Shorter and Fred Plaut. *A Critical Dictionary of Jungian Analysis*, Routledge: New York, 1986.

Sears, John. 'Crawling from the Wreckage: *The Language of Sharks* by Pat MacEnulty.' *Pop Matters.* May 11, 2004, viewed 20 January, 2010. http://www.popmatters.com/review/language-of-sharks/.

Steinberg, Laurence. *Adolescence.* New York: Knopf, 1985.

Terr, Lenore. *Too Scared to Cry: Psychic Trauma in Childhood.* New York: Harper Collins, 1990.

Van der Kolk, Bessel and Onno Van Der Hart. 'The Intrusive Past: the Flexibility of Memory and the Engraving of Trauma.' In *Trauma: Explorations in Memory,* edited by Cathy Caruth. 158–182. Baltimore: The Johns Hopkins University Press, 1995.

Vickroy, Laurie. *Trauma and Survival in Contemporary Fiction.* Charlottesville: University of Virginia Press, 2002.

White, James and G. David Batty. 'Intelligence across Childhood in Relation to Illegal Drug Use in Adulthood: 1970 British Cohort Study.' *Journal of Epidemiology and Community Health 66* (2012): 767–774.

Whitehead, Anne. *Trauma Fiction.* Edinburgh: Edinburgh University Press, 2004.

CHAPTER 7

What Enables Resilience after Traumatic Childhood Experiences?

Monica Hinton

1 Introduction

> If we think we are fragile and broken, we will live a fragile, broken life. If we believe we are strong and wise, we will live with enthusiasm and courage; the way we name ourselves colours the way we live.[1]

During my Master of Social Work (MSW) clinical practicum placement, my thoughts on the nature of my research study came into focus. My clinical caseload at the Child Abuse Service, at the Alberta Children's Hospital (in Calgary, AB, Canada), comprised predominantly boys under the age of 10 who had experienced abuse at the hands of family members. During my clinical placement, I met a seven-year-old permanent ward of the state. The social worker assigned him under Permanent Guardianship Order discussed with me her thoughts on how this boy was destined to live a life of crime. After having known him for a year, she deemed him beyond help. After our conversation, I questioned my role as a play therapist in this seven-year-old's life. What is the point of working with those who have experienced abuse, if there is no hope, I asked myself. This case sparked my research question regarding resilience, despite experiences of childhood trauma/abuse. Despite the extent of those who experience CSA in Canada, research did not seem to reflect people's actual lived experience. I wondered why research on those doing well did not widely exist. How, as clinicians, would we know their story, as we work in agencies that resilient individuals may not access? According to the Committee on Sexual Offences Against Children and Youths, among the adult Canadian population, 53% of women and 31% of men are sexually abused as children.[2] Despite

1 Wayne Muller, *How Then, Shall We Live? Four Simple Questions That Reveal the Beauty and Meaning of Our Lives* (New York: Bantam Books, 1996), 16.

2 Robin Badgley, Canada, Department of Justice and Canada, Health and Welfare Canada, *Sexual Offences Against Children in Canada: Report of the Committee on Sexual Offences Against Children and Youths* (Ottawa: Supply and Services Canada, 1984), 1–2.

 | DOI:10.1163/9789004385931_008

such significant rates of abuse, I believed in people's resilience, and I wanted to find out how they developed resilience.

2 Prevalence of Child Sexual Abuse

Over the last few decades, a plethora of research on the prevalence of childhood sexual abuse (CSA) has established that it is not only a common experience,[3] but also an international dilemma.[4] A survey of adult, nonclinical populations across at least 19 countries, including 10 national probability samples, has confirmed that 7%-36% of women and 3%-29% of men have experienced CSA.[5] Variations in methodologies, definitions, techniques for garnering data, samples and questions used, along with the cultural and economic situation in the assortment of countries in which studies take place, can account for the diversity in prevalence rates between studies. In accordance with the global focus on the issue of childhood sexual abuse – a longstanding crisis – the World Health Organization announced the international importance of childhood sexual abuse and its 'silent health emergency.'[6]

Childhood sexual abuse has always existed, in all cultures and at all times. Florence Rush's historical work ascertains that CSA has been tolerated and endorsed at official levels[7] and according to Finkelhor, 'children are arguably the most criminally victimised people in society.'[8] Even today, in times of poverty, war or stress, children are abandoned or sold, often into forms of sexual

3 J.C. Anderson, et al., 'The Long-Term Impact of the Physical, Emotional and Sexual Abuse of Children: A Community Study,' *Child Abuse & Neglect* 20.1 (1996): 11–12; John Briere, Kathy Smiljanich and Diane Henschel, 'Sexual Fantasies, Gender, and Molestation History,' *Child Abuse & Neglect* 18.2 (1994): 133; David Fergusson, Michael Lynskey and John Horwood, 'Childhood Sexual Abuse and Psychiatric Disorder in Young Adulthood: I. Prevalence of Sexual Abuse and Factors Associated with Sexual Abuse,' *Journal of the American Academy of Child and Adolescent Psychiatry* 35.10 (1996): 1355.

4 David Finkelhor, 'The International Epidemiology of Child Sexual Abuse,' *Child Abuse & Neglect* 18.5 (1994): 409; Elya Moore, et al., 'The Prevalence of Childhood Sexual Abuse and Adolescent Unwanted Sexual Contact Among Boys and Girls Living in Victoria, Australia,' *Child Abuse & Neglect* 34.5 (2010): 379–380.

5 Finkelhor, 'The International Epidemiology,' 411.

6 Paulo Sergio Pinheiro, 'Independent Expert For The United Nations Secretary-General's Study on Violence Against Children,' *World Report on Violence against Children* (2006): 117.

7 Florence Rush, *The Best Kept Secret: Sexual Abuse of Children* (New York: McGraw Hill, 1980), 116.

8 David Finkelhor, *Childhood Victimization: Violence, Crime and Abuse in the Lives of Young People* (New York: Oxford University Press, 2008), 3.

slavery.[9] In North American and Australian professional literature, the issue of child sexual abuse received little attention until the late 1970s and only in the 1980s has the issue been recognised in Northern Europe.[10]

Multiple and varied definitions of childhood sexual abuse exist but none nationally or internationally agreed upon for the phenomenon. The difficultly in defining the sexual abuse of children relates to culturally specific and time-bound ideas based on the beliefs and values of individuals, professional organisations and society at large.[11] No universal definition of 'child sexual abuse' exists and 'sexual exploitation,' 'sexual misuse' and 'sexual assault' are frequently used interchangeably. Within countries like Canada and Australia, legal definitions differ between provinces/states, territories, jurisdictions and agencies.[12] Health Canada defines child sexual abuse occurs when a child is used for sexual purposes by an adult or adolescent.[13] It involves exposing a child to any sexual activity or behaviour and most often involves fondling. It could also include the invitation to touch or be touched sexually. Other forms of sexual abuse consist of sexual intercourse, juvenile prostitution and sexual exploitation through child pornography.[14] In Canada, this offence outlined in the Criminal Code of Canada is defined in the Canada Evidence Act.[15] Childhood sexual abuse, as defined in the Medical Journal of Australia, consists of sexual contact (fondling to penetration), before age 12 with a person 5 or more years older, regardless of consent and all unwanted or distressing sexual contact between the ages of 12 and 16 with a person five or more years older.[16] The

---

9 Jean-Claude Chesnais, *History of Violence (In the West From 1800 to the Present)* (Paris: The National Research Institute, 1981), 201–202.

10 Christopher Bagley and Kathleen King, *Child Sexual Abuse: The Search for Healing* (London: Tavistock/Routledge, 1990), 37; J. Stanley and C. Goddard, *Hearing Only Half of the Story by Leaving Out Half of the Violence*, Australian Government, Australian Institute of Family Studies, 2003, 1.

11 C. Henry Kempe and Patricia Beezley Mrazek, *Sexually Abused Children and Their Families* (New York: Pergamon Press, 1981): 5–7; Karen O'Hagan, *Working with Child Sexual Abuse: A Post-Cleveland Guide to Effective Principles and Practice* (Milton Keynes: Open University Press, 1989): 49–50.

12 Australian Bureau of Statistics, *Sexual Assault in Australia: A Statistical Overview* (Canberra: ABS, 2004), 8.

13 Health Canada, 1997, 'National Clearinghouse on Family Violence,' *National Clearinghouse on Family Violence/Health Canada*, Ontario, 1–2.

14 Ibid., 1.

15 Colin Mangham, Graham Reid and Miriam Stewart, 'Resilience in Families: Challenges for Health Promotion,' *Canadian Journal of Public Health-Revue Canadienne de Sante Publique* 87.6 (1996): 373–374.

16 J.M. Fleming, 'Prevalence of Childhood Sexual Abuse in a Community Sample of Australian Women,' *The Medical Journal of Australia* 166.2 (1997): 67.

Australian Bureau of Statistics released an information paper, 'Sexual Assault in Australia: A Statistical Overview,' which contained a wide definition of sexual assault. This paper designates sexual assault as

> unwanted behaviour of a sexual nature directed towards a person: which makes that person feel uncomfortable, distressed, frightened or threatened, or which results in harm or injury to that person; to which that person has not freely agreed or given consent, or to which that person is not capable of giving consent; in which another person uses physical, emotional, psychological or verbal force or (other) coercive behaviour against that person.[17]

The definition of CSA varies in detail and in criteria from research study to research study in both the general prevalence literature and in reviews of specific populations. Some studies include non-body contact such as exposure and others define CSA in terms of body contact only. The age criterion, with respect to the age that defines a child and the difference in age between victim and perpetrator, also varies from study to study. Additionally, some studies define history as one incident while others investigate the actual number of times and duration of the abuse.[18]

Issues arise when the criteria for defining an experience differs. For example, in one particular study, Peters, Wyatt and Finkelhor recalculated Wyatt's prevalence rate using Finkelhor's and Russell's criteria.[19] In Finkelhor's study, sexual experiences between a child and an older person included intercourse, simulated intercourse or attempted intercourse, fondling of the genitals, exhibitionistic display of the genitals, kissing, hugging, fondling in a sexual way and overt sexual overtures, for example being asked to show genitals, with no contact.[20] Furthermore, this study included three categories of relationships based on age.[21] Intrafamilial child sexual abuse was defined as any kind of sexual contact

---

17 Australian Bureau of Statistics, *Sexual Assault in Australia,* 8.

18 C. Bagley and R.J. Thomlison, *Child Sexual Abuse: Critical Perspectives on Prevention, Intervention and Treatment* (Toronto: Wall & Emerson, 1991): 79–120.

19 S. Peters, Gail Wyatt and David Finkelhor, *Prevalence: A Sourcebook on Child Sexual Abuse,* ed. D. Finkelhor (Beverly Hills: Sage Publications, 1986): 15–59; Gail Wyatt, 'The Sexual Abuse of Afro-American and White-American Women in Childhood,' *Child Abuse and Neglect* 9 (1985): 507–519; Diana Russell, 'The Incidence and Prevalence of Intrafamilial and Extrafamilial Sexual Abuse of Female Children,' *Child Abuse & Neglect* 7.2 (1983): 133–146.

20 David Finkelhor, *Sexually Victimized Children* (New York: The Free Press, 1979), 54.

21 Ibid., 54.

between relatives, regardless of how distant, before age 18.[22] Russell defined extrafamilial CSA as experience(s), one or more, with those unrelated by blood and/or marriage.[23] Wyatt defined sexual abuse as contact of a sexual nature ranging from non-body contact, for example exhibitionism, to body contact, fondling, intercourse and oral sex for example, prior to age 18 and involving any perpetrator, be they family, acquaintances or strangers.[24] An age difference of 5 years was needed to define the experience as abuse, unless coercion occurred between those with less than a 5-year age difference.[25] Wyatt, Russell and Finkelhor's criteria differed in a variety of areas from Russell's. When Finkelhor's criteria were used, Wyatt's incident rate of 62% dropped to 54% and when Russell's criteria were used, her prevalence rate dropped to 53%.[26] As Finkelhor's actual rate was 19%, other factors must also be involved in the occurrence rate differences.[27] This one study demonstrates the difficulties inherent in having varied standards of defining childhood sexual abuse.

In addition to the struggles with definitions, many researchers believe that reported cases of CSA represent only a fraction of the actual rates of occurrence, as only the most severe cases are reported to legal authorities and social agencies.[28] According to the Australian Institute of Criminology, 1 in 4 girls and 1 in 7 boys are sexually abused in Australia.[29] 'Sexual assault includes offences such as rape, sodomy, oral sex, incest, carnal knowledge, unlawful sexual intercourse, indecent assault, and assault with intent to rape or commit unnatural offence; and it excludes pornography and prostitution.'[30] According to the Australian Childhood Foundation Report, child victims fall under the age of 14 with the highest percentage of all child victims under the age of 10.[31]

22 Diana Russell, *Lives of Courage: Women for a New South Africa* (New York: Basic Books, 1989): 1–10.

23 Ibid., 1–10.

24 Wyatt, 'The Sexual Abuse,' 510–511.

25 Ibid., 511.

26 Wyatt, 'The Sexual Abuse,' 507–519.; Russell, *Lives of Courage*, 1–10; Finkelhor, *Sexually Victimized Children*, 131–140.

27 Finkelhor, *Sexually Victimized Children*, 131–140.

28 Juliette Goldman and Usha Padayachi, 'Some Methodological Problems in Estimating Incidence and Prevalence in Child Sexual Abuse Research,' *The Journal of Sex Research* 37.4 (2000): 305–314.

29 B. Cook, F. David and A. Grant, 'Sexual Violence in Australia,' *Research and Public Policy Series No. 36*, (Canberra: Australian Institute of Criminology, 2001) viewed 1 November 2012, http://www.aic.gov.au/publications/rpp/36/index.html.

30 Ibid., 5.

31 Ibid., 5–6.

Almost half of the sexual assaults reported to police, for both male and female children, occurred between the child and non-family members.[32] A national Canadian survey, found that 17.6% of adult females and 8.2% of adult males recalled 'unwanted' sexual touching or assault prior to their 17th birthday.[33] Also, the United Nations Secretary-General's Study on Violence against Children estimated that the experience of non-consensual sexual intercourse and/ or other sexual violence encounters occur to 150 million girls and 73 million boys under the age of 18.[34]

3 Effects of Child Sexual Abuse

The physical, emotional, cognitive and social developmental impact of trauma has a devastating impact.[35] Study findings suggest that exposure to childhood sexual abuse leads to a wide range of effects including depression,[36] anxiety,[37] substance abuse problems,[38] attempted suicide[39] and deliberate self-harm[40]

32 Ibid., 5–6.

33 Christopher Bagley, 'Prevalence and Correlates of Unwanted Sexual Acts in Childhood in a National Canadian Sample,' *Canadian Journal of Public Health* 80 (1989): 295–296.

34 United Nations General Assembly, *Report of the Independent Expert for the United Nations Study on Violence Against Children* (Place of Publication: United Nations, 2006): 9–10.

35 Bruce Perry, 'Childhood Experience and the Expression of Genetic Potential: What Childhood Neglect Tells Us About Nature and Nurture,' *Brain and Mind* 3 (2002): 88.

36 Joseph Beitchman, et al., 'A Review of the Long-Term Effects of Child Sexual Abuse,' *Child Abuse & Neglect* 16.1 (1992): 106–107; Angela Browne and David Finkelhor, 'Impact of Child Sexual Abuse: A Review of the Research,' *Psychological Bulletin* 99.1 (1986): 68; M.A. Cerezo-Jimenez, and D. Frias, 'Emotional and Cognitive Adjustment in Abused Children,' *Child Abuse & Neglect* 18.11 (1994): 924.

37 Denise Allen and Kenneth Tarnowski, 'Depressive Characteristics of Physically Abused Children,' *Journal of Abnormal Child Psychology* 17.1 (1989): 8; John Briere and Marsha Runtz, 'Multivariate Correlates of Childhood Psychological and Physical Maltreatment Among University Women,' *Child Abuse & Neglect* 12.3 (1988): 331; Audrey Burnam, 'Sexual Assault and Mental Disorder in a Community Population,' *Journal of Consulting and Clinical Psychology* 56.6 (1988): 843.

38 Briere and Runtz, 'Multivariate Correlates,' 331; Burnam, 'Sexual Assault,' 843; J.C. Anderson, et al., 'The Long-Term Impact,' 12.

39 Briere and Runtz, 'Multivariate Correlates,' 331; J.C. Anderson et al., 'The Long-Term Impact,' 7–8; Mary Sedney and Barbara Brooks, 'Factors Associated With a History of Childhood Sexual Experience In a Nonclinical Female Population,' *Journal of the American Academy of Child Psychiatry* 23.2 (1984): 217.

40 James Beck and Bessel van der Kolk, 'Reports of Childhood Incest and Current Behaviour of Chronically Hospitalized Psychotic Women,' *The American Journal of Psychiatry* 144.11 (1987): 1474; David Goldston, Dawn Turnquist and John Knutson, 'Presenting Problems of Sexually Abused Girls Receiving Psychiatric Services,' *Journal of Abnormal Psychology* 98.3 (1989): 316; David Herzog, et al., 'Childhood Sexual Abuse in Anorexia Nervosa and

and a range of other adverse psychological outcomes.[41] Many sexually abused children often suffer well after the abuse has ceased. The injury of CSA takes many forms including guilt, feeling responsible for the abuse, shame, fear, grief, helplessness, depression and more. Children may stop seeing the world as a safe and friendly place; they may mourn the loss of their sense of innocence and freedom; they may experience intense and uncontrollable anger through which they lash out at people, themselves or a pet. Several studies report that those who have experienced abuse report feelings of negative self-image, depression, anxiety, feelings of isolation and stigma, substance abuse, a tendency towards revictimisation and issues in their interpersonal relationships.[42] Others have documented the severe and long-term psychological consequences of childhood sexual abuse, which includes difficulty in emotional, behavioural, social and sexual functioning in adulthood.[43] Later in adult life, an individual who has experienced CSA may encounter on-going low self-esteem, difficulty with relationships and sexuality, negative feelings about his/her body and issues parenting his/her own children. For example, both Bagley and Ramsay and Sedney and Brooks report much higher levels of depression amongst adult women abused in childhood than in the female population as a whole.[44] Sexual abuse research also consistently reports experiences of more invasive abuse, such as anal, oral or vaginal intercourse as associated with more psychological symptoms. The use of force by an abuser, as well as the duration of abuse and degree of atypicality such as the use of sexual torture, multiple perpetrators and satanic rituals, count among the variables that most clearly explain the negative psychological reactions by victims.[45] Russell reported that

---

Bulimia Nervosa: A Pilot Study,' *Journal of the American Academy of Child and Adolescent Psychiatry* 32.5 (1993): 964.

41 Briere and Runtz, 'Multivariate Correlates,' 331–332.

42 Angela Browne and David Finkelhor, 'Initial and Long Term Effects: A Review of the Research,' *A Source Book on Child Sexual Abuse,* ed. David Finkelhor (Beverly Hills: Sage Publications, 1986): 15; Christine Courtois, 'Healing The Incest Wound: A Treatment Update with Attention to Recovered Memory Issues,' *American Journal of Psychotherapy* 51.4 (1997): 467–470; Patricia Mrazek and David Mrazek, 'Resilience in Child Maltreatment Victims: A Conceptual Exploration,' *Child Abuse and Neglect,* 11.3 (1987): 357–359.

43 Beitchman, et al., 'A Review,' 115; Kathleen Kendall-Tackett, Linda Williams and David Finkelhor, 'Impact of Sexual Abuse on Children: A Review and Synthesis of Recent Empirical Studies,' *Psychological Bulletin,* 113.1 (1993): 173–177.

44 Christopher Bagley and R. Ramsay, 'Sexual Abuse in Childhood: Psychosocial Outcomes and Implications for Social Work Practice,' *Journal of Social Work and Human Sexuality* 4 (1986): 33–47; Mary Sedney and Barbara Brooks, 'Factors Associated With a History of Childhood Sexual Experience,' 215–218.

45 Judy Chew, *Women Survivors of Childhood Sexual Abuse: Healing Through Group Work* (New York: The Haworth Press, Inc, 1998), 1–8; Scott Ketring and Leslie Feinauer,

the most psychologically damaging sexually abusive relationship exists when the father figure is the abuser.[46]

The reactions of parents and family, the response from professionals and their interventions, if any, can also contribute to the trauma. One incident may be experienced as dire but the potential negative effects of the experience may be aggravated by the reaction of family or professionals to a disclosure.[47] Finkelhor and Browne provide a model of factors that affect trauma, based on the reactions of the survivor, rather than on external criteria.[48] They mention the four trauma causing factors, or in Finkelhor and Browne's words 'traumagenic dynamics,' namely traumatic sexualisation, betrayal, powerlessness and stigmatisation.[49] The interplay between these four concepts combines to render the trauma of sexual abuse as distinct from other types of abuse. According to Finkelhor and Browne, these dynamics alter a child's cognitive and emotional view of the world and generate trauma by altering a child's self-concept, worldview and emotional capacity. Each dynamic engenders a collection of harmful effects with a common theme. These four factors, they explain, should function as broad categories useful for informing our understanding of the results of sexual abuse.[50] Traumatic sexualisation, the first concept, refers to the 'process in which a child's sexuality (including sexual feelings and attitudes) is shaped in a developmentally inappropriate and interpersonally dysfunctional manner as a result of sexual abuse.'[51] According to Finkelhor and Browne, children traumatically sexualised emerge from their experiences with a variety of inappropriate sexual behaviours, distortions about their sexual self-concepts and atypical emotional links to sexual activities. A child may cope by becoming promiscuous or by developing an aversion to sex. These reactions represent a failure to develop 'normal' sexual relationships.[52] Betrayal, the second aspect, acts as a dynamic in which 'children discover that someone upon whom they were vitally dependent has caused them harm.'[53] Children can experience

---

'Perpetrator-Victim Relationships: Long-Term Effects of Sexual Abuse for Men and Women,' *American Journal of Family Therapy* 27 (1999): 111.

46 Diana Russell, *The Secret Trauma: Incest in the Lives of Girls and Women* (New York: Basic Books, 1986): 25.

47 Linda Sanford, *The Silent Children: A Parent's Guide to the Prevention of Child Sexual Abuse* (New York: McGraw-Hill, 1980): 40.

48 David Finkelhor and Angela Browne, 'The Traumatic Impact of Child Sexual Abuse: A Conceptualization,' *American Journal of Orthopsychiatry* 55.4 (1985): 530.

49 Ibid., 530.

50 Ibid., 531.

51 Ibid., 531.

52 Ibid., 534.

53 Ibid., 531–532.

betrayal not only at the hands of the offenders, but also family members who did not protect them. The degree of betrayal, in their estimation, also relates to the response to the child's disclosure.[54] This could produce a wounded ability to trust other people in a variety of life situations, especially those involving interpersonal relationships.[55] Powerlessness, a third facet, refers to the 'process in which the child's will, desires and sense of efficacy is continually contravened.'[56] According to Finkelhor and Browne, a basic kind of powerlessness occurs in sexual abuse when a child's space and body are repeatedly invaded against the child's will.[57] The feeling may be enhanced by the force and intimidation the offender may impose as part of the abuse process.[58] According to Bagley and King, prolonged assaults may lead to a sense of powerlessness in the survivor that seems endless.[59] The final feature, stigmatisation, refers to 'the negative connotations communicated to the child around the experiences and that then become incorporated into the child's self-image.'[60] Stigmatisation can be reinforced by attitudes that the survivor construes or deduces from the words or actions of others in the family or outside of the family. Keeping the secret that one is a survivor of sexual abuse might increase the sense of shame, as it supports the sense of being different.[61]

Studies investigating the effects of CSA, however, have tended to use clinical samples, which may apply to non-clinical populations.[62] More recently, meta-analytic reviews have suggested that the general population does not necessarily associate CSA with significant psychological maladjustment[63] and that the link between histories of CSA and adult symptomatology are considerably starker in clinical populations.[64] Studies involving small samples of highly specific populations, such as follow-up studies of sexually abused children, have generated

54 Ibid., 535.
55 Bagley and Ramsey, *Child Sexual Abuse: The Search for Healing*, 116.
56 Finkelhor and Browne, 'The Traumatic Impact,' 532.
57 Ibid., 536.
58 Ibid., 532.
59 Bagley and Ramsey, *Child Sexual Abuse: The Search for Healing*, 116.
60 Finkelhor and Browne, 'The Traumatic Impact,' 532–533.
61 Ibid., 535.
62 Beitchman, et al., A Review of The Long-Term Effects, 102.
63 Bruce Rind and Philip Tromovitch, 'A Meta-Analytic Review of Findings from National Samples on Psychological Correlates of Child Sexual Abuse,' *The Journal of Sex Research* 34.3 (1997): 237–255.
64 Debra Neumann, et al., 'The Long-Term Sequelae of Childhood Sexual Abuse in Women: A Meta-Analytic Review,' *Child Maltreatment* 1.1 (1996): 6–16.

the evidence of the harmful effects of CSA.[65] Also, observations of adult women in psychotherapy seem to be the main source of the reported impact of CSA experiences.[66] Until recently, written work outlining the effects of CSA involved clinical reports that presented alleged effects, often in small samples, without reporting true measurement of the consequences.[67] Such reports are useful in giving a context for discovery. Without measurement or control procedures, however, they fail to show with any certainty how well children manage following sexual abuse and what may account for such functioning.[68] Without actual data describing the consequences, variation in outcomes across cases and change in the effects across time, it is difficult to establish the reliability and/or representativeness of the findings.

Research on outcomes relies on experiences of both past and present. The effects category of CSA has more variables and drawbacks than any other aspect of research in CSA. Research into long-term effects falls short in providing adequate information about the type of sexual abuse perpetrated against the child, the social and family context in which the abuse took place and the ways and means of intervention by agency personnel who become involved. Without reliable empirical evidence, no one can say with certainty which sexually abused child is the most vulnerable to abuse, nor what social and family context intensifies the hurt.[69] One cannot establish with certainty to what degree the behavioural chaos a child displays following sexual abuse results directly from the abuse, and not some other behaviour that already existed and rendered the child more susceptible to sexual abuse. Similarly, the data do not enable us to distinguish longstanding difficulties from more recent responses to emotional trauma. Other experiences in the child's history occurring before the sexual abuse may also account for some of the psychopathology observed.[70] Estimating the effects of sexual abuse consists in an enormously complex task due to the variety of factors involved, including 'age, frequency, amount of associated aggression, relationship of participants, total family dynamics and object-relations before and after the act of abuse, sub-cultural

65 Gail Wyatt, 'The Aftermath of Child Sexual Abuse of African American and White American Women: The Victim's Experience,' *Journal of Family Violence* 5.1 (1990): 61–81.

66 Judith Herman, *Father Daughter Incest* (Cambridge: Harvard University Press, 1981): 22–24; Mavis Tsai and Nathaniel Wagner, 'Therapy Groups for Women Sexually Molested as Children,' *Archives of Sexual Behavior* 7.5 (1978): 417–427.

67 Ida Nakishima and Gloria Zakus, 'Incest: Review and Clinical Experience,' *Pediatrics* 60.5 (1977): 696–697.

68 Jon Conte and John Schuerman, 'The Effects of Sexual Abuse on Children: A Multidimensional View,' *Journal of Interpersonal Violence* 2.4 (1988): 380–390.

69 O'Hagan, *Working with Child Sexual Abuse*, 47–55.

70 B. Gomes-Schwartz, J. Horowitz and A.P. Cardarelli, *Child Sexual Abuse: The Initial Effects* (California: Sage Publications, 1990), 104.

customs and environmental responses.'[71] Possibly few outcomes of abuse exist without other harmful factors involved beyond 'simple' sexual interactions.[72]

Researchers in the area of child sexual abuse comment on their field being in the beginning stages and that many critical areas need more research.[73] This does exclude the saturation of research focussed on CSA and the little to no attention given to the question of its value to practitioners.

4 Resilience

Despite the abundance of research that implies inevitable and hurtful outcomes of sexual abuse, one must remember that reactions vary. Even though nearly 40% of all individuals who have experienced childhood sexual abuse might suffer effects serious enough to require therapy in adulthood, millions lead successful lives without any formal therapy.[74] Lynskey and Fergusson delineate success as individuals who do not suffer from symptoms of trauma or struggle with issues of anxiety, substance use issues, conduct disorders or mood disorders.[75] According to Valentine and Feinauer, success includes the ability to have stable careers, healthy personalities and having relationships with others.[76] More recently, researchers have begun to apply the concept of resilience to these more positive experiences of coping. Traditionally, the term resiliency has described the ability to manage or cope with adversity or stress in ways not only helpful, but resulting in a better ability to respond to future suffering.[77] Hence, within this conceptualisation, resiliency does not function

---

71 C. Henry Kempe and Patricia Beezley Mrazek, *Sexually Abused Children and Their Families* (New York: Pergamon Press, 1981), 232.

72 Ibid.,.

73 Kendall-Tackett, Williams and Finkelhor, 'Impact of Sexual Abuse,' 173–177; National Research Council, *Understanding Child Abuse and Neglect: Panel on Research on Child Abuse and Neglect*, (Washington, D.C.: National Academy Press, Washington, 1993): 15.

74 Frances Grossman, et al., *With the Phoenix Rising: Lessons from Ten Resilient Women Who Overcame the Trauma of Childhood Sexual Abuse* (San Francisco: Jossey-Bass, 1999): vii; Michael Lynskey and David Fergusson. 'Factors Protecting Against the Development of Adjustment Difficulties in Young Adults Exposed to Childhood Sexual Abuse,' *Child Abuse & Neglect* 21.12 (1997): 1179; LaNae Valentine and Leslie Feinauer, 'Resilience Factors Associated with Female Survivors of Childhood Sexual Abuse,' *The American Journal of Family Therapy* 21.3 (1993): 216–217.

75 Lynskey and Fergusson, 'Factors Protecting Against,' 1184–1185.

76 Valentine and Feinauer, 'Resilience Factors,' 218–222.

77 George Bonanno, Anthony Papa and Kathleen O'Neill, 'Loss and Human Resilience,' *Applied & Preventive Psychology* 10.3 (2001): 193; Norman Garmezy, 'Resiliency and Vulnerability to Adverse Developmental Outcomes Associated with Poverty,' *American Behavioral Scientist* 34.4 (1991): 419–420; Suniya Luthar, Pamela Brown, and Jeanette

as a static characteristic, but a process of coping. It is dynamic, in that successful coping in one instance reinforces the ability to deal with other difficulties in the future.[78]

One ground-breaking research study described how a group of 700 children encountered resilience despite difficult living conditions at birth. Emmy Werner and Ruth Smith followed 700 children born into serious high-risk conditions including mentally ill, alcoholic, abusive, or criminal parents, or those living in poor communities. Their longitudinal study found that 50%, often closer to 70%, of their study participants developed social competence despite exposure to severe stress and they prevailed over their experiences and environment to lead 'successful' lives. Werner and Smith began studying all of the children born on the island of Kauai, Hawaii, in 1955. Of 700 individuals born, 70 seemed 'invulnerable' to the multiple risk-factors at birth and developed no issues. Two main reasons for this, according to Werner and Smith's research, include the fact that these individuals were born with outgoing and social dispositions and could engage supportive resources. The other 2/3rds of the 700 babies developed issues but were doing well by their 30s. The study participants explained that they 'bounced back' because someone, at some point in their life gave them the message, 'You matter'/'I believe in you.'[79]

Throughout the resilience literature, no universal guidelines exist to direct the definitions of risk, resilience and competence. Also, very few research methodologies and data analysis techniques are standardized.[80] When comparing studies on resilience, the results and conclusions are occasionally conflicting and it is difficult to generalize findings.[81] Research and methodological issues in studies on resiliency include: definitions, sample selection, confounding factors, determining a sufficient comparison group, protective factors and processes, source of data, type of data and methodology.[82] As well, definitional

---

Sawyer, 'Conceptual Issues in Studies of Resilience,' *Annals of the New York Academy of Sciences* 1094.1 (2006): 105.

78 Colin Mangham, Miriam Stewart and Graham Reid, 'Fostering Children's Resilience,' *Journal of Pediatric Nursing* 12.1 (1997): 25; Ann Masten, M. O'Dougherty Wright and K.H. Nuechterlein, 'Norman Garmezy (1918–2009),' *The American Psychologist* 66.2 (2011): 140.

79 Emmy Werner and Ruth Smith, eds., *Overcoming the Odds: High Risk Children from Birth to Adulthood* (New York: Cornell University Press, 1992): 173–189.

80 Kim Anderson, 'Uncovering Survival Abilities in Children Who Have Been Sexually Abused,' *Families in Society: The Journal of Contemporary Human Services* (1997): 592–593.

81 Ibid., 593.

82 Suniya Luthar and Edward Zigler, 'Vulnerability and Competence: A Review of Research on Resilience in Childhood,' *American Journal of Orthopsychiatry* 61 (1991): 6–22.

issues and the lack of longitudinal studies limit the conclusions that can be drawn.[83]

The concept of resiliency represents a paradigm shift from a disease model, with its focus on pathology, to a strengths-based model.[84] Thinking about the area of childhood sexual abuse generally and specifically from a resiliency perspective proves especially meaningful for social workers whose training and philosophy emphasise a wellness approach to counselling and while that recognises and builds upon the strengths of their clients they serve.[85] A complex process, according to researchers, resiliency involves the interplay between biological, psychological and social factors. These factors combine to mend the impact of stressful events and encourage adaptation over time in an individual's life.[86] According to O'Connell-Higgins, resilience is 'the active process of self-righting and growth.'[87] She defined resiliency as the ability to negotiate significant developmental challenges that confront individuals as they grow.[88] Ong, Bergeman and Chow also define resilience as 'positive adaptation' in the context of 'risk' or adversity.[89] Ryff, Singer, Love and Essex report that resilience contributes to the maintenance, recovery or improvement in mental or physical health following a challenge.[90] They explain that the definition goes beyond the absence of illness and argue that it centres on psychological well-being along with physical health.[91]

83 Gina O'Connell-Higgins, *Resilient Adults: Overcoming a Cruel Past* (San Francisco: Jossey-Bass, 1994), 1.

84 Kim Anderson, 'Uncovering Survival Abilities in Children Who Have Been Sexually Abused,' *Families in Society: The Journal of Contemporary Human Services* (1997): 592–593.

85 Ibid., 593.

86 Suniya Luthar and Edward Zigler, 'Vulnerability and Competence: A Review of Research on Resilience in Childhood,' *American Journal of Orthopsychiatry* 61 (1991): 6–22.

87 Gina O'Connell-Higgins, *Resilient Adults: Overcoming a Cruel Past* (San Francisco: Jossey-Bass, 1994), 1.

88 Ibid., 1.

89 Anthony Ong, C.S. Bergeman and Sy-Miin Chow, 'Positive Emotions as a Basic Building Block of Resilience in Adulthood,' *Handbook of Adult Resilience*, eds. John Reich, Alex Zautra and Stuart Hall. (New York: The Guilford Press, 2009): 81–93.

90 Carol Ryff, et al., 'Resilience in Adulthood and Later Life: Defining Features and Dynamic Processes,' *Handbook of Aging and Mental Health*, ed. J. Lomranz (New York: Springer Science + Business Media, 1998): 69–96.

91 Carol Ryff, 'Happiness is Everything, Or Is It? Explorations on the Meaning of Psychological Well-Being,' *Journal of Personality and Social Psychology* 57.6 (1989): 1069–1081; Carol Ryff and Corey Lee Keyes, 'The Structure of Psychological Well-Being Revisited,' *Journal of Personality and Social Psychology* 69.4 (1995): 719–727.

The concept of resilience emerged almost by chance from longitudinal developmental studies of 'at risk' groups of children.[92] The epidemiological studies investigated the incidence of disease and pathology. Interest grew in what Rutter (1990) called the 'phenomenon of individual difference in people's responses to stress and adversity.'[93] Instead of focussing on individual shortcomings, the new approach focussed on individual and community strengths and the concept of resilience emerged in psychological texts.[94]

The majority of research on resilience focuses on individual factors and characteristics.[95] Specifically, past studies investigated the factors that separated individuals exposed to childhood sexual abuse who developed problems of adjusting, from those who did not. A range of factors, including personality traits, family characteristics and community influences have been identified as important determinants of resilience following the experience of CSA.[96]

Recently, the role of contextual factors on resilience has gained the attention of researchers. Studies that have investigated this process of resilience explore the effects of contextual factors on resilience.[97] This research investigates the effects of such factors including the stress of parenting,[98] community

---

92 Werner and Smith, *Overcoming the Odds*, 1–17.

93 Michael Rutter, 'Psychosocial Resilience and Protective Mechanisms,' *Risk and Protective Factors In the Development of Psychopathology*, eds. J. Rolf, Ann Masten, Dante Chichetti, K.H. Nuechterlin and S. Weintraub (New York: Cambridge University Press, 1990): 181–214.

94 Sue Howard and Bruce Johnson, 'What Makes the Difference? Children and Teachers Talk about Resilient Outcomes for Children "At Risk,"' *Educational Studies* 26.3 (2000): 321–337.

95 Howard and Johnson, 'What Makes the Difference,'322; Elizabeth Kandel, et al., 'IQ as a Protective Factor for Subjects at High Risk for Antisocial Behavior,' *Journal of Consulting and Clinical Psychology* 56 (1988): 224–226; Patricia Moran and John Eckenrode, 'Protective Personality Characteristics Among Adolescent Victims of Maltreatment,' *Child Abuse & Neglect* 16.5 (1992): 743–754.

96 Brent Morrow and Gwendolyn Sorell, 'Factors Affecting Self-Esteem, Depression, and Negative Behaviours in Sexually Abused Female Adolescents,' *Journal of Marriage and the Family* 51.3 (1989): 677–686; S.E. Romans et al., 'Factors That Mediate Between Child Sexual Abuse and Adult Psychological Outcome,' *Psychological Medicine* 25 (1995): 127–142; Steve Spaccarelli and Soni Kim, 'Resilience Criteria and Factors Associated with Resilience in Sexually Abused Girls,' *Child Abuse & Neglect* 19.9 (1995): 1171–1182.

97 Grossman, et al., *With the Phoenix Rising*, 20.

98 Carol Ryff, et al., 'My Children and Me: Midlife Evaluations of Grown Children And of Self,' *Psychology and Aging* 9.2 (1994): 195–205; Kristen Kling, Marsha Seltzer and Carol Ryff, 'Distinctive Late-Life Challenges: Implications for Coping and Well-Being,' *Psychology and Aging* 12.2 (1997): 288–295.

relocation,[99] care giving,[100] marital transitions,[101] growing up with an alcoholic parent,[102] having a child diagnosed with Down syndrome[103] and the effects of position in the socioeconomic hierarchy.[104]

5 Resilience and Child Sexual Abuse

The finding that not all children exposed to sexual abuse develop troubles of adjustment later in life prompted interest and research into the factors that may protect against the effects of experiencing childhood sexual abuse.[105] Over time, general resiliency research has focused less on the attributes of resilient children and more on the processes of resilience. As the research has attempted to understand the processes associated with resilience, one important finding suggests that rather than avoiding risks, resilient children take substantial risk to cope with stressors, leading to what Cohler called 'adaptation and competence.'[106] Over the past 25 years, research on a variety of at-risk populations has identified both individual and contextual factors that ameliorate

99 Kristen Kling, Carol Ryff and Marilyn Essex, 'Adaptive Changes in the Self-Concept During a Life Transition,' *Personality and Social Psychology Bulletin* 23.9 (1997): 981–990; Kling, 'Distinctive Late-Life Challenges,' 288–289; Nancy Smider, Marilyn Essex and Carol Tyff, 'Adaptation to Community Relocation: The Interactive Influence of Psychological Resources and Contextual Factors,' *Psychology and Aging* 11.2 (1996): 362–372.

100 Lydia Li, Marsha Seltzer and Jan Greenberg, 'Change in Depressive Symptoms Among Daughter Caregivers: An 18-Month Longitudinal Study,' *Psychology and Aging* 14.2 (1999): 206–219; Nadine Marks and James Lambert, 'Marital Status Continuity and Change Among Young and Midlife Adults: Longitudinal Effects on Psychological Well-Being,' *Journal of Family Issues* 19.6 (1998): 652–686.

101 Marks and Lambert, 'Marital Status Continuity and Change,' 652–686.

102 Sandra Tweed and Carol Ryff, 'Adult Children of Alcoholics: Profiles of Wellness Amidst Distress,' *Journal of Studies on Alcohol and Drugs* 52.2 (1991): 133–141.

103 Marcia Van Riper, Carol Ryff and Karen Pridham, 'Parental and Family Well-Being in Families of Children With Down Syndrome: A Comparative Study,' *Research in Nursing & Health* 15.3 (1992): 227–235.

104 Michael Marmot, Carol Ryff, Larry Bumpass, Martin Shipley and Nadine Marks, 'Social Inequalities in Health: Next Questions and Converging Evidence,' *Social Science & Medicine* 44.6 (1997): 901–910; Carol Ryff, et al.,, 'Forging Macro-Micro Linkages In The Study of Psychological Well-Being,' *The Self and Society in Aging Processes,* eds. Carol Ryff and V.W. Marshall (New York: Springer, 1999): 247–278.

105 Patricia Moran and John Eckenrode, 'Protective Personality Characteristics Among Adolescent Victims of Maltreatment,' *Child Abuse & Neglect* 16.5 (1992): 743–744; Romans, et al., 'Factors That Mediate,' 127–128; Spaccarelli and Kim, 'Resilient Criteria,' 1171–1172.

106 Glicken, *Learning from Resilient People*, 81.

the link between risk and competence.[107] These factors include the individual qualities of intellectual functioning,[108] appealing, sociable, easy going disposition, self-efficacy, self-confidence, high self-esteem, talents, faith, and a close relationship to a caring parent figure.[109] Research on the environmental factors that mediate the relation between risk and competence found that authoritative parenting, warmth, structure, high expectations, socioeconomic advantages, connections to extended supportive family networks, bonds to prosocial adults outside the family, connections to prosocial organisations and attending effective schools exist in cases of functional competence.[110] While research has paid some attention to contextual factors as well as individual factors in the general adult resiliency reporting, not enough research has addressed the contextual factors that might contribute to resilience and the contributions of community and neighbourhood to understanding resilience in relation to CSA.[111] My research focussed on how the factors of community and neighbourhood affect the process of resilience in those who experienced CSA. For each participant I interviewed the role of sport, community and/or neighbourhood impacted how they remained resilient despite their experiences of abuse. Many reflected that the interaction with others, the shared community of sport or of their neighbourhood created a support network that acted as a positive shield amidst the traumatic encounters. As Peter Bray explains in his research on the role of Holotropic breath work as a therapeutic intervention, I suspect that the role of breathing during sport activities and playing music acted as a means of releasing parts of the traumatic experiences

107 Ann Masten and Douglass Coatsworth, 'The Development of Competence in Favorable and Unfavorable Environments: Lessons from Research on Successful Children,' *American Psychologist* 53.2 (1998): 205–216.

108 Kandel, et al., 'IQ as a Protective Factor,' 224–226; Ann Masten, Karin Best and Norman Garmezy, 'Resilience and Development: Contributions From the Study of Children who Overcome Adversity,' *Development and Psychopathology* 2 (1990): 425–426; Jennifer White, Terrie Moffitt and Phil Silva, 'A Prospective Replication of the Protective Effects of IQ in Subjects at High Risk for Juvenile Delinquency,' *Journal of Consulting and Clinical Psychology* 57.6 (1989): 721–723.

109 National Research Council, *Understanding Child Abuse and* Neglect, 16; Emmy Werner and Ruth Smith, *Vulnerable But Invincible: A Study of Resilient Children* (New York: McGraw-Hill, 1982): 55; Norman Garmezy, et al., 'The Structure and Coherence of Competence from Childhood Through Adolescence,' *Child Development* 66.6 (1995): 1653–1656.

110 R.J. Haggerty, et al., *Stress, Risk and Resilience in Children and Adolescents: Processes, Mechanisms, and Interventions* (Cambridge: Cambridge University Press, 1994): 354; Werner and Smith, *Vulnerable But Invincible,* 61; Werner and Smith, *Overcoming the Odds*, 173–180.

111 Carol Ryff and Burton Singer, 'Flourishing Under Fire: Resilience As a Prototype of Challenged Thriving,' *Flourishing: Positive Psychology and The Life Well-Lived*, eds. Corey Keyes and Jonathan Haidt (Washington: American Psychological Association, 2003): 15–36.

of participants. For my research participants, the sense of being a part of a community (sport or neighbourhood) acted as a protective factor, and being part of something larger gave a sense of purpose, provided a physical outlet, an emotional outlet and was seen as a social network of belonging. Regarding the gap in the research on adults and resiliency, Ryff and Singer suggest that research must study how individuals find routes out of difficulties that occur over time. They also report that useful data is garnered from studying the lives of individuals who have experienced CSA. Rather than simply studying which individual assets and social resources are associated with positive adaptation, researchers have shown a growing awareness of the need to consider how such factors contribute to resilience in spite of challenges.[112]

6 My Master's Research

My Master's exploratory grounded theory research on resiliency uncovered what participants believed fostered their resiliency despite the experience of CSA. I analysed the research data was analysed using grounded theory, which included open, axial and selective coding. As a methodology, grounded theory centres on issues of importance in peoples' lives,[113] through a process of data collection described as inductive in nature.[114] A grounded theory study begins with a general subject area and from this initial opening, the study becomes continually focussed towards a particular area of interest.[115] My decision to use grounded theory as a method was deliberate as it has been embraced widely as a potential means of bridging the theory-practice divide. It offers clinicians and academics a systematic and interpretive means of generating a theory from data that has the potential to explain, interpret and guide practice.[116] The chosen central phenomenon that emerged from the data collection was the perception that participants' experiences of childhood sexual abuse were traumatic and three categories of strategies used to address this phenomenon were identified. These categories were regulating the traumatic experience,

112 Ong, Bergeman and Chow, *Positive Emotions As a Basic Building Block*, 81–93.

113 Ryff, et al., *Resilience in Adulthood*, 69–96; Ryff and Singer, *Flourishing Under Fire*, 15–36.

114 Janice Morse, 'Using Shadowed Data,' *Qualitative Health Research 11* (2001): 291–292.

115 M. Jones, George Kriflik and M. Zanko, 'Grounded Theory: A Theoretical and Practical Application in the Australian Film Industry,' *Proceedings of the International Qualitative Research Convention* (*QRC05*), eds. A. Hafidz and Bin Hj (Malaysia: Qualitative Research Association of Malaysia, 2005) 48.

116 Jenna Breckenridge and Derek Jones, 'Demystifying Theoretical Sampling in Grounded Theory Research,' *The Grounded Theory Review* 8 (2009): 113–126.

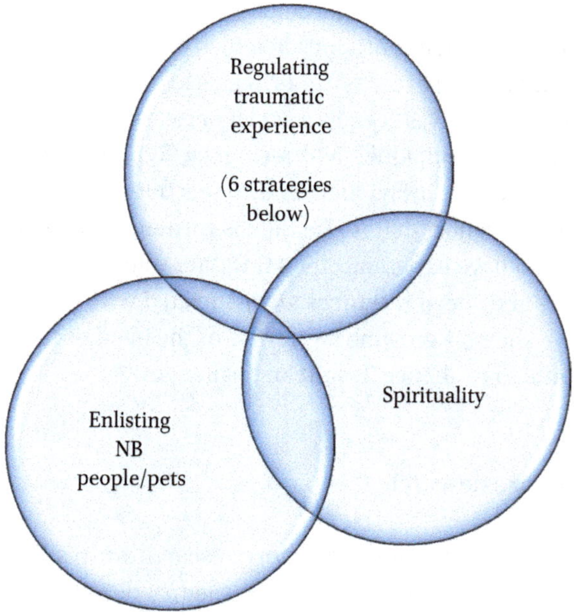

ILLUSTRATION 7.1 MSW grounded theory: Strategies for addressing the phenomenon.

ILLUSTRATION 7.2 Strategies to regulate the traumatic experience.

enlisting important individuals/pets and spirituality (Illustration 7.1). Comparisons between participants showed that many used the same strategies to remain resilient, including humour, self-preservation, imagination, choice and 'unhealthy' strategies (Illustration 7.2). The results indicated degrees of resiliency, a process as well as shared similarities and differences among the participants.[117]

7 My PhD Research

Embarking on my PhD grounded theory research, I hoped to discover more about the process involved in resiliency despite childhood trauma, with the goal of informing clinical practice. Following my first interview, the idea of sport and pushing oneself to the limit arose (Illustration 7.3). Through theoretical sampling, I honed my next interview questions to investigate the potential emerging theme of sport/pushing oneself to the limit. The ebb and flow between data collection and analysis over the past year has led to my discovery of creating distance from memories, from self, from others and from location, which encapsulates the process and a time component consistent in all 15 interviews (Illustration 7.4). Currently, I am immersed in discovering the core concept related to the process of resilience, over time, of those who have experienced the trauma of CSA. My research will address how one's context – including but not limited to community, neighbourhood, family, and school – affects the dynamic process of resilience in those who have experienced CSA. According to Ryff et al., and Ryff and Singer, focussing on how individuals remain resilient despite hardship is paramount to understanding resilience as a dynamic process.[118] My study employed a non-pathology exploration of resilience and will, using a grounded theory approach, develop a theory with the intent of informing the clinical practice field.

This research moves beyond examining individual traits to uncover what maintains or fosters one's resilience over time, by investigating the importance of context, as well as environmental and community influences on the processes of resilience. Knowledge of the factors and processes which lead to resilience, especially in the face of an abusive and/or neglectful environments and experiences, matters crucially for the development of intervention and prevention programs that aim to foster resiliency.[119]

117 Monica Hinton, 'Factors That Foster Resiliency in Adult Women Who Have Experienced Childhood Sexual Abuse' (MSW thesis, University of Calgary, 2004): 81–91.

118 Ryff, et al., *Resilience in Adulthood*, 69–96; Ryff and Singer, *Flourishing Under Fire*, 15–36.

119 Heller, et al., 'Research on Resilience,' 334.

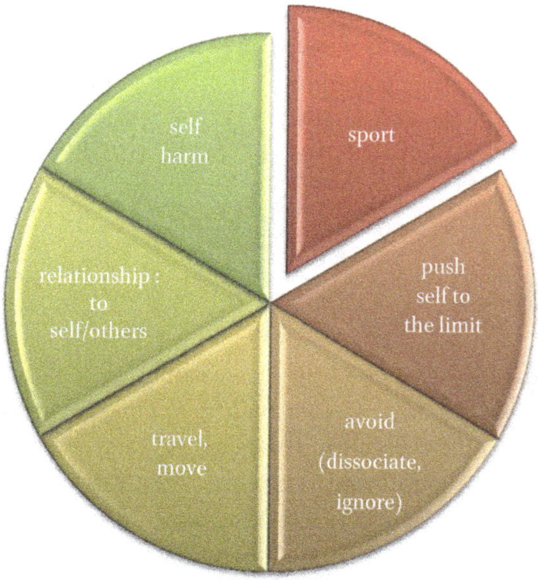

ILLUSTRATION 7.3 Pictorial representation of first PhD interview memo.

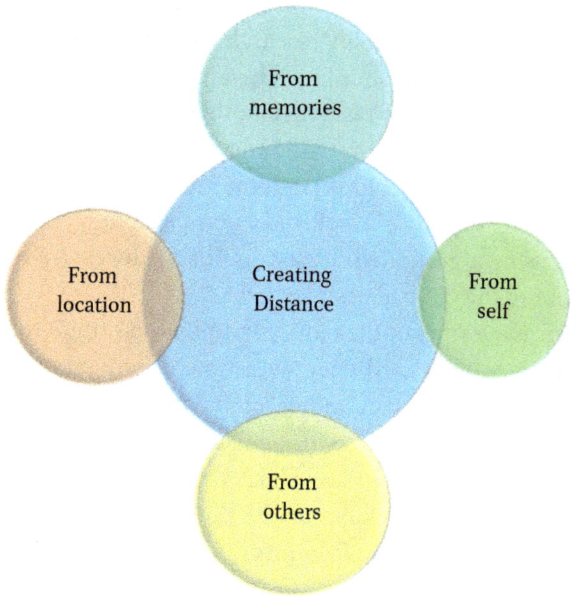

ILLUSTRATION 7.4 First PhD concept creating distance.

8 Practice Implication of Research Findings

According to Benard, the characteristics that alter and/or reverse potential negative outcomes for individuals living in at-risk conditions consist of three broad categories: caring relationships, high expectations and opportunities for meaningful participation[120] Bonnie Benard explained that expressing compassion, understanding, respect and interest, listening, and establishing safety and basic trust positively affects those living in difficult situations.[121] To clinicians, she explained that believing in a client's innate resilience, looking for his/her strengths and assets, as opposed to problems and deficits, offers protection. Benard went on to explain that providing opportunities for valued responsibilities, for making decisions and for contributing one's talents to the community deflects the possible negative results of living in high risk conditions.[122] A familiar example of Bonnie Benard's research on protective factors appears in our winter season routine. We regularly try to protect ourselves from contracting the flu by wearing hats, gloves, scarves, by taking vitamin C, and by getting ample sleep but we cannot eliminate the virus. According to Benard, a major implication for practice stems from these findings.[123] The research findings in both my MSW and PhD research echo Benard's research. Participants expressed that participation in sports activities, team-type activities (like music) and community/neighbourhood involvement helped in their process of resilience despite traumatic experiences of abuse. As reflected in Marie France Forcier's personal account of the role of movement in how she noticed the effects of her traumatic experiences, the use of body in sport activities or music was a factor that helped to foster participant's resilience. Interviewees discussed the role of important individuals in their lives and of how having someone believe in them were paramount in their ability to remain resilient. If we hope to nurture socially competent people who have a sense of their own identity, and can make decisions, set goals, and believe in their future, then we must focus on meeting their basic human needs for respect, caring, connectedness, challenge, power, and meaning.[124]

120 Bonnie Benard, 'Fostering Resiliency in Kids: Protective Factors in the Family, School, and Community,' *Northwest Regional Educational Laboratory* (1991): 15–18.

121 Ibid., 19–20.

122 Ibid., 19–20.

123 Bonnie Benard, *Resiliency: What We Have Learned* (San Francisco: WestEd, 2004): 113–117.

124 Ibid., 113–117.

9 Conclusion

Mary Richmond, a pioneer in the field of social work, addressed the strengths and resiliencies of individuals. Almost a hundred years later, it seems as though our clinical focus has shifted away from seeing our client's strengths to seeing their deficits and issues. It is my objective and practice to validate the innate resilience in clients and I aim to bridge the gap between resilience theory, research and practice. A clinical focus on strengths acts as a unique way of working with our clients to empower them, which will bring about a change that will reconnect us to our social work roots of practice.

Bibliography

Allen, Denise and Kenneth Tarnowski. 'Depressive Characteristics of Physically Abused Children.' *Journal of Abnormal Child Psychology* 17.1 (1989): 1–11.

Anderson, Kim. 'Uncovering Survival Abilities in Children Who Have Been Sexually Abused.' *Families in Society: The Journal of Contemporary Human Services* (1997): 592–599.

Anderson, J.C., J.L. Martin, P.E. Mullen, S.E. Romans and G.P. Herbison. 'The Long-Term Impact of the Physical, Emotional and Sexual Abuse of Children: A Community Study.' *Child Abuse & Neglect* 20.1 (1996): 7–21.

Australian Bureau of Statistics. *Sexual Assault in Australia: A Statistical Overview*. Canberra: ABS, 2004.

Badgley, Robin F. *Sexual Offences against Children in Canada: Report of the Committee on Sexual Offences Against Children and Youths*. Ottawa: Supply and Services Canada, 1984.

Bagley, Christopher 'Prevalence and Correlates of Unwanted Sexual Acts in Childhood in a National Canadian Sample.' *Canadian Journal of Public Health* 80 (1989): 295–296.

Bagley, Christopher and Kathleen King. *Child Sexual Abuse: The Search for Healing*. London: Tavistock/Routledge, 1990.

Bagley, Christopher and R.J. Thomlison. *Child Sexual Abuse: Critical Perspectives on Prevention, Intervention and Treatment*. Toronto: Wall & Emerson, 1991.

Beck, James, and Bessel van der Kolk. 'Reports of Childhood Incest and Current Behaviour of Chronically Hospitalized Psychotic Women.' *The American Journal of Psychiatry* 144.11 (1987): 1474.

Beitchman, Joseph, Kenneth Zucker, Jane Hood, Granville daCosta, Donna Akman and Erika Cassavia. 'A Review of the Long-Term Effects of Child Sexual Abuse.' *Child Abuse & Neglect* 16.1 (1992): 101–118.

Benard, Bonnie. 'Fostering Resiliency in Kids: Protective Factors in the Family, School, and Community.' *Northwest Regional Educational Laboratory* (1991): 5–31.

Benard, Bonnie. *Resiliency: What We Have Learned*. San Francisco: WestEd, 2004.

Bonanno, George, Anthony Papa and Kathleen O'Neill. 'Loss and Human Resilience.' *Applied & Preventive Psychology* 10.3 (2001): 193–206.

Breckenridge, Jenna and Derek Jones. 'Demystifying Theoretical Sampling in Grounded Theory Research.' *The Grounded Theory Review* 8 (2009): 113–126.

Briere, John and Marsha Runtz. 'Multivariate Correlates of Childhood Psychological and Physical Maltreatment among University Women.' *Child Abuse & Neglect* 12 (1988): 331–341.

Briere, John, Kathy Smiljanich and Diane Henschel. 'Sexual Fantasies, Gender, and Molestation History.' *Child Abuse & Neglect* 18.2 (1994): 131–137.

Browne, Angela and David Finkelhor. 'Impact of Child Sexual Abuse: A Review of the Research.' *Psychological Bulletin* 99 (1986a): 66–77.

Browne, Angela and David Finkelhor. 'Initial and Long Term Effects: A Review of the Research.' *A Source Book on Child Sexual Abuse*, edited by David Finkelhor, xx-yy. Beverly Hills: Sage Publications, 1986b.

Burnam, Audrey. 'Sexual Assault and Mental Disorder in a Community Population.' *Journal of Consulting and Clinical Psychology* 56.6 (1988): 843–850.

Cerezo-Jimenez, Angeles and Dolores Frias. 'Emotional and Cognitive Adjustment in Abused Children.' *Child Abuse & Neglect* 18.11 (1994): 923–932.

Chesnais, Jean-Claude. *History of Violence (In the West From 1800 to the Present)*. Paris: The National Research Institute, 1981.

Chew, Judy. *Women Survivors of Childhood Sexual Abuse: Healing Through Group Work*. New York: The Haworth Press, Inc, 1998.

Cohler, B.J. 'Adversity, Resilience, and the Study of Lives.' *The Invulnerable Child*, edited by E.J. Anthony and B.J. Cohler, 363–424. New York: The Guilford Press, 1987.

Conte, Jon and John Schuerman. 'The Effects of Sexual Abuse on Children: A Multidimensional View.' *Journal of Interpersonal Violence* 2.4 (1988): 380–390.

Cook, B, F. David and A. Grant. 'Sexual Violence in Australia.' *Research and Public Policy Series no. 36*. Canberra: Australian Institute of Criminology, 2001. Viewed on 1 November 2012 http://www.aic.gov.au/publications/rpp/36/index.html.

Courtois, Christine. 'Healing the Incest Wound: A Treatment Update with Attention to Recovered Memory Issues.' *American Journal of Psychotherapy* 51.4 (1997): 464–496.

Dufour, M.H., L. Nadeau and K. Bertrand. 'Les Facteurs de Resilience chez les Victims d'Abus Sexuel: Etat de la Question.' *Child Abuse and Neglect* 24.6 (2000): 781–797.

Feiring, Candice, Lynn Taska and Michael Lewis. 'Social Support and Children's and Adolescents' Adaptation to Sexual Abuse.' *Journal of Interpersonal Violence* 13.2 (1998): 240–260.

Fergusson, David, Michael Lynskey and John Horwood. 'Childhood Sexual Abuse and Psychiatric Disorder in Young Adulthood: I. Prevalence of Sexual Abuse and Factors Associated with Sexual Abuse.' *Journal of the American Academy of Child and Adolescent Psychiatry* 35.10 (1996): 1355–1364.

Finkelhor, David. *Sexually Victimized Children*. New York: The Free Press, 1979.

Finkelhor, David. 'Early and Long-Term Effects of Child Sexual Abuse: An Update.' *Professional Psychology: Research and Practice* 21.5 (1990): 325–330.

Finkelhor, David. 'The International Epidemiology of Child Sexual Abuse.' *Child Abuse & Neglect* 18.5 (1994): 409–417.

Finkelhor, David. *Childhood Victimization: Violence, Crime and Abuse in the Lives of Young People*. New York: Oxford University Press, 2008.

Finkelhor, David and Angela Browne. 'The Traumatic Impact of Child Sexual Abuse: A Conceptualization.' *American Journal of Orthopsychiatry* 55.4 (1985): 530–541.

Finkelhor, David and Jennifer Dzuiba-Leatherman. 'Victimization of Children: 1.' *The American Psychologist* 49.3 (1994): 173–183.

Finkelhor, David, Hotaling Gerald, I.A. Lewis and Christine Smith. 'Sexual Abuse in a National Survey of Adult Men and Women: Prevalence, Characteristics, and Risk Factors.' *Child Abuse & Neglect* 14.1 (1990): 19–28.

Fleming, J.M. 'Prevalence of Childhood Sexual Abuse in a Community Sample of Australian Women.' *The Medical Journal of Australia* 166.2 (1997): 65–68.

Garmezy, Norman. 'Resiliency and Vulnerability to Adverse Developmental Outcomes Associated with Poverty.' *American Behavioral Scientist* 34.4 (1991): 416–430.

Garmezy, Norman, Douglas Coatsworth, Jennifer Neemann, Scott Gest, Auke Tellegen and Ann Masten. 'The Structure and Coherence of Competence from Childhood through Adolescence.' *Child Development* 66.6 (1995): 1635–1659.

Glaser, Barney. *Theoretical Sensitivity*. Mill Valley: The Sociology Press, 1978.

Glaser, Barney and Anselm Strauss. *The Discovery of Grounded Theory*. Chicago: Aldine, 1967.

Glicken, Morley D. *Learning from Resilient People: Lessons We Can Apply to Counselling and Psychotherapy*. Thousand Oaks: SAGE Publications, 2006.

Goldston, David, Dawn Turnquist and John Knutson. 'Presenting Problems of Sexually Abused Girls Receiving Psychiatric Services.' *Journal of Abnormal Psychology* 98.3 (1989): 314–317.

Gomes-Schwartz, B., J. Horowitz and A.P. Cardarelli. *Child Sexual Abuse: The Initial Effects*. California: Sage Publications, Inc, 1990.

Grossman, Frances, Alexandra Cook, Selin Kepkep, and Karestan Koenen. *With the Phoenix Rising: Lessons from Ten Resilient Women Who Overcame the Trauma of Childhood Sexual Abuse*. San Francisco: Jossey-Bass, 1999.

Haggerty, R.J. L.R. Sherrod, Norman Garmezy, and Michael Rutter. *Stress, Risk and Resilience in Children and Adolescents: Processes, Mechanisms, and Interventions*. Cambridge: Cambridge University Press, 1994.

Health Canada, 1997, 'National Clearinghouse on Family Violence,' *National Clearinghouse on Family Violence/Health Canada*, Ontario: Publisher.

Heller, Sheryl, Julie Larrieu, Rhonda D'Imperio and Neil Borris. 'Research on Resilience to Child Maltreatment: Empirical Considerations.' *Child Abuse and Neglect* 23.4 (1999): 321–338.

Herman, Judith. *Father Daughter Incest*. Cambridge: Harvard University Press, 1981.

Herzog, David, Janet Staley, Susan Carmody, Wendi Robbins, and Bessel van der Kolk. 'Childhood Sexual Abuse in Anorexia Nervosa and Bulimia Nervosa: A Pilot Study.' *Journal of the American Academy of Child and Adolescent Psychiatry* 32.5 (1993): 962–966.

Hinton, Monica. 'Factors That Foster Resiliency In Adult Women Who Have Experienced Childhood Sexual Abuse.' MSW thesis, University of Calgary, 2004.

Howard, Sue and Bruce Johnson. 'What Makes the Difference? Children and Teachers Talk About Resilient Outcomes for Children "At Risk."' *Educational Studies* 26.3 (2000): 321–337.

Johnson, Bret and Mary Beth Kenkel. 'Stress, Coping, and Adjustment in Female Adolescent Incest Victims.' *Child Abuse & Neglect* 15.3 (1991): 293–305.

Jones, M., George Kriflik and M. Zanko. 'Grounded Theory: A Theoretical and Practical Application in the Australian Film Industry.' *Proceedings of the International Qualitative Research Convention* (QRC05). Edited by A. Hafidz and Bin Hj. Malaysia: Qualitative Research Association of Malaysia, 2005.

Jumper, Shan. 'A Meta-Analysis of the Relationship of Child Sexual Abuse to Adult Psychological Adjustment.' *Child Abuse & Neglect* 19.6 (1995): 715–728.

Kandel, Elizabeth, Sarnoff Mednick, Lis Kirkegaard-Sorenson, Barry Hutchings, Joachim Knop, Raben Rosenberg, and Fini Schulsinger. 'IQ as a Protective Factor for Subjects at High Risk for Antisocial Behavior.' *Journal of Consulting and Clinical Psychology* 56 (1988): 224–226.

Kashani, Javad and Gabrielle Carlson. 'Seriously Depressed Preschoolers.' *The American Journal of Psychiatry* 144.3 (1987): 348.

Kempe, C. Henryand Patricia Beezley Mrazek. *Sexually Abused Children and Their Families*. New York: Pergamon Press, 1981.

Kendall-Tackett, Kathleen, Linda Williams and David Finkelhor. 'Impact of Sexual Abuse on Children: A Review and Synthesis of Recent Empirical Studies,' *Psychological Bulletin* 113.1 (1993): 164–180.

Ketring, Scott and Leslie Feinauer. 'Perpetrator-Victim Relationships: Long-Term Effects of Sexual Abuse for Men and Women.' *American Journal of Family Therapy* 27 (1999): 109–120.

Kling, Kristen, Carol Ryff and Marilyn Essex. 'Adaptive Changes in the Self-Concept During a Life Transition.' *Personality and Social Psychology Bulletin* 23.9 (1997a): 981–990.

Kling, Kristen, Marsha Seltzer and Carol Ryff. 'Distinctive Late-Life Challenges: Implications for Coping and Well-Being.' *Psychology and Aging* 12.2 (1997b): 288–295.

Kolko, David. 'Individual Cognitive Behavioural Treatment and Family Therapy for Physically Abused Children and their Offending Parents: A Comparison of Clinical Outcomes.' *Child Maltreatment* 1.4 (1996): 322–342.

Kolvin, I., F.J.W. Miller, M. Fleeting and P.A. Kolvin. 'Social and Parenting Factors Affecting Criminal-Offense Rates: Findings from the Newcastle Thousand Family Study.' *British Journal of Psychiatry* 152 (1988): 80–90.

Li, Lydia, Marsha Seltzer and Jan Greenberg. 'Change in Depressive Symptoms Among Daughter Caregivers: An 18-Month Longitudinal Study.' *Psychology and Aging* 14.2 (1999): 206–219.

Luthar, Suniya and Edward Zigler. 'Vulnerability and Competence: A Review of Research on Resilience in Childhood.' *American Journal of Orthopsychiatry* 61 (1991): 6–22.

Luthar, Suniya, Pamela Brown and Jeanette Sawyer. 'Conceptual Issues in Studies of Resilience.' *Annals of the New York Academy of Sciences* 1094.1 (2006): 105–115.

Luthar, Suniya, Dante Cicchetti and Bronwyn Becker. 'The Construct of Resilience: A Critical Evaluation and Guidelines for Future Work.' *Child Development* 71.3 (2000): 543–562.

Lynskey, Michael and David Fergusson. 'Factors Protecting Against the Development of Adjustment Difficulties in Young Adults Exposed to Childhood Sexual Abuse.' *Child Abuse & Neglect* 21.12 (1997): 1177–1190.

Mandleco, Barbara and Craig Peery. 'An Organizational Framework for Conceptualizing Resilience in Children.' *Journal of Child and Adolescent Psychiatric Nursing* 13.3 (2000): 99–112.

Mangham, Colin, Graham Reid and Miriam Stewart. 'Resilience in Families: Challenges for Health Promotion.' *Canadian Journal of Public Health-Revue Canadienne de Sante Publique* 87.6 (1996): 373–374.

Mangham, Colin, Miriam Stewart and Graham Reid. 'Fostering Children's Resilience.' *Journal of Pediatric Nursing* 12.1 (1997): 21–31.

Mannarino, Anthony and Judith Cohen. 'Abuse-Related Attributions and Perceptions, General Attributions, and Locus of Control in Sexually Abused Girls.' *Journal of Interpersonal Violence* 11.2 (1996): 162–180.

Marks, Nadine and James Lambert. 'Marital Status Continuity and Change Among Young and Midlife Adults: Longitudinal Effects on Psychological Well-Being.' *Journal of Family Issues* 19.6 (1998): 652–686.

Marmot, Michael, Carol Ryff, Larry Bumpass, Martin Shipley and Nadine Marks. 'Social Inequalities in Health: Next Questions and Converging Evidence.' *Social Science & Medicine* 44.6 (1997): 901–910.

Masten, Ann. 'Ordinary Magic: Resilience Processes in Development.' *American Psychologist* 56.3 (2001): 227–238.

Masten, Ann and Douglas Coatsworth. 'The Development of Competence in Favorable and Unfavorable Environments Lessons from Research on Successful Children.' *American Psychologist* 53.2 (1998): 205–220.

Masten, Ann, Karin Best and Norman Garmezy. 'Resilience and Development: Contributions from the Study of Children who Overcome Adversity.' *Development and Psychopathology* 2 (1990): 425–444.

Masten, Ann, M. Wright O'Dougherty and K.H. Nuechterlein. 'Norman Garmezy (1918–2009).' *The American Psychologist* 66.2 (2011): 140.

Miller-Perrin, C.L., and R.D. Perrin. *Child Maltreatment: An Introduction*. 2nd. ed., Thousand Oaks: Sage Publications, 2007.

Moore, Elya, Helena Romaniuk, Craig Olsson, Yasmin Jayasinghe, John Carlin, and George Patton. 'The Prevalence of Childhood Sexual Abuse and Adolescent Unwanted Sexual Contact among Boys and Girls Living in Victoria, Australia.' *Child Abuse & Neglect* 34.5 (2010): 379–385.

Moran, Patricia and John Eckenrode. 'Protective Personality Characteristics among Adolescent Victims of Maltreatment.' *Child Abuse & Neglect* 16.5 (1992): 743–754.

Morrow, Brent and Gwendolyn Sorell. 'Factors Affecting Self-Esteem, Depression, and Negative Behaviours in Sexually Abused Female Adolescents.' *Journal of Marriage and the Family* 51.3 (1989): 677–686.

Morse, Janice. 'Using Shadowed Data.' *Qualitative Health Research 11* (2001): 291–292.

Mrazek, Patricia and David Mrazek. 'Resilience in Child Maltreatment Victims: A Conceptual Exploration.' *Child Abuse and Neglect*, 11.3 (1987): 357–366.

Mullen, P.E., J.L. Martin, J.C. Anderson, S.E. Romans, and G.P. Herbison. 'The Long-Term Impact of the Physical, Emotional and Sexual Abuse of Children: A Community Study.' *Child Abuse & Neglect* 20.1 (1996): 7–21.

Muller, Wayne. *How, Then, Shall We Live? Four Simple Questions That Reveal the Beauty and Meaning of Our Lives*. New York: Bantam Books, 1996.

Nakishima, Ida and Gloria Zakus. 'Incest: Review and Clinical Experience.' *Pediatrics* 60.5 (1977): 696–697.

National Research Council, *Understanding Child Abuse and Neglect: Panel on Research on Child Abuse and Neglect*, Washington, D.C.: National Academy Press, Washington, 1993.

Neumann, Debra, Beth Houskamp, Vicki Pollock and John Briere. 'The Long-Term Sequelae of Childhood Sexual Abuse in Women: A Meta-Analytic Review.' *Child Maltreatment* 1.1 (1996): 6–16.

O'Connell-Higgins, Gina. *Resilient Adults: Overcoming a Cruel Past*. San Francisco: Jossey-Bass, 1994.

O'Dougherty-Wright, M., and Ann Masten. 'Vulnerability and Resilience in Young Children.' *Handbook of Child and Adolescent Psychiatry: Vol. 1 Infancy and Preschoolers:*

Development and Syndromes, edited by J.D. Noshpitz, S. Greenspan, S. Wieder, and J. Osofsky, xx-yy. New York: Wiley, 1997b.

O'Dougherty-Wright, M., Ann Masten, A. Northwood and J.J. Hubbard. 'Long-Term Effects of Massive Trauma: Developmental and Psychobiological Perspectives.' *Rochester Symposium on Developmental Psychopathology: Vol. 8, Developmental perspectives on Trauma,* edited by Dante Cicchetti and S.L. Toth, xx-yy. New York: University of Rochester Press, 1997a.

O'Hagan, Karen. *Working with Child Sexual Abuse: A Post-Cleveland Guide to Effective Principles and Practice.* Milton Keynes: Open University Press, 1989.

Ong, Anthony, C.S. Bergeman and Sy-Miin Chow. 'Positive Emotions as a Basic Building Block of Resilience in Adulthood.' *Handbook of Adult Resilience,* edited by John Reich, Alex Zautra and Stuart Hall, 81–93. New York: The Guilford Press, 2009.

Pelcovitz, David, Sandra Kaplan, Barbara Goldenberg, Fran Mandel, Julie Lehane, and James Guarrera. 'Post-Traumatic Stress Disorder in Physically Abused Adolescents.' *Journal of the American Academy of Child and Adolescent Psychiatry* 33.3 (1994): 305–312.

Perry, Bruce 'Childhood Experience and the Expression of Genetic Potential: What Childhood Neglect Tells us About Nature and Nurture.' *Brain and Mind* 3 (2002): 79–100.

Peters, S., Gail Wyatt and David Finkelhor. 'Prevalence.' *A Sourcebook on Child Sexual Abuse,* edited by David Finkelhor, xx-yy. Beverly Hills: Sage Publications, 1986.

Pinheiro, Paulo Sérgio. 'Independent Expert for the United Nations Secretary-General's Study on Violence against Children.' *World report on violence against children* (place: publisher, 2006): p. 117.

Rind, Bruce and Philip Tromovitch. 'A Meta-Analytic Review of Findings From National Samples on Psychological Correlates of Child Sexual Abuse.' *The Journal of Sex Research* 34.3 (1997): 237–255.

Romans, S.E., J.L. Martin, J.C. Anderson, M.L. O'Shea, and P.E. Mullen. 'Factors That Mediate Between Child Sexual Abuse and Adult Psychological Outcome.' *Psychological Medicine* 25 (1995): 127–142.

Rush, F. *The Best Kept Secret: Sexual Abuse of Children.* New York: McGraw Hill, 1980.

Russell, Diana. 'The Incidence and Prevalence of Intrafamilial and Extrafamilial Sexual Abuse of Female Children.' *Child Abuse & Neglect* 7.2 (1983): 133–146.

Russell, Diana. *The Secret Trauma: Incest in the Lives of Girls and Women.* New York: Basic Books, 1986.

Russell, Diana. *Lives of Courage: Women for a New South Africa.* New York: Basic Books, 1989.

Rutter, Michael. 'Psychosocial resilience and protective mechanisms.' *Risk and protective factors in the development of psychopathology,* edited by J. Rolf, Ann Masten, Chichetti Dante, K.H. Nuechterlin and S. Weintraub, 181–214. New York: Cambridge University Press, 1990.

Rutter, Michael. 'Resilience Concepts and Findings: Implications for Family Therapy.' *Journal of Family Therapy* 21 (1999): 119–144.

Ryff, Carol. 'Happiness is everything, or is it? Explorations on the Meaning of Psychological Well-Being.' *Journal of Personality and Social Psychology* 57.6 (1989): 1069–1081.

Ryff, Carol and Corey Lee Keyes. 'The Structure of Psychological Well-Being Revisited.' *Journal of Personality and Social Psychology* 69.4 (1995): 719–727.

Ryff, Carol and Burton Singer. 'Flourishing Under Fire: Resilience As a Prototype of Challenged Thriving.' *Flourishing: Positive Psychology and The Life Well-Lived,* edited by Corey Keyes and Jonathan Haidt xx-yy. Washington, DC, US: American Psychological Association, 2003.

Ryff, Carol, Young Hyun Lee, Marilyn Essex and Pamela Schmutte. 'My Children and Me: Midlife Evaluations of Grown Children and of Self.' *Psychology and Aging* 9.2 (1994): 195–205.

Ryff, Carol, W. Magee, Kristen Kling and E. Wing. 'Forging Macro-Micro Linkages in the Study of Psychological Well-Being.' *The Self and Society in Aging Processes,* edited by C.D. Ryff and V.W. Marshall, xx-yy. New York: Springer, 1999.

Ryff, Carol, Burton Singer, Gayle Love and Marilyn Essex. 'Resilience in Adulthood and Later Life: Defining Features and Dynamic Processes.' *Handbook of Aging and Mental Health,* edited by J. Lomranz, xx-yy. New York: Springer Science + Business Media, 1998.

Sanford, Linda. *The Silent Children: A Parent's Guide to the Prevention of Child Sexual Abuse*. New York: McGraw-Hill, 1980.

Sedney, Mary Anne and Barbara Brooks. 'Factors Associated with a History of Childhood Sexual Experience in a Nonclinical Female Population.' *Journal of the American Academy of Child Psychiatry* 23.2 (1984): 215–218.

Silbert, Mimi and Ayala Pines. 'Sexual Child Abuse as an Antecedent to Prostitution.' *Child Abuse and Neglect* 5.4 (1981): 407–411.

Spaccarelli, Steve and Soni Kim. 'Resilience Criteria and Factors Associated with Resilience in Sexually Abused Girls.' *Child Abuse & Neglect* 19.9 (1995): 1171–1182.

Stanley, J. and C. Goddard. *Hearing Only Half of the Story by Leaving Out Half of the Violence,* Melbourne: Australian Institute of Family Studies, 2003.

Strauss, Anselm and Juliet Corbin. *Basics of Qualitative Research: Grounded Theory Procedures and Techniques*. Thousand Oaks: Sage, 1998.

The Canadian Badgley Royal Commission, Report on Sexual Offenses Against Children and Youths. *Child Sexual Abuse,* 1984.

Tsai, M. and N. Wagner. 'Therapy Groups for Women Sexually Molested as Children.' *Archives of Sexual Behavior* 7 (1978): 417–429.

Tweed, Sandra and Carol Ryff. 'Adult Children of Alcoholics: Profiles of Wellness Amidst Distress.' *Journal of Studies on Alcohol and Drugs* 52.2 (1991): 133–141.

United Nations General Assembly. *Report of the Independent Expert for the United Nations Study on Violence Against Children*. (2006): 1–34.

Valentine, LaNae and Leslie Feinauer. 'Resilience Factors Associated with Female Survivors of Childhood Sexual Abuse.' *The American Journal of Family Therapy* 21.3 (1993): 216–224.

van der Kolk, Bessel, Christopher Perry and Judith Herman. 'Childhood Origins of Self-Destructive Behaviour.' *The American Journal of Psychiatry* 148.12 (1991): 1665–1671.

Van Riper, Marcia, Carol Ryff and Karen Pridham. 'Parental and Family Well-Being in Families of Children with Down Syndrome: A Comparative Study.' *Research in Nursing & Health* 15.3 (1992): 227–235.

Werner, Emmy. 'Resilience in Development.' *Current Directions in Psychological Science* 4.3 (1995): 81–85.

Werner, Emmy and Ruth Smith. *Vulnerable but Invincible: A Study of Resilient Children.* New York: McGraw-Hill, 1982.

Werner, Emmy and Ruth Smith, eds. *Overcoming the Odds: High Risk Children from Birth to Adulthood.* New York: Cornell University Press, 1992.

White, Jennifer, Terrie Moffitt and Phil Silva. 'A Prospective Replication of the Protective Effects of IQ in Subjects at High Risk for Juvenile Delinquency.' *Journal of Consulting and Clinical Psychology* 57.6 (1989): 719–724.

de Wilde, E.J., I.C. Kienhorst, R.F. Diekstra and W.H. Wolters. 'The Relationship between Adolescent Suicidal Behaviour and Life Events in Childhood and Adolescence.' *The American Journal of Psychiatry* 149.1 (1992): 45–51.

Wolfe, David, L. Sas, and C. Wekerle. 'Factors Associated with the Development of Post-traumatic Stress Disorder among Child Victims of Sexual Abuse.' *Child Abuse & Neglect* 18.1 (1994): 37–50.

Wolfe, Vicky, Carole Gentile and David Wolfe. 'The Impact of Sexual Abuse on Children: A PTSD Formulation.' *Behaviour Therapy* 20.2 (1989): 215–228.

Wyatt, Gail. 'The Sexual Abuse of Afro-American and White-American Women in Childhood.' *Child Abuse and Neglect* 9.4 (1985): 507–519.

Wyatt, Gail. 'The Aftermath of Child Sexual Abuse of African American and White American Women: The Victim's Experience.' *Journal of Family Violence* 5.1 (1990): 61–81.

Wyatt, Gail, Donald Guthrie and Cindy Notgrass. 'Differential Effects of Women's Child Sexual Abuse and Subsequent Sexual Revictimization.' *Journal of Consulting and Clinical Psychology* 60.2 (1992): 167–173.

Zimmerman, Marc and Revathy Arunkumar. 'Resiliency Research: Implications for Schools and Policy.' *Social Policy Report: Society for Research in Child Development* 3.4 (1994): 1–20.

Zuravin, Susan and Cynthia Fontanella. 'The Relationship between Child Sexual Abuse and Major Depression among Low-Income Women: A Function of Growing Up Experiences?' *Child Maltreatment* 4.1 (1999): 3–12.

CHAPTER 8

Investigating the Post-Traumatic Lens in the Choreographer's Work

Marie France Forcier

1 Introduction

1.1 *Personal Background*

I have now lived with the aftereffects of trauma for fifteen years. I was diagnosed with Post-Traumatic Stress Disorder (PTSD) a full 15 months after being the victim of a number of overlapping psychologically traumatic events.[1] 'At that point, I consulted a mental health professional for complications I was experiencing in developing new personal relationships'.[2] The PTSD diagnosis came as a relief. During the period between the trauma and the diagnosis, I had felt detached, depressed, misunderstood, judged, unable to relate, emotionally unstable and physically dissociated. It was reassuring to hear that my state resulted from a condition; that contrary to what I had burdened myself with believing, it wasn't *my fault*. I had not been manufacturing my feelings for self-destructive purposes, but rather had simply been suffering from a condition also affecting countless others. With the help of a cognitive-behavioural therapist, I learned to make new sense out of life moving forward.[3]

That held until recently. As a dancer-choreographer by profession, I began to notice elements characteristic of dissociation arising in my work.[4]

'It is important to note that it was not the traumatic events themselves that appeared to manifest in my choreographic work, but rather my long repressed post-traumatic symptoms'.[5] As such, in this context, it was deemed irrelevant to provide further information on the nature of those events.[6]

1 Marie France Forcier, 'Creating Contemporary Choreography Through the Post-Traumatic Lens' (MFA thesis, York University, 2014). This chapter was developed in parallel to my Master of Fine Arts thesis research and, as such, I paraphrased or quoted directly from the thesis.

2 Ibid., 1.

3 Ibid., 1.

4 Ibid., 1.

5 Ibid., 2.

6 Ibid., 2.

 | DOI:10.1163/9789004385931_009

1.2 *Choreographic Background*

While a student in the last year of my professional dance training at the time of the incidents, I sustained a trauma that had a substantial impact on my physical performance. I experienced a noticeable technical regression due to, among others, a loss of proprioception and the inability to concentrate.[7] 'This was devastating at the time, because I had trained for a career as a performer since childhood, and did not understand what was happening to my body'.[8] My psychological distress was amplified tenfold when teachers and potential employers who used to praise me reacted critically to my regression, as though it manifested laziness on my part.[9] 'This destroyed my confidence as a performer, and to this day, I feel the somatic repercussions of what happened to me then'.[10] Aware that dance remained my way of existing in the world in spite of those hardships, I stayed the course and recovered professionally in the years following by focusing on choreography instead of performance. I went on to create *Forcier Stage Works* (FSW), a contemporary dance company that employs a returning group of collaborators and presents my choreography as the core of its programming.[11]

When first establishing myself as a professional dance creator, my preferred aesthetics were strongly based in athleticism, which I approached from a mechanical standpoint.[12] Creatively during those early years, *states*, those particular mental conditions that affect the quality, the physical origin and the very purpose of human movement, were of little interest to me.[13] 'Compositionally, I prioritized structure over malleability; I created technically polished works and directed dancers in ways that ensured exact duplication'.[14] My creative means were mostly directorial; in process or in performance, I did not give the dancers much freedom to follow their impulses. All elements of my work were calculated, exact and rigid; in hindsight, they reflected trust issues inherent to my personal post-traumatic life of the time. I followed the traditional hierarchical ways established by ballet, at a time when the trend in Western contemporary choreography was established as a democratic platform – dancers were encouraged to collaborate creatively with choreographers.[15] This style

7 Ibid., 2.
8 Ibid., 2.
9 Ibid., 2.
10 Ibid., 2.
11 Ibid., 2–3.
12 Ibid., 3.
13 Ibid., 3.
14 Ibid., 3.
15 Ibid., 3.

prevailed in my work until 2011 when, faced with a sustained lack of inspiration, I recognized that I had reached a plateau. To remedy my lingering sense of creative and professional stagnation, I challenged myself with a project revolving around the creation of solo pieces, an intimidating form for which I then felt very little natural affinity. I began to create a series of one-person studies as a result, and this turned into the first developmental phase for a new full-length group work, ultimately titled *Lab Rats*.[16]

Following my established creative habits, I initiated the first of these studies with an output of athletic movement following musical structure. Two or three days into the process, while watching my dancer rehearse, I had an uncharacteristic moment of clarity about my work. My choreography revealed itself as though I was seeing it clearly for the first time.[17] Through this new lens, "I saw it as a *forced* expanse of energy, executed with no impetus other than obeying a randomly imposed set of physical rules".[18] In processing this perspective, I recognized that my body of choreography had up to then been devoid of genuine communicative substance; it consisted in a mere exercise in virtuosity safely designed to impress.[19] In response to that artistic epiphany, over the course of the following year, I went on in my studio work to create *Lab Rats*' remaining choreography, dramaturgical arc and staging. This time, I experimented with encouraging the expression of my dancers' and my own instincts within an established frame, and found it surprisingly natural to follow my unconscious mind's suggestions.[20] A creatively freer work resulted from the exercise; a work lucid enough for me to discern suggestions of PTSD-related elements when I first saw it performed. For example, in several instances, the performers looked straight through the audience with a vacant focus while carrying-out the physical movement.[21] 'This was breaking the established choreographic convention where the dancer's eye is trained to go where the body goes'.[22] I realized that, unbeknownst to me, I had directed my dancers to perform dissociative states characterized by this vacant focus.[23]

In the winter of 2013, shortly after the professional presentation of *Lab Rats,* I went back to the studio creating a new piece, *Portraiture/Wreckage*, as part of an MFA course work assignment. After being in process for less than a week

16 Ibid., 3–4.
17 Ibid., 4.
18 Ibid., 4.
19 Ibid., 4.
20 Ibid., 4.
21 Ibid., 4–5.
22 Ibid., 5.
23 Ibid., 5.

with my undergraduate student dancers, I noticed that my choreographic practice was insisting on guiding them to embody dissociative-like states.[24] 'Without premeditation, I was repeating certain of the directorial demands I had placed on my dancers in *Lab Rats*'.[25] In retrospect, I seemed fixed on engineering dissonance; I could no longer ignore the impetus. More specifically, I was striving to repeat both a visual disconnection with one's own body and environment, and touches of violent action bursting through eerily calm energy: two insistent choreographic patterns.[26]

Almost immediately after presenting *Portraiture/Wreckage*, I went back to the creative process, again as part of my academic work, with new undergraduate dancers. For *Pool Party*, I deliberately chose to direct the students to perform dissociative-like states. The action was staged among a series of large inflatable props and I guided the dancers to interact with those props and with one another by focusing on an unstated purpose, in visually idle ways. I was compelled to further investigate this choreographic direction less intuitively, more analytically. By this point, I had recognized with growing certitude that my experience of PTSD had been infiltrating my creative work.[27] My instincts compelled me to let the phenomenon happen and to develop it consciously. While guiding dancers to perform dissociation felt complex and delicate, I was truly interested in the aesthetic dissonance it could create for the audience.[28] 'By the end of the creative process for this new piece, I had made the decision to dedicate my MFA thesis investigation to the expression of PTSD through contemporary choreography'.[29]

1.3 *Methodology*

In preparation for my practical research, I consulted a number of publications on psychological trauma from various sources and disciplines in order to get a comprehensive picture of the existing research on the topic. This enabled me

24 Ibid., 5.

25 Ibid., 5.

26 Ibid., 5.

27 Although the intent behind my creative work in this context was not therapeutic, I believe that my processes bore catalytic similarities between Danielle Schaub's phototherapy, as reported in this volume. Schaub's creative photo-collage act visually confronted her family, which prompted subsequent analytic and story telling acts, in turn leading her to 'put the traumas behind and focus on the present and the future without dwelling on the past wounds'. Similarly, my choreographic act with *Lab Rats* allowed me to externally witness my dissociative history for the first time, unravelling the process and outcomes that I outline in this chapter. Danielle Schaub, 'Reading Myself and Worlds: Coping Strategies in the Face of Cumulative Trauma', in this volume.

28 Ibid., 5–6.

29 Ibid., 6.

to recognize the symptoms of PTSD most germane to what had been transpiring in my own choreography.[30] 'This literature review also enabled me to identify the disciplines and theories most pertinent to the exploration I was interested in pursuing creatively'.[31] I recognized through my readings that the focus of my investigation did not rest on the contributions made by dance therapy. While expressive arts therapy is incontestably valuable in theory and practice, the questions I wanted to answer academically concerned the use of PTSD as a lens for staging dances, and not the investigation of choreography as a means to achieve catharsis. As a creator, I deemed important to avoid the edge where artistic expression plummets towards self-indulgence. Forcing an audience to witness a personal breakthrough voyeuristically is a selfish act and, to me, art should be foremost altruistic. Consequently, rather than helping me unearth commonalities and develop a hybrid form between dance therapy exercises and choreographic methodologies, my readings helped me refine my understanding of psychological trauma's psychic and physical repercussions, in order to create informed choreographic worlds. This new theoretical knowledge, paired with a decade's worth of my own post-traumatic somatic embodiment, fuelled the creative processes for my Master of Fine Arts' choreographic assignments.[32]

In this chapter, I outline the creation processes behind two of these pieces – an autobiographical solo and a proscenium group work – and, within each, 'the discoveries I have made in regards to my own artistry and to the various ways in which the embodiment of PTSD can be used to generate choreographic meaning'.[33]

2 Creative Processes

2.1 *Autobiographic Solo:* Little Guidebook for Using Your Suffering Wisely

2.1.1 Intention

Towards the beginning of September 2013, I read *What Doesn't Kill Us,*[34] the work of Dr. Stephen Joseph on Post-Traumatic Growth (PTG). Exposing the shinier flipside of an otherwise very dark coin without falling into the self-help genre's clichés, I found his research to have a catalytic effect on my creativity.

30 Ibid., 6.
31 Ibid., 7.
32 Ibid., 7–8.
33 Ibid., 8.
34 Stephen Joseph, *What Doesn't Kill Us: The New Psychology of Posttraumatic Growth* (New York: Basic Books, 2011).

From my perspective, publications of the self-help genre cater to impressionable people desperate for a pick me up. A money-grab, those publications tend to be filled with motivational lingo devoid of substantial foundation.[35]

> For example, in his best seller, *The Power of Now*, Eckhart Tolle declares: "If you cannot be present even in normal circumstances, such as when you are sitting alone in a room, walking in the woods, or listening to someone, then you certainly won't be able to stay conscious when something goes wrong".[36] In practical terms, what does he mean by "being present"? To the person suffering from dissociative symptoms, to be "present" is infinitely more complex than Tolle makes it out to be, and his generalization comes across as inconsiderate and misinformed.[37]

I entered the process for *Little Guidebook for Using your Suffering Wisely*, an autobiographical solo, with the concept of PTG and reflections on the unfortunate marketability of self-help publications in mind. As its title foreshadows, *Little Guidebook* integrated ironic and culturally dissonant ideas while being based in dark humour within a Western contemporary dance framework.[38] 'Conceptually, the work unfolds as a character, closely moulded on myself, embarks on a journey towards healing her PTSD, guided by a self-help audiobook narrator'.[39] As the character falls apart struggling to follow the book's step-by-step programme, it becomes obvious that it is emotionally dangerous and socially irresponsible to suggest that generic and impersonal formulas could heal an individual from their post-traumatic symptoms.[40]

2.1.2 Creative Process Trajectory

Traditionally for me, in creation, kinaesthetic elements came first, and content and structure came second. Up until that point indeed, the choreographic act for me had started with chance-based improvisations from which revelatory elements would emerge. The entry point to my creative processes was somatic rather than intellectual. I never really knew what my work would deal with until a theme revealed itself over the course of those kinaesthetic improvisations.

35 Forcier, 'Creating Contemporary Choreography', 9.
36 Eckhart Tolle, *The Power of Now: A Guide to Spiritual Enlightenment* (Vancouver: Namaste Publishing, 1997), 47.
37 Forcier, 'Creating Contemporary Choreography', 9.
38 Ibid., 9–10.
39 Ibid., 10.
40 Ibid., 10.

The movement I was producing would spark an idea and a given work's structure would develop from there.[41]

Uncharacteristically with this piece, my plan for the structure and content developed *before* I entered the studio. As previously mentioned, my overarching idea for the work was sparked during my readings on PTG. I began by scripting a fictional self-help audiobook and then solicited a voice-over actor's help to record the lines overtop a new-age musical environment. Once in the dance studio, guided by that pre-set soundscape and dramaturgical outline, the movement flowed out of me with exceptional ease, and the piece was choreographed in an unusually short amount of time.[42] Upon reflection, I suspect that the movement came lucidly because I was moving from experience, physically expressing what I had somatically stored and intimately known for years.[43]

2.1.3 Juxtaposing Dissonant Ideas

From the onset, I instinctively took a humorous angle for the work – an ironic one certainly, but a humorous one nonetheless. I did not question this inclination until a fellow graduate student asked me whether it reflected my own coping mechanisms in response to PTSD. Though I could not be completely objective in the matter, I recognized that it did. In most social situations, to diffuse tension or to keep my depressive tendencies in check, I tend to play the clown, something I do not recall doing before the trauma.[44] For me, this realization confirmed my taking an appropriate direction with *Little Guidebook*, answering the autobiographical component of the assignment on yet another level.[45] In her analysis of American performance artist Lisa Kron's work on generationally transmitted Holocaust-related trauma, author Ann Cvetkovich reminds us that 'humor is much easier than tears, and while it often seems to displace other emotions, it would be more accurate to see it as a way of expressing what cannot be expressed otherwise'.[46] I believe that in

41 Ibid., 10.

42 Ibid., 10.

43 Ibid., 11.

44 In her scholarly article investigating resilience following traumatic childhood experiences, Monica Hinton observes that, for childhood sexual abuse victims, humour functions as a recurring strategy to remain resilient. Although my particular history of trauma unfolded in adulthood, I believe that humour helped me to build and maintain resilience as a result of a similar instinct. Monica Hinton, 'What enables Resilience after Traumatic Childhood Experiences?', in this volume.

45 Ibid., 13.

46 Ann Cvetkovitch, *An Archive of Feelings* (Durham: Duke University Press, 2003), 25.

any performing art, there emerges much power in juxtaposing comedy and tragedy. Such juxtaposition creates moral and emotional incongruity for an audience: having allowed themselves to laugh at or with a character before the revelation of his/her underlying sorrowful reality, they now have to pause in the face of their dissonant reaction. Having to reconsider their values, however briefly, holds them responsible for their experience, engaging them more actively in a given work.[47]

> According to Cvetkovich, when employed to address a traumatic topic, "humor can seem especially taboo or transgressive";[48] culturally, when reacting to others' trauma, there is an expectation for appropriate emotional reactions, hence the dissonance of humour-trauma and its inherent artistic power.[49]

I believe that dissonance emerges with much the same strength when beauty is adjacent to trauma, a pairing similarly subject to an expectation for appropriate affects. How conflicting is it to allow oneself the pleasure that comes with experiencing beauty when the core of what is witnessed is traumatic in essence and involves another human being's distress?[50]

'Such juxtaposition takes contrast to an extreme as a compositional element, at the very least in the emotional range, perhaps explaining the synergy that beauty and sadness create when combined'.[51] Choreographically for me, contrast has always been a preferred compositional strategy, and I capitalized on it when creating *Little Guidebook*. I exploited a clear beauty-sorrow contrast in two obvious instances: by wearing an airy costume while performing helplessness, and by releasing a colourful confetti shower atop myself while uncomfortably forcing a smile to the point of tears.[52] 'Adding to the overall sense of contrast and tonal instability in the piece, my character was constantly shifting on the scale of awareness'.[53] She went back and forth between retreating to her inner world and focusing uncomprehendingly on a part of her body or environment.[54] While this type of flux could have confused the viewer,

47 Forcier, 'Creating Contemporary Choreography', 13–14.

48 Cvetkovitch, *Archive of Feelings*, 26.

49 Forcier, 'Creating Contemporary Choreography', 14.

50 Ibid., 14.

51 Ibid., 14.

52 Ibid., 14.

53 Ibid., 14.

54 A parallel can be drawn here between the soloist character of *Little Guidebook* and Kate Burton's understanding of Pat MacEnulty's characters who 'exist in a dimension where they live their lives in a state of dissociation born from an environment of instability

ILLUSTRATION 8.1 Marie France Forcier in *Little Guidebook for Using your Suffering Wisely*, ©David Hou, 2013.

its unpredictability was as compelling as a ticking bomb. A large contributor to this success, I believe, is the embodied fashion with which I performatively approached the fluctuation.[55] From experience, I knew what it felt like 'to

due to traumatic experience'. Much as in Burton's account of MacEnulty's *Sweet Fire*, my choreographic choices here led to non-linear, fragmented narratives reflective of the soloist's traumatic memories and state of inner turmoil. Kate Burton, 'Shaping Personality Through Suffering: The Transformative Writing of Pat MacEnulty', in this volume.

55 Ibid., 14–15.

dissociate, to mentally fluctuate from presence to absence in uncontrollable ways. I was simply kinaesthetically amplifying a known feeling until it became perceptible through movement'.[56]

2.1.4 Performing Dissociative States

Isolating the choreographic and performance task is perhaps impossible in a context like this one, where the choreographer is also the performer, and where the work is heavily autobiographical in nature. Certainly in the studio, I sensed the imperative to be in performance-mode while generating movement. In a sense, being in a state of performance was necessary to generate PTSD related material.[57] 'For curiosity, fear, confusion, frustration and dissociation to come across, I needed to genuinely put myself through those states before they could literally move me'.[58]

> Of all the processes I have undertaken as a choreographer over the course of my career, this one was by far the quickest to produce a satisfactory work. In comparison with my experience in the studio for previous works, the movement here flowed straight out of me and I knew almost instantaneously whether it was right or wrong for the work; a significantly larger-than-normal proportion of my initial material output was actually used in the final product. I attribute this phenomenon to the fact that my body had been internalizing those states for a decade by the time I reached the studio, developing an intimate [somatic] understanding of their nature and subtleties over time. My movement-generating process was simply an externalization and amplification of that long repressed [somatic] knowledge.[59]

I divided the choreographic content into sections corresponding to the audiobook narrator's guiding commentary. I found that each of the narrator's comments evoked a different emotional state, and I could identify their analogous loci within my physical body.[60] For instance, 'a section about confronting triggers activated superficially: the surface of my skin tingled, and I followed my instinct to let that part of my body initiate the movement'.[61] I recruited those bodily trauma-host sites constantly when performing the work. To me,

56 Ibid., 15.
57 Ibid., 15.
58 Ibid., 15.
59 Ibid., 15–16.
60 Ibid., 16.
61 Ibid., 16.

these components were as essential to the piece's integrity as its compositional structure.[62]

> By the time I presented *Little Guidebook* to an audience, subjecting myself to the required emotional range felt controllable and safe, largely because I had approached the creative process as a performer and by then had confirmed that I was able to get through it repeatedly without breaking down.[63] Moreover, performing material that I had recognized to be an authentic physical trace of my PTSD appeared to increase my confidence on stage. Being the sole bearer of my own somatic history, I was convinced of my work's validity beyond doubt. My usual insecurities surrounding my performance skills were almost entirely gone. In terms of practice, this was self-affirming.[64]

2.2 *Proscenium Group Work:* The Snow Globe

2.2.1 Intention

For this group choreographic process, I worked with undergraduate dance students from York University's pre-professional dance company, the York Dance Ensemble (YDE). Although I understood that working with students in the trauma-research context would require different considerations and choreographic sensitivities on my part, I thought that the exercise would lead to my development. Not only would it allow me to rehearse on campus, a geographically convenient location, but it would also sharpen my knowledge-facilitating skills. By audition and through consultation with the department's faculty, I selected six dancers based on their physical abilities, open-mindedness and apparent stage presence.[65]

My initial objective for this process was to explore trauma from the collective angle.[66] It is estimated that 75% of all people will experience some form of trauma over the course of their lives.[67] 'In light of that statistic, and because I had a relatively large group of performers at my disposal, I was interested in

62 Ibid., 16.

63 I sense that re-experiencing my physical reaction to trauma rather than the experience of trauma itself contributed substantially to my ability to perform the work while avoiding re-traumatisation, much alike to the Holotropic breathers' experience as suggested by Grof and Grof. Peter Bray, 'Holotropic Breathwork as a Therapeutic Intervention for Survivors of Trauma: An Autoethnographic Case Study', in this volume.

64 Ibid., 16–17.

65 Ibid., 26.

66 Ibid., 26.

67 Joseph, *What Doesn't Kill Us*, 21.

exposing the universality of trauma through choreography'.[68] About half way through the process, I acknowledged that the material produced felt forced and misinformed. I reasoned that this resulted from my lack of first-hand knowledge about my intended sub-topic.[69] 'Having never personally experienced or witnessed *collective* trauma, I did not have enough insight to contribute to a cohesive choreographic statement'.[70] I discerned that, although the experience of trauma itself may be somewhat universal, it rarely has a collective impact. Whereas a single event can traumatize many, the ways in which its aftermath manifests can differ greatly from one individual to the next.[71]

My own PTSD certainly unfolded in a place of deep solitude, at the collective's antipode. Drawing from this known history of isolation to create a congruent work made better sense. To achieve that, I went back to the drawing board and re-contextualized my previously developed material in order to reveal the isolated reality brought upon by PTSD. One of the dancers became the work's protagonist, and I directed her to embody a different state of awareness than her counterparts'. A survivor's self-perceived inability to relate to his/her post-traumatic world became the new basis for our creative exploration.[72]

Even with this change, I kept struggling. I yet had to find my work's spine, the element that would artistically bind and contextualize everything else. Luckily, I fell upon a lost and forgotten quote highlighted during my literature review.[73] On page 22 of *What Doesn't Kill Us*, Stephen Joseph draws the following analogy:

> Imagine a Christmas snow globe. Shake it and the snow flurries. Over time, it settles. How long the snow remains unsettled depends on how vigorously the globe was shaken in the first place. So it is, with the trauma that shakes up our mental world.[74]

Having intended to use falling theatrical snow as a feature of the work for months without quite knowing why, I now had my answer, my work's spine. I had unconsciously been choreographing the insides of that snow globe.[75]

---

68 Forcier, 'Creating Contemporary Choreography', 26.
69 Ibid., 27.
70 Ibid., 27.
71 Ibid., 27.
72 Ibid., 27.
73 Ibid., 27–28.
74 Joseph, *What Doesn't Kill Us*, 22.
75 Forcier, 'Creating Contemporary Choreography', 28.

2.2.2 Creative Process Trajectory

To develop the actual movement for the piece, I used a kinaesthetic-exploration-first creative strategy. Having identified early on that my young dancers' strengths stemmed from their technique and that they could not yet physicalise emotional states with confidence, I initiated the creative process by developing movement-based vocabulary to capitalize on their abilities.[76] Unfortunately, what was produced through that approach left me neutral when I first watched it from the audience's vantage point at an *in-process* showing.[77] 'Although compositionally valid, what I had created thus far did not relate to my research in any informative way, and that upset me'.[78]

On the positive side, seeing the work on the proscenium stage half way through the process allowed me to discover that I could afford choreographing in subtler ways, with micro-movement. Contrary to what I had previously assumed, for instance, *shaking* was perceptible from afar. This discovery, paired with my growing dissatisfaction towards my work's insipidity, made me abandon the great majority of our existing vocabulary and revise my movement-generating approach.[79]

Back in the studio with my research question as first priority, I focussed on developing state-based movement fit for the proscenium space. I let the dancers experiment with directions such as *imagine that world around you no longer makes sense*, or *feel cold*, or *reminisce an experience of loss … and let that shape the way in which you execute the material.* This came with a number of challenges, but at least it elicited more genuine physical responses, and I felt I was taking constructive risks towards answering my research questions.[80]

2.2.3 Staging an Environment for Choreographic Context

For years, I had developed an artistic interest in populating the vertical space on proscenium stages. Contrary to the black box theatre, the proscenium stage offers a clear spatial separation from its audience and this allows for the shaping of distinctly separate environments. An open sky-like illusion can be created because of the proscenium arch, an advantage on which I intended to capitalize with this piece.[81]

In continuation of my dissonant imagery explorations in *Little Guidebook*, I was interested in staging ideas of morbid fear in a beautiful, seemingly

76 Ibid., 28.
77 Ibid., 28.
78 Ibid., 28–29.
79 Ibid., 29.
80 Ibid., 29.
81 Ibid., 29–30.

peaceful environment. I have personally undergone much cognitive dissonance when experiencing near-death in blissful surroundings.[82] I know that, when one has freshly survived a traumatic event, it may be challenging to reconcile 'how one's outer world can remain beautiful while one's inner landscape is being blown to pieces, realities clashing'.[83] 'I have returned from a world beyond knowledge and must now unlearn for otherwise I clearly see I can no longer live', said Holocaust survivor Charlotte Delbo.[84] Her sense of cognitive incongruity epitomizes what I was aiming to recreate scenically and choreographically in *The Snow Globe*.[85]

Falling snow, I believe, is universally considered as beautiful. As such, as previously mentioned, I had been planning on using theatrical snow to create a blissful environment against which to set my piece long before I even re-discovered Joseph's snow globe analogy.[86] 'I anticipated that staging a post-traumatic scene under gently floating snowflakes would create contrast and reinforce dissonance, making the beauty more striking and the desperation more poignant for the audience'.[87]

ILLUSTRATION 8.2 York Dance Ensemble in *The Snow Globe*, ©David Hou, 2014.

82 Ibid., 30.
83 Ibid., 30.
84 Delbo, Charlotte, *Auschwitz and After* (New Haven: Yale University Press, 1995), 230.
85 Forcier, 'Creating Contemporary Choreography', 30.
86 Ibid., 30.
87 Ibid., 30.

2.2.4 Challenges Inherent to Working with Student Performers

Asking under-experienced young dancers to generate genuine state-based work brought on a series of complications. Used to taking a movement – rather than state-based approach when directing pre-professional students, I had no previous experience from which to draw to elicit the subtle emotional and physical responses I needed. I also struggled to gauge the appropriateness of my requests to them.[88]

I identified three major interplaying obstacles to contend with in this process: 'our hierarchic dancer-to-choreographer relationship; my own fear of bringing them to unsafe emotional places; and their still-developing interpretative skills'.[89]

> Over the last few years, when developing state-based work with professional dancers, I had grown accustomed to working collaboratively [...], in settings where it is commonly understood that, regardless of our respective roles, our individual contributions bear equal weight. In such scenarios, if one pushes him/herself too far emotionally, it does not result from having obeyed a person in power, but from having willingly taken part in a personal exploration within a mutually beneficial artistic exchange. Working among peers in this type of environment breeds mutual trust and allows the artists involved to support one another towards greater risk-taking for what is understood as being the common good.[90]

With the YDE dancers, the creative process unfolded amid a very different social climate, and this had a significant impact on its outcome. Unavoidably, in the studio, a distinct sense of hierarchy emerged.[91] A 'student-teacher type of relationship arose between us, in which they apparently felt compelled to apply every single one of my directions literally and diligently'.[92] *To please me* appeared to be their foremost intent.[93] This presented a problem because 'one cannot engage in genuine state-based work if one's motivation is external and if one is feeling a pressure to *do it properly*'.[94]

To elicit the responses I needed from them, I had to be extremely descriptive. I also had to nudge them to take initiatives. Taking on such a shepherding

88 Ibid., 30–31.
89 Ibid., 31.
90 Ibid., 31.
91 Ibid., 31.
92 Ibid., 31.
93 Ibid., 32.
94 Ibid., 32.

role reinforced my impression that I bore responsibility for conserving their well-being. Trauma affords such a loaded reality to access somatically that I was struggling with moral reservations towards potentially causing them emotional harm for my own creative purposes.[95] By the time I finally acknowledged for myself that the dancers, as rational young adults, had the right to reject my directions and that my overprotectiveness was impairing their depth of exploration, *The Snow Globe*'s theatrical presentation was imminent.[96]

With little rehearsal time left, I could no longer afford to workshop new state-embodied material with the students. I did find the time, however, to fine-tune our existing work. In light of my new understanding of their limits, I altered my directive vocabulary to accommodate a more universal frame of lived experiences. I stopped bringing up the intimidating *trauma* as a descriptive word. Instead, I guided the dancers to imagine living in a snow globe that had just been shaken beyond their control, to picture their world as newly unrecognizable. These simpler suggestions seemed to enable the dancers to draw from their actual physical memories. As a result, this subtilized their interpretation; they *acted less* and *embodied more* when performing the piece.[97]

> In retrospect, I realize that when developing state-based work, mature performers do for themselves exactly what I had to do for the young YDE dancers: they adapt the choreographer's directions for their own frame of reference, until they create an imaginative landscape to which they can physically relate and from which they can draw genuine, embodied reactions.[98]

3 Outcomes

3.1 *Fundamental Change in Preferred Methods and Interests*

I originally expected my academic research to yield one of two possible outcomes for my choreographic practice, whether focussing on creating dances exclusively inspired by trauma would allow the persisting emergence of PTSD-related imagery to run its course, or it would confirm that a fundamental change had taken place in my artistic priorities. With four years of perspective since its conclusion, I have realised that the latter has occurred, rather than the former.[99] Indeed, the transformation that my creative direction and

95 Ibid., 32.
96 Ibid., 32.
97 Ibid., 32–33.
98 Ibid., 33.
99 Ibid., 34.

methodology have undergone feels momentous in nature. I have no interest in reverting to my prior hierarchical ways in studio. I cannot foresee ever again finding relevance in polishing technique in the pursuit of genuine and honest work. I have gained far too much insight into the power of memory-informed movement to return to my earlier choreographic dispositions.[100]

> Being transparent about my post-traumatic psychological landscape and its influence on my choreographic work has enabled me to embrace that reality for its potential. This led me to make bolder compositional and interpretative choices, which, according to the feedback I collected, resulted in clearer choreographic intent and greater resonance for the audience.[101]

As a creator I found it self-affirming to bring years of repressed psychological scenery to the surface in my work. Self-identified trauma survivors in attendance at various shows reached out to express having found deep personal connections to the performances. This hints at the significantly greater implications that the trauma-related choreographic exercise had rather than simply having produced enjoyable works.[102] It 'suggests that, for people affected with PTSD, choreography can instil or reinforce the reassuring sense that they are not alone; that they are acknowledged and understood'.[103]

3.2 *Findings*

3.2.1 Movement-Related

The two outlined choreographic processes generated much movement. Several constants surfaced from generating such a large bank of movement from one single focus, two of which being particularly noteworthy.[104] In the first place, 'the tasks of choreography and performance may be inseparable when developing state-based movement related to trauma and/or embodied memories'.[105] Because I was simultaneously acting as performer and choreographer at the time, this appeared most obviously with *Little Guidebook*; yet, the suggestion re-surfaced while I worked on *The Snow Globe*.[106] From what

100 Ibid., 34.
101 Ibid., 34.
102 Ibid., 34–35.
103 Ibid., 35.
104 Ibid., 35.
105 Ibid., 35.
106 Ibid., 35.

I garnered, 'the movement instigator, whether he/she is the choreographer or the creatively contributing performer, needs to be in a performance mode in order to generate genuine state-based vocabulary'.[107] Movement may lack specificity and/or feel false if its instigator does not approach the task with complete emotional investment.[108] Additionally, undertaking the creative process this way may be favourable because early onset emotional investment fosters 'a gradual acclimatization to the work's emotional demands, promoting a greater sense of control and preventing unfortunate breakdowns once in actual performance'.[109] Secondly, investing the necessary time to warm the dancers' emotional-physical connection up before running a work through pays off. I indeed noticed that, on days when memory-recall exercises were performed prior to rehearsing, the outcomes were noticeably more satisfying than on those when I had not taken that step with myself, or with the dancers. Attuning the somatic body in conjunction with recall seems to homogenize the group's state of awareness while helping individual performers to take greater emotional risk.[110]

3.2.2 Composition-Related

Other noteworthy constants emerged compositionally.[111] 'Psychological trauma being heavy, dark and emotional in essence, trauma-related art could easily be monotone, inaccessible and/or overly disturbing'.[112] I found the following two compositional strategies successful in conserving poignancy while avoiding these potential pitfalls.[113]

> I discovered that as a general rule, emotionally distressing elements bear more resonance when balanced with neutral or positively perceived ones. For example, beauty or humour when tactfully applied can warm an audience up emotionally, increasing their receptiveness to a work's otherwise difficult content. Additionally, the dissonance created by emotional contrast emulates the inner landscape of the traumatized for the audience, contributing further to the work's relevance.[114]

107 Ibid., 35.
108 Ibid., 35.
109 Ibid., 36.
110 Ibid., 36.
111 Ibid., 37.
112 Ibid., 37.
113 Ibid., 37.
114 Ibid., 37.

I also determined that familiar staging elements contribute to contextualize a work in reality.[115] 'Because contemporary dance is abstract, state-based work is somatic, and psychological trauma, private and internal, trauma-based choreographic work could easily look as though it portrays an alternate reality'.[116] Integrating easily recognisable man-made or organic props (here confetti and snow) to a work grounds it in the contemporary world. Such juxtaposition reinforces the notion of trauma as an undeniable part of reality; it holds an audience responsible for acknowledging its actuality.[117]

3.2.3 Challenges and Resolutions

The challenges inherent to this research process were either linked to the closeness of my own relationship to the topic, or to the development of my collaborators' understanding of the task.[118] 'Finding perspective in the creative process when making a choreographic work sourced from a deeply personal experience is a conundrum'.[119] Of course, an artist can never attain full objectivity towards his/her own work. Yet, the degree of separation between the artist and his/her work divides tenfold when the inspiration stems from a core personal issue. Considering the works as though *descriptive* exercises proved helpful in my case.[120] 'Of course, any work of art will reflect a point of view, whether it is its creators' intention or not'.[121] However, to stay clear of interweaving a personal agenda into choreography seemed to grant greater emotional objectivity, somewhat neutralising the creative task.[122]

Although *I* have an intimate and pervasive understanding of living with PTSD, my performers did not necessarily share this appreciation. Adding them to the trauma-based choreographic equation added to the operation's complexity.[123]

> Ethically, in the context of this research, I could not select my cast members based on their previous experience with psychological trauma. This made establishing a common level of comprehension challenging.

115 Ibid., 37.
116 Ibid., 37.
117 Ibid., 37.
118 Ibid., 38.
119 Ibid., 38.
120 Ibid., 38.
121 Ibid., 38.
122 Ibid., 38.
123 Ibid., 38.

> Simplifying the directive language by referring to regular psychological states such as "shaken up" instead of referring to infrequent, albeit more accurate, ones such as "dissociated" proved helpful in promoting our homogenous understanding.[124]

3.3 *Further Development*

The comprehensive outcome of my practice-based research did not complement my choreographic identity, but rather re-organised it entirely, down to its most basic components. This overall metamorphosis has laid for me a fertile bed in which to grow as a creator.[125] I still benefit from those gains in my professional life to this day.

I sense that much further depths need exploring below the base understanding I have laid out for myself over the course of this creative experiment. There exists much post-traumatic, artistic and embodied information left to unearth, to funnel and to share.[126] Several questions related to the choreographic relationships I had initially set to clarify also remain unanswered. Foremost, I am curious to contextualize my experience as an artist working with the post-traumatic cognitive landscape. Are there universal ways in which the artist's work is influenced or changed by trauma? What are the commonalities among the ways in which trauma affects the dancing body?[127] Is the post-traumatic lens indelible?

Bibliography

American Psychiatric Association. *Diagnostic and statistical manual of mental disorders* (5th ed.). Arlington: American Psychiatric Publishing, 2013.

Cvetkovitch, Ann. *An Archive of Feelings.* Durham: Duke University Press, 2003.

Delbo, Charlotte. *Auschwitz and After.* New Haven: Yale University Press, 1995.

Marie France Forcier, 'Creating Contemporary Choreography Through the Post-Traumatic Lens'. MFA Thesis, York University, 2014.

Halprin, Daria. *The Expressive Body in Life, Art and Therapy: Working with Movement, Metaphor and Meaning.* London: Kingsley, 2003.

Hanna, Judith Lynne. *Dance and Stress: Resistance, Reduction and Euphoria.* New York: AMS Press, 1988.

124 Ibid., 38.
125 Ibid., 39.
126 Ibid., 40.
127 Ibid., 40.

Joseph, Stephen. *What Doesn't Kill Us: The New Psychology of Posttraumatic Growth.* New York: Basic Books, 2011.

Levy, Fran J. *Dance and Other Expressive Art Therapies: When Words Are Not Enough.* New York: Routledge, 1995.

Terr, Lenore. *Too Scared to Cry.* New York: Basic Books, 1990.

Tolle, Eckhart. *The Power of Now: A Guide to Spiritual Enlightenment.* Vancouver: Namaste Publishing, 1997.

CHAPTER 9

Reading Myself and Worlds: Coping Strategies in the Face of Cumulative Trauma

Danielle Schaub

1 Introduction

When starting in the years during which the self takes shape, childhood trauma leaves its scars on the sites of formation in the child's developmental trajectory. In my case, the continuous geographical and linguistic disruptions caused by my father's peripatetic working life foregrounded language as a site of traumatisation and insecurity in early years. Such insecurity only signals one trauma this body experienced repeatedly. The various traumatic experiences that inform me include cumulative trauma resulting from parental symbiosis underplaying a child's existence; unprepared-for displacement and translation of identity; abandonment in a convent at the age of three; untimely death of a parent believed healthy without post-factum psychological or emotional support; death of an underage sibling. I thought I had managed to bounce back after the debilitating experiences, proving capable of resilience. To some extent I had; otherwise I would not have functioned, but since the experiences haunted me with a nagging, unsettling feeling for years, I found myself pondering over my reactions, behaviours, responses to specific stressful situations. With time and much ink, as Boris Cyrulnik notes, I have come to terms with the past and perceive what once felt life threatening as less devastating.[1] With creative pieces involving the textual and the visual in combination or on their own, the chapter illustrates and theorises the process undertaken to cope with traumas as well as the understanding of patterns adopted to disconnect from the traumatic sources.

Biblio-, photo- and scriptotherapy have no doubt played an extremely important role in my working through. Bibliotherapy, 'a therapeutic approach using texts as a basis for discussion of emotional and/or social problems,' consists in 'the interaction with fictional and/or poetic texts reflecting emotions, situations and relational issues of patients'; the bibliotherapeutic interaction 'engages the latter's emotions in the safe distance of other bodies, other places,

1 Boris Cyrulnik, *Un merveilleux malheur* (Paris: Odile Jacob, 1999), 7–23.

 | DOI:10.1163/9789004385931_010

other times and frees them, allowing productive unconscious work on the self at a remove.'[2] Different from its homonym used for medical conditions, phototherapy here involves addressing photographs that stir emotions, affording insights into suppressed past experiences. Scriptotherapy, on the other hand, refers to writing enabling healing. I use all three with patients and in my own work with or without a therapist. As a photographer, while interacting with the negatives in the dark room and recently with digital photographs, I engage in a dialogue with the unconscious motives for capturing a person, scene, or landscape, as well as with the emotional impact of the finished product. Likewise when reading or writing poetry, fiction and non-fiction, I also open a dialogue with the material.

While exemplifying and explaining the process followed to overcome the detrimental effects of traumas, this chapter sometimes repeats itself, illustrating how trauma returns to haunt its victim and how its multiple ramifications reach out in multiple directions, thus presenting the same facet of an impact in different areas. In this respect Rafael E. López-Corvo has helped me understand the haunting linguistic anxieties and fear of abandonment informing me by differentiating 'pre-conceptual traumas' and 'conceptual traumas'; occurring in early childhood before the emergence of a mind 'containing and endowing them with meaning,' pre-conceptual traumas 'become an eternal "now" ... continuously projected everywhere,' 'thereby determining not only all forms of psychopathology, but also the idiosyncrasy of every individual.'[3] I now understand that circumstantial distress went back to pre-conceptual traumas that had scribbled layers of anxiety over loss and abandonment, each spreading like ink over wet paper. Amongst the behavioural and mental reactions fed by traumatic overflow, I recognise fear of not belonging, over-achievement for attention, perfectionism for approval, need to programme life, multi-tasking to face all situations, creation of stress to re-experience the original stressor, overarching self-criticism, existing at the edge, never fully controlling situations, never fully informed, never fully knowledgeable. The remnant of the harrowing curse, these whirling mental and behavioural responses swell, leaving nothing untouched, explaining their visit in all fields of experience. However, on-going work has enhanced the resilience that at first kept this body functioning sometimes at speeds defying human understanding. Today, though stress and excess of activities still inform me, I can avoid plunging in the doing mode and remain in the being mode for extensive periods.

---

2 Danielle Schaub, 'Michel Deville's *La Lectrice*: Honouring or Deriding Freud's Theories Through Bibliotherapy?' *International Journal of Psycho-Analysis* 89 (2008): 1238.

3 Rafael E. López-Corvo, *Traumatised and Non-Traumatised States of the Personality: A Clinical Understanding Using Bion's Approach* (London: Karnac, 2014).

2 Language, a Matter of Life and Death

Raised all over the world because of my father's geological postings, I grew up with many languages, an asset in the long run no doubt, but certainly a source of insecurity at the time. In order to secure acceptance among the locals wherever we lived, I viewed language as a threat to existence. Jean-Bertrand Pontalis discusses the omnipotence of language and the 'impossibility of satisfying its demands,' relating it to the loss of the maternal.[4] In my case, language captured a double loss: loss of the maternal and exclusion from parental symbiosis. Each time a new language translated the self, it involved another loss, probably so unbearable as to feel life threatening. For those raised in only one place, such perception may sound disproportionate, but for the child forever feeling like an outsider, how best to fit in if not by mimicking the locals, including their linguistic peculiarities? Julia Kristeva captures the distress of the exiled 'living with resonances and reasoning ... cut off from the body's nocturnal memory, from the bittersweet slumber of childhood'; she further comments on the exiled as 'bearing within oneself like a secret vault, or like a handicapped child – cherished and useless – that language of the past that withers without ever leaving.'[5] Such reality exists in me but magnified by the number of languages, further complicated by the choice to distance myself from the mother tongue in which I suffered abandonment by a father dying too early and a mother needing mothering. The further negation of the mother tongue through the choice of another to raise my children incurred more losses. Given the reality and unending quality of mourning Pontalis ascribes to language, my considering language a matter of life and death becomes understandable.[6] Luckily, I must have had enough secure attachment not to negate language and not to develop what Dana Amir terms 'concrete language' and 'pseudo language,' 'the former rendering psychic discourse ... impossible,' the latter rendering 'psychic discourse ... barren and empty, high brow, and false.'[7]

Interestingly enough, in the country I chose to raise my children, I have not managed to reach a linguistic level meeting my expectations. In part this inadequacy stems from decisions made at the time of emigrating. When we moved

4 Jean-Bertrand Pontalis 'Mélancolie du langage,' *Perdre de vue* (Paris: Gallimard, 1988), 252 (translation mine).

5 Julia Kristeva, *Strangers to Ourselves*, trans. Leon S. Roudiez (New York: Columbia University Press, 1991), 15. For a potent description of the rupture in linguistic knowledge and apprehension born of exile, see Eva Hoffman, *Lost in Translation: A life in a New Language* (New York and London: Penguin, 1989).

6 Pontalis, *Perdre de vue*, 252.

7 Dana Amir, *Cleft Tongue: The Structures of Psychic Language* (London: Karnac, 2014), 4.

to Israel with our young children, my partner and I did not use the rights we could have benefitted from to adjust faster, such as free linguistic tuition. We did not even realise that we forwent these, so eagerly did we jump into our new lives. Rather than learning the language in an immersion centre as most immigrants, we proceeded with our new professional occupations that required no Hebrew. As part of an English Department, I only needed to master English. But each time a document in Hebrew required my attention, I felt as helpless as my younger self must have. Later when I decided to train as a bibliotherapist at the university, the nightmare started all over again. There I studied a new field whose Hebrew jargon I did not master. Most papers I could write in English, but at times I had to write in Hebrew, which redoubled the stress exerted. My youngest daughter, who trained as a psychologist at the time, would type and polish what I dictated to her. When I had to deal with textual analysis of peers' reports from therapy sessions, in order to relate their content and form to psychoanalytical theories, I had to translate the reports, an unwelcome addition to an otherwise packed load. Confronted with a text in Hebrew I could not retain its information nor its phrasing long enough to comment on; I saw nothing worth highlighting. I *had* to translate the reports – sometimes with the invaluable help of my youngest daughter – if I wanted to engage in the exercise properly and learn from the experience. Why train in a field without learning how to use the tools of the trade? And so I did translate the reports till the early hours in the morning, enduring frustration to the power n.

It took me long to understand that what I experienced as illiteracy in the language I had chosen to live in tapped into the helplessness I must have felt at the age of three when, because my baby brother's life was at risk, I ended up in a convent shortly after having moved to Venezuela. I remember next to nothing of that period, except for two images stuck in the deep recesses of my mind: my hiding behind an open door for fear of the black nun running after me and the helpless look on my father's face as he stood on the threshold of the convent. Abandoned at the hands of eagle-like creatures from a different planet, a different religion, a different culture and a different language, I could not even find protection in my god-like father … Presumably, my three-year-old self registered her new environment with bewilderment. Without a word of the local language, intelligible communication could not exist, throwing the already distraught dispensed-with, disposed-of, disavowed child into the deeper wretchedness of incomprehension. I must have felt perturbed not to understand the nuns, intent on taming the wild child running in five directions at once. I now believe that though circumstantial, my inability to master the Hebrew language in reading and writing suggests another phenomenon: I needed to relive the helplessness of the three-year-old in order to process the traumatic experience.[8] With time I realised that I had chosen to treat children not only because I could get by without academic command of the language, but mostly because unconsciously I needed to understand what I had undergone as a child.[9] I also wanted to prevent children from growing with unsolved psychological issues. It took me many years to even consider jumping what felt like a sharp divide to the world of adult patients. Had it not been for a student's request to recommend a bibliotherapist for a therapeutic centre where she worked to finance her studies, I might not have crossed the divide.[10] Slowly but surely, I started abandoning the 'crutches' of transliteration and began reading Hebrew texts in the original version.[11]

Even though my optimist self tried to look for the advantage of multicultural and multilingual education, the multiple displacements without emotional preparation that my younger self faced constitutes a major cumulative trauma, forever projecting before public lectures, conferences, exhibition openings where I turn up feeling unprepared for want of secure grounds afforded by the assurance that my words will flow in utter perfection. My reaction to the challenge of presenting my textual identity during my bibliotherapy training signalled the anguish of the life-and-death threat behind reading in a language inadequately mastered. The sheet informed me verbally and visually through extracts of texts and poems from different languages that I had translated into Hebrew and then pasted on one of the photographs from my 'Interior Views' project. The negative of tree roots I had chosen as background completed my textual identity insisting on the intermingling quality of the vision created. 'Just as tree roots that unrelentingly weave, rift, suck from and feed the ground, the words invite the imagination to explore hidden interwoven layers of consciousness laying bare previously unconscious shapes, figures and constellations of the psyche.'[12]

For the first time ever I tried to read Hebrew texts aloud. I felt like my much younger self when in a new country I fought to mind my p's and my q's so as not to betray my foreignness. No matter how caring my fellow students were, the old menace choked my sense of security. As the lecturer arrived late, I reacted like a child enraged because an adult has cut down the time allotted for an activity, losing control and cracking up even before reading my heartrending

---

8 To understand this need, see Bessel A. van der Kolk's 'The Compulsion To Repeat the Trauma: Re-enactment, Revictimization, and Masochism,' *Psychiatric Clinics of North America* 12: 2 (June 1989), 389–411.

9 Therapists undoubtedly benefit from treating others. Winnicott captures the impact of patients on therapists with the dedication 'To my patients who have paid to teach me,' see Donald W. Winnicott, *Playing and Reality* (Harmondsworth: Penguin, 1971), n.p.

10 I am most grateful to her for having empowered me.

11 I borrow this term from my son David.

12 Danielle Schaub, *Interior Views: Photopoetry* (Edmonton: Rubicond, 2009), n.p.

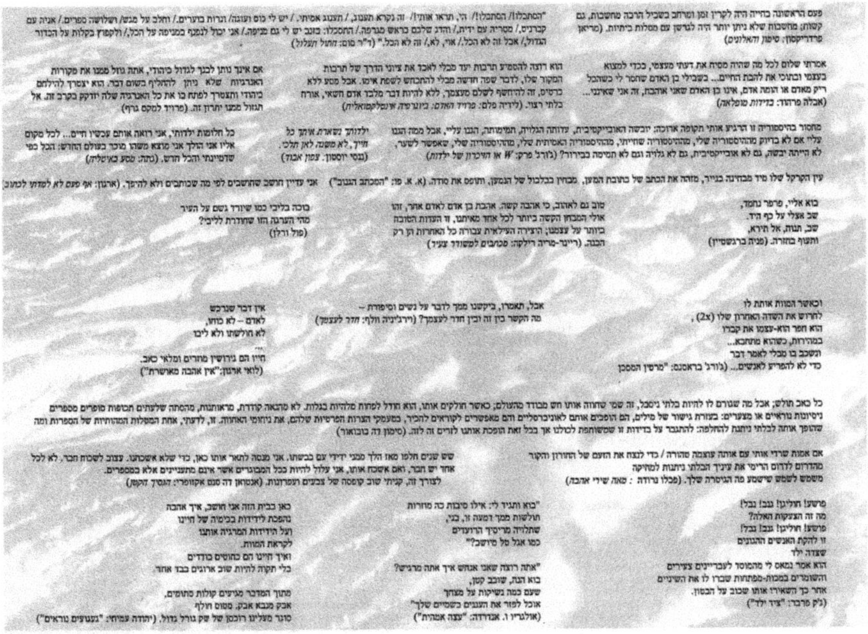

ILLUSTRATION 9.1 Textual Identity.

texts. The adult had lost her mask; the child spluttered the words like a rusty machine coughing hot blistering slime. I could have taken the teacher's life buoy and swum in the original languages of the texts but the threatened child must have wanted to measure herself up and see whether she could survive the shame of ignorance, the shame of difference. I did and then at the request of the students I read a few of the texts in their original languages, modulating another voice – unshaken, untroubled, unstrained. And yet, even the adult voice felt insecure, for in its eclectic linguistic knowledge it suffers from less grounding than that of a monolingual.

My attempt to capture the daunting linguistic whirl caused by multiple displacements and unexplained riddance to the darkness of religious zeal at an age when language sets in throws light on its remaining awe-inspiring or paralysing effect:

dancing languages

a child in constant t e a r
with   no   country or   too
many to offer a single
web of words and certitude
you understand the need
to dance between languages

as life's choreographer
requires rehearsals more
local than the locals can
even manage

the split in you never shows
cultures and languages
inform you as a photo composite
with layers and layers of
self moulded and disassembled
at equal speed
the child in you forever
under the threat of
betrayal
difference a bonus or
a minus for no
perceptible reason

you live in the country
of your choice but no longer
obey the choreographer
language not dancing on
your tongue a daily memory
of religious darkness
in a convent whose wimples
and black robes threatened
you like so many hawks racing
to feed guilt on you

their strange sounds like
their myths and rites
mean nothing to you
but no one explains why
you have to be there
darkness waltzing with fear
to pursue you till adulthood
the cross filling you with despair
lest your hands and feet be
nailed in black solidarity

today your inability to
read and write the language

of your desired life
throws you back daily in
the hopeless pit of
childhood helplessness
the mask of competence
refusing to fit tongue and face
you rehearse fears not fathomed
signing your death sentence

heart rapping at expeditive speed
each time an achievement calls you
slows destination for fear of the dark
eye blazing reproach at all times and
in all places at the convent its sting
still stifling your simplest thought
your mind roams in wild circles
faster and faster incapable of
holding thoughts long enough
for shaped thoughts to emerge

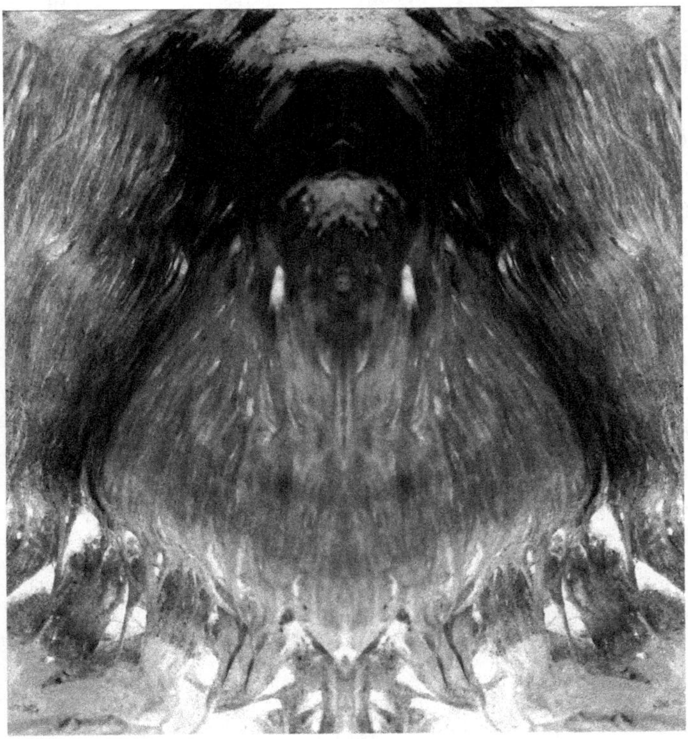

ILLUSTRATION 9.2 Dancing languages.

3 Perfection, the Cursed Solution

Children learn early how to secure approval from their caregivers, adopting behaviours that will reward them with the expected response.[13] After events with a harrowing impact they may even give their undivided attention to specific details as though to ward off the evil eye. The summer after my father's death, when kitchen duty fell on me at the family camp where my mother joined childhood friends, I would set the table where my family and close friends would sit with utter care as though I followed a manual of etiquette. I would choose the same design for all the plates – carefully selected for their mint condition – and would do the same for glasses and cutlery, setting them at the precise position in front of the chairs previously set at equal distance from one another. I now understand after years of therapeutic work on myself and others that, to my child's mind, the perfection of the table would keep the family together, would not allow further departures; any imperfection, even the slightest, could bring about the disposal of one person, very much in line with the nursery rhyme entitled 'Ten Green Bottles Hanging on the Wall.' Life to me felt as arbitrary as the bottles falling off the wall for no specific reason. Having attended to the table of family and close friends, I would usher them, directing them to the right table, taking great pride when people noticed the difference between the table I had set and the ones others also on duty had set. Just as high achievers securing resilience by 'having a sense of control in their work-related activities,' I found protection from childhood depression through control gained from the perfection of table setting.[14]

With time such small achievements did not suffice. Every activity, every enterprise required perfection. An idiosyncratic response to the early trauma of abandonment magnified by parental loss, the search for excellence has inhabited my whole existence, often leading to unachievable goals that I sometimes end up not pursuing, regardless of their appealing challenge. However, how can one possibly excel at everything? There lies the source of much tension my younger self went through. Striving after perfection did not bring satisfaction as long as the goal remained out of reach. And goals multiplied, forever more ambitious. To some extent my present self still suffers from excessive stimulation and appetite for endeavours, but with less pressure and more enjoyment. I no longer see tasks and projects as musts, but more as desired, and

13 Donald W. Winnicott, 'The theory of the parent-infant relationship,' *International Journal of Psycho-Analysis* 41 (1960): 585–595 and 'Mirror role of mother and family in child development,' In Donald W. Winnicott, *Playing and Reality* (Harmondsworth: Penguin, 1971), 130–138.

14 Mustafa Sarkar and David Fletcher, 'Ordinary Magic, Extraordinary Performance: Psychological Resilience and Thriving in High Achievers,' *Sport, Exercise, and Performance Psychology* 3:1 (2014), 52.

joy derives from each. Before, once I had accomplished a task, it no longer mattered. I remember that when my first authored book came out, it did not bring much satisfaction; I merely ticked the slot on my list of achievements. Once I embarked on the creative, my approach changed, in part because through it I accessed pent-up feelings and engaged in scripto- and phototherapy, in part because I had started working on myself. I delighted in each publication, whether of a story, a poem or my considerable *Reading Writers' Reading*.[15] For the first time, when a colleague and friend emphatically praised my photographs I acquiesced. Taking pleasure in one's achievement did not belong to the unspoken law our parents enforced; my family advocated modesty, indeed banned manifestations of pride at personal achievements. I imagine that by then the philosophy of my husband and our elder daughter had rubbed off on me – they lived not boastingly but out of genuine pleasure by the famous saying of Hillel the Elder, 'If I am not for myself who is for me? And being for my own self what am I? If not now when?'[16] Unlike common practice in my own family, the community had not forced them to erase themselves, but they knew the importance of their contribution to it. I still needed to come to terms with the obliterated sources of my inability to sustain pleasure and happiness. A poem that emerged around the phrase 'à la guerre comme à la guerre,' served as our daily bread, captures how the scar left by past misery that our elders endured stamped us without regard for our right to breathe unharmed:

> à la guerre comme à la guerre
>
> when the unstable stability shattered
> we were served daily sayings
> like herbs sprinkled
> on our lives' dishes
> ironically bursting out like grace
> 'another meal the Boches won't
> snatch from us' alternated with
> 'at war just as at war'
> to coax us to put up with
> some unpleasantness
> or if wasteful we had to swallow
> the reproof 'you haven't lived the war'

15 Danielle Schaub, ed., *Reading Writers Reading: Canadian Authors' Reflections* (Edmonton: University of Alberta Press and Jerusalem: Magnes Press, 2006).

16 *Sayings of the Jewish Fathers* (1:14). Internet Sacred Trans. Charles Taylor, Sacred Text Archive, 1897. Viewed on 27 December 2014. http://www.sacred-texts.com/jud/sjf/sjf03.htm.

the daily spray of allusions
showered remembrance
of a war throwing
our elders in hiding or
captivity the war becoming
ours too
its losses engraved on
our minds like jewellers'
stamps deep enough
to feel their scars but
not enough for the
visible eye to see

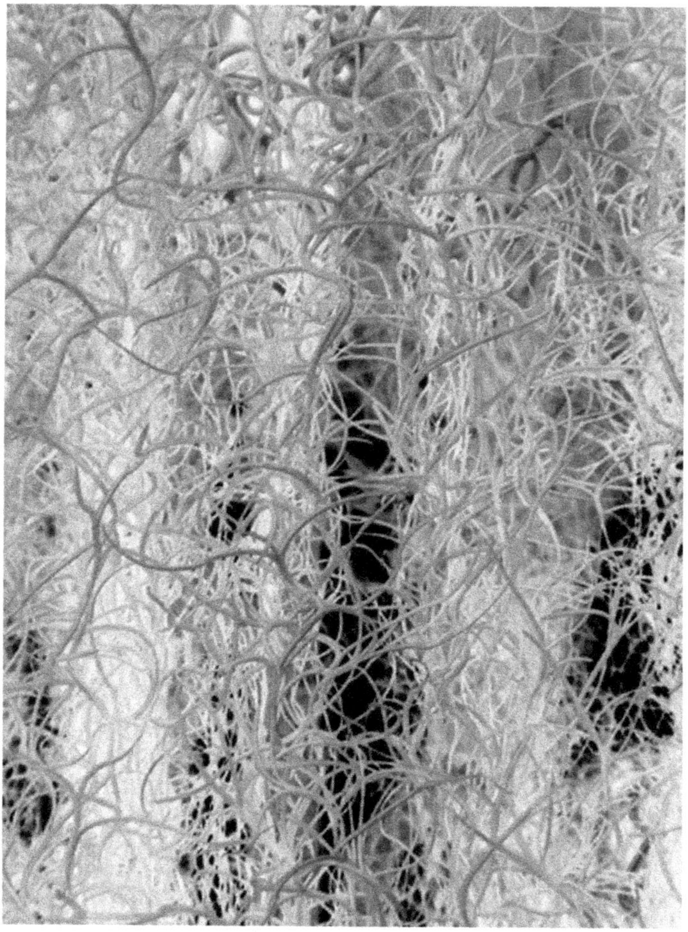

ILLUSTRATION 9.3 À la guerre comme à la guerre.

4 Helplessness, My Other Self

No matter how unpleasant, the linguistic insecurity only signals one trauma this body experienced repeatedly in early childhood. Other traumas were to harrow each one of us, sometimes collectively, sometimes privately. At the age of three, I ended up in a world different from any experience I had had before. When only a few-weeks old, my baby brother nicknamed Kiko caught Asiatic flu. His life was at risk and the three-year-old 'brat' who had already once drunk liquid wax when unsupervised had to be placed somewhere. The kindergarten of my father's company catered for four-year-olds and up. The local convent agreed to take a three-year-old; it was run in Spanish – a language I did not speak then – by nuns in black garb and wimples, a headgear made of white starched cloth folded so as to resemble horns (hence 'cornettes' in French). Lack of memory from this period has fed an obsession, causing the two images at first stuck in the darker crannies of my mind to spring repeatedly like so many pictures in pop-up books: my hiding behind an open door for fear of the black eagle-like creature ready to swoop and the helpless look on my father's face as he stood on the threshold of the convent. Abandoned at the hands of eagle-like creatures from a different planet, a different culture and a different language, I could not even find protection in my god-like father … I had a mirror experience at the age of eight: one day, after leaving school early for a private French class, I bumped into a drunkard slurring on the pavement near a crossroad. For weeks I refused to walk on that side of the street for fear of the helplessness I felt in front of the man's total loss of control. The scene would probably have passed unnoticed to many, but it left a strong mark on the child marked with the hot iron of helplessness so that it functioned as a screen memory, not recording 'the relevant experience itself' but 'another psychical element closely associated with the objectionable one.'[17] The screen memory actually helped me uncover the long-forgotten convent episode, which I later tried to recover through guided imagination, but it only led to a dark cellar with myself on the ground, impaled, just a transposition of the distress and powerlessness felt in an environment governed by rigid discipline.

Feelings of helplessness have submerged me for a long time, causing me to lose ground, to perceive goals as unreachable so that I would eventually decline an offer to perform or at best wait till the last minute before undertaking the task. By procrastinating, I would inevitably raise the level of stress in myself and those around me. I addressed such issues in therapy and later in

17 Sigmund Freud, 'Screen Memories,' *The Standard Edition of the Complete Psychological Works of Sigmund Freud, Volume III (1893–1899): Early Psycho-Analytic Publications*, 307.

training. Luckily when I trained as a bibliotherapist many weekly assignments involved writing in response to a text, a psychoanalytical theory, a psychopathology discussed. To such homework I turned with a creative mind and wrote poems or nonfiction that helped me unravel the knots I had tied around my 'story bag' in an attempt to stifle the harrowing experiences and to consign them to oblivion.[18] By doing so I managed to unearth the sources of helplessness that sometimes overwhelmed me. In other words, I tested the tools of the trade on myself while engaging in bibliotherapeutic and scriptotherapeutic work for the papers assigned.

5 A Family on the Road

For one of the courses offered, the students took turns to present their families and lives. Mine I started with a photograph I had worked on to understand the nature of my family.[19]

ILLUSTRATION 9.4 Family re-captured.

18 For an explanation of the metaphorical phrase 'story bag,' see Kim So-un, 'The Story-Bag,' *The Story-Bag: A Collection of Korean Folk Tales*, Translated by Setsu Higashi (Rutland, Vermont: Charles E. Tuttle Co., 1955), 3–10.

19 The following text offers a slightly revised section of the family history presented during my training.

To begin with, a house with no family album and no access, for lack of a private plane, to the collection of albums stored in another place.

To produce a family photograph I must turn to the collage of photos in the frame that used to hang in my mother's bedroom. It summed up her life and kept together what she wished intact as if death and departures had not dug holes in the family fabric like so many moths feeding on blood. Eventually I decide to fill the holes in the family photo my mother took in transit between two lives in our world peregrinations and to paste part of a photo my father took in yet another transitional place some years before. How appropriate that transit marks both photos for a family never grounded in space except for the final destination death imposed … Though the collage has my parents smile at the viewer, they in fact smile at each other, a trace of the symbiotic bond that strengthened their weave but weakened it when on different grounds each took a layer of the fabric. The smiles leave the children out, mere embroidered decorations marking their love.

My deliberate tampering with the original photograph encourages reflection. My photographic collage attempts at recapturing the family picture as I lived it and at engaging in mourning for the lost ones and the lost past.[20] That I chose to paste my mother in the gap between my sister and myself may surprise: one would assume that enamoured spouses would stand next to each other, but given the nature of the bond between my parents their closeness need no physical representation. Besides by closing the gap, I create a close-knit unit that would otherwise not transpire. The original gap marks a distance between my sister and the rest of the children, a spatial allusion to her different father. However, by virtue of my father's gesture towards my baby brother whose pushchair handle extends towards her, the photograph also alludes to my father's *de facto* adoption of my sister beyond legal permissibility. The position I give my mother also hints at her presence on the shoulders of both my sister and myself even if I set my mind at peace by cutting the umbilical cord when leaving Europe and later when working out my relationship to her through analysis. By adding her in the picture, I ascribe her the 'physical presence of an embodied and solid individual,' thereby offering a link between the past and the present retrieval of a unified family.[21] The triangular positioning of the two tallest and the smallest subject matters that emerges from

20 For an eye-opening discussion of the processes, see Marianne Hirsch, 'Reframing the Human Family Romance,' *Family Frames: Photography, Narrative and Postmemory* (Cambridge, MA: Harvard University Press, 1997), 41–77 and 'Mourning and Postmemory,' ibid. 17–40.

21 Linda Haverty Rugg, *Picturing Ourselves: Photography and Autobiography* (Chicago: University of Chicago Press, 1997), 2.

the tampering, namely the father, the mother and the baby boy, almost stand apart, future presences-in-absence for the remaining children.

The looks on the faces of the living siblings – my sister Nicole, left, my brother Kiko, right, and myself in the middle – symptomatically evoke each child's approach to life or to the family. With her open face, my sister marks the optimism that still fuels her even though her life thousands of kilometres away from her partner must generate tensions and disruption. Already then attentive to our parents' moods, she went on sharing with our mother her life's happiness and distress with no reserve. Sticking his tongue out, my brother had already years of rebellion against any system behind him. He would go on showing his objection to any established order by quitting school and studying much more education material in a small environment than at school out of a need for a wider vision than the two history pages a week, for instance. After starting Medicine at university, he added History of Art and Archaeology and then dropped Medicine, eventually opening his own school of parallel teaching after trying his hand at other jobs. As for the sandwiched girl, the look on her face shouts her anguish, her dissatisfaction, her anger. Already then did she not have enough space and felt misunderstood, ill-appreciated.

It took me until the age of fifteen to internalise my childhood incomprehension that legally Nicole was only my half-sister. I remember an incident at school when, at the age of seven, I went to her homeroom teacher to receive homework for her to catch up while ill at home. The teacher looked at my school apron – a pink dress-like outfit with my name embroidered – and declared that my sister did not study in her class. I insisted, fighting like a small devil, saved only when one of my sister's friends confirmed that I was 'Nicole's sister.' Until my sister turned seventeen she never visited her father because he lived too far away. Her father still worked in Indonesia and my mother did not want my sister to travel so far unaccompanied. Her father must have seen her whenever he had meetings in Europe but I did not take that in. I realised my sister had another father the year I turned twelve, when her other half-sister joined me at a scouts' camp. But only much later did I understand by noticing my sister's name on the door bell (I usually pressed it without looking) that the reaction of her homeroom teacher had nothing to do with rejection, just ignorance of our family details – just the same as mine, for that matter. In a philosophy class at school, a pupil once mentioned in a debate that her half-siblings had told her she could be either a full sibling or a stranger. Then I reflected on my parents' incredible feat of raising us all without a difference. To this day my sister considers herself more a child of my father's than of her biological father, who could not fight his jealous wife and give a respectful place in his life to my sister, forever considered a second-class relative in his family though he admired her greatly. Each time such a blow hit my sister, I rallied with her, angry at her rejection when she herself proved generous to a fault. When her father died only she left in the middle of the night and drove 300 kilometres to support her cruel stepmother, while the woman's own daughter took her time to arrive from elsewhere, postponing the funeral on that account.

My brothers played a crucial role in my life. Kiko, the child who sandwiched me, was both a partner and an enemy in games. Several of my scars go back to fights we had and yet I would not give him up for the world. To this day we share a lot. Secretive and talkative at the same time, we confide in each other. Just before his wedding, we spent a day moving furniture and fixing his house as if carved from the same stone. We did not need to talk; we moved in unison. I lost him somehow to his wife at first, but in recent years both he and his wife have become real friends to me. I know they do not quite take to my partner, but that no longer bothers me. As for my baby brother, Marc, my baby doll, we paired as Kiko and Nicole paired, Nicole always protecting Kiko, just as I protected Marc.

6 Retracing My Family History for Grounding[22]

My parents' background lacks interest in comparison with our immigrant itinerary and adjustment to a new world. Both grew up in educated environments, my father the son of a Swiss university professor in zoology, who brought snakes and all sorts of other animals home to further his research, and a German woman who never talked about her origins and proceeded raising her children as everybody else around her. My mother's father, an architect, designed many houses and buildings in Brussels while her mother made *haute couture* her profession though not throughout her married life. Together with her two sisters, my grandmother started working after her own mother had died prematurely and went back to it for survival at the end of WWII when my grandfather had died. With such examples both my parents went to university, my father becoming a geologist, my mother a teacher. They met in New Guinea where my elder sister was born. Dissatisfied with their respective married lives, they each decided to divorce their partners without knowing if they would ever reconnect. My mother left for Belgium and stayed with her mother so as to get help with my two-year-old sister when she went teaching. A year-long

22 Also slightly revised, this section presents a further section of the family history I exposed in class.

correspondence from the antipodes reinforced my parents' feelings for each other. After a visit to receive the blessing of my grandmother and her entire circle of friends – can you believe this? – my father eventually welcomed my mother in Borneo where he had transferred and they married locally. The civil ceremony set the nonreligious character of the education they would give us and functioned as an example of adaptation. Wherever we lived we mixed with the locals, never looking for compatriots, and adjusting to the local customs and those of the expatriate community they inevitably mixed with professionally. We ended growing up without any religion but with a taste for many different customs, languages and foods. In the same manner, displacement caused us to grow up with no family history; we heard so few stories of the past that my family history reads like a hidden story with more holes than substance. Searching for roots in such a context proves disquieting.

As a result of my father's multiple postings, each child was born in a different continent: my sister in Oceania, I in Asia, my brother in Central America and my baby brother in South America. Faced with European parents married in Asia and four children born all over the world, municipal administrations lost their senses. What about us? Did we also lose our senses? Did we have a sense of belonging anywhere? I cannot vouch for my siblings but I certainly did even if it split me all over the map; wherever I lived I was more local than the locals. Even today after having chosen Israel as my home, my heart has strong ties with as many places as Argentina, Belgium, Canada, England, France, India and Switzerland. Some of these places belong to my itinerary as an adult, not as a child. Some of these places I have visited repeatedly rather than having really lived in them. This means I easily adopt places as my own on account of affinity. Of course, the multiplicity of ties reduces the depth of roots. But it has certainly helped me adjust to any situation and circumstance, turning me into a chameleon of sorts. Plunge me into a new culture and I will start humming songs along with the locals as if I had drunk them with my mother's milk.

7 Night Travel

When back in Cambridge for a sabbatical with my children and their father, after having anticipated the pleasure of sharing my past at university with them, I found myself less happy than I had imagined. I passed the whole year engulfed in books, spending nights reading. I had reached a turning point. Just as spoken words could cause sadness, anger, anguish, terror, enthusiasm or happiness in real life, words in a text had a reinforced emotional impact on me. Reading became bibliotherapeutic. As I witnessed other lives, I indirectly got in touch with my inner self. It helped me sort out problems, uncover knots, face repressed thoughts/emotions and blockages that prevented a feeling of fulfilment and happiness. By revealing other people's experiences and thoughts, books generated a confrontation with my unconscious through situations or images powerful enough to bring pent-up feelings and thoughts to the surface. Images in a text moved me to tears even though I saw no connection between these and any of my own experiences. When reading Lee Maracle's *Bobby Lee*, for instance, a tremor rippled through me as if I recognised the abusive experiences she had suffered; yet I had known nothing close to these in my sheltered childhood as a white child in a bourgeois context.[23] But her text spoke of traumas that could not be spoken. Bobby Lee unleashed the monsters, allowing me to address emotions. So when I read Aritha van Herk's *The Tent Peg*, I cried myself to pieces over Mackenzie's final spoken words to J.L.: his apologetic phrase – 'I'm sorry, I'm sorry' – sounded like words my father, also a geologist, was saying to me, begging for forgiveness at having abandoned the family.[24]

The ending of *The Tent* Peg allowed me to reconnect with the Ensorian masquerade that greeted me at the age of ten, after years of displacements without emotional preparation. It brought back the momentous experience when shortly after having moved to Gabon, we went to the airport to welcome my father after a professional trip to Europe. He did not return, then or ever. My mother took lock, stock and barrel, bundling us in winter clothes. Gone were the days of pleasure under the tropical sun, gone the security afforded by a job as an anchor. We flew off to uncertainty. After a traumatic visit to the hospital, we relocated with an aunt in yet another country. Death deprived me of my father; I heard of it after the funeral. To lighten my mother's weight, I learnt to mould my life on hers, never expressing sadness, fears, anxieties, silencing unpleasant feelings. I imposed a mask on myself, a mask of strength and triumph. Previous and subsequent losses haunted me, for I had to bottle up all wrecking experiences. In hindsight, I understand why I wrote 'Night Travel.'[25] The context encouraged me to revisit the past. I had indeed returned to the place that had shaped me in my twenties when I took a distance from my family – geographically, linguistically, emotionally – and I spent most of the year with my children, then aged eight and ten, as their father kept going back and forth to his *alma mater* in Brussels to fulfil his professional duties. I had witnessed my children's reactions to the unsettling adjustment to a new place in a far-off

23 Lee Maracle, *Bobby Lee: Indian Rebel – Struggles of a Native Canadian Woman* (Richmond, BC: LSM Press, 1975).

24 Aritha Van Herk, *The Tent Peg* (Toronto: McClelland and Stewart, 1987), 222.

25 Danielle Schaub, 'Night Travel,' *Open Letter: A Canadian Journal of Writing and Theory* 10:8 (Spring 2000) [Part Two of a special issue on 'The Body Chronic']: 53–59.

country and had tried to help them face the change by responding to their distress. A new phase opened up – I could engage in scriptotherapy and unleash the emotions long erased. I typed the story with my eyes sprinkling the atmosphere with mist so thick that I could not see the keys on the keyboard, or the text on the screen. My writing literally transplanted me back to the airport to welcome my father after a professional trip to Europe. The context demanded to adjust, not just to a new country, a new language, and new faces. We had to adjust to the pit of loss, irretrievable loss in a climate ever so foreign to that of the tropical countries we had grown in. The white snow pervaded, freezing our hearts.

8 Another Heart

Ten years later, as if fate had not served enough indigestible food, it served another heart. At age eleven, while at camp on the coast, our younger brother Marc entered into a deep coma after a car had knocked him over. Eleven days of anxious visits at the hospital warned us that if he did survive, he would probably come through blind or suffer some neurological impairment. Again no one spoke lest inappropriate ears would hear and bring bad luck.

Imagine that one day while in the intensive care unit next to your brother's bed in the top emergency room, you notice an irregularity in the heart rate. The two nurses in charge of only his case have not even noticed. You call them immediately and they whisk to stabilise the heart. From then on, you take turns next to him constantly.

Then again one day the heart falls flat when you happen to sit in the intensive care unit. The doctor darts in immediately and pumps the heart violently. Another doctor comes in and they alternate their efforts. After forty-five minutes that feel like five and an eternity at once, the doctors proclaim the end. You run out and yell like a wounded cub. You do not want to lose your baby brother, the brother who'd come to your room early on Sundays not to wake your mother and who would enter your bed for warmth and a story.

The doctors hush you. They give you a heavy dose of Valium, which your mother lifts out of your palm, and you drink the glass of water given you without anything.

Swallowing hard, you pull the shutter of emotions shut and adopt the mask of comfort for everyone. You spend the night cradling your mother, whispering words of unnatural wisdom learnt in past lives.

At the funeral, wearing a red suit, you greet relatives and friends, thanking them for their support on behalf of your mother as if at a cocktail party. You shed no tear for fear of the waterfall that a crack in the dam may unleash.

You cannot hear words of condolence. You block them out. Nothing has happened.

The next day rather than staying with the family you take the oral exam assigned in your exam timetable. You must show that life goes on. You take one exam, two exams and finish the year with honours as if nothing had disturbed the course of life.

In the summer a year later, you stay behind when the family leaves for holidays. You must write your thesis. But cannot write. Your mind is blank.

You must ask for an extension and go to the university counsellor, a family friend. He greets you and asks what he can do for you. The dam unexpectedly cracks and you collapse. All of a sudden the counsellor fathoms the extent of your sorrow, of the un-mourned deaths, of the repeated pattern.

The caring ear soothes you. After the meeting, extension recommendation in hand, you fly, the words pouring out on the page, meeting the new deadline.

Mourning obviously did not belong to my apprehension of death. By not mourning I somehow negated death, but alienated myself from reality and the recognition of loss. Just as with the death of my father, I went on leading a life of pretence, feigning normalcy as the cumulative pre-conceptual traumas had taught me to do. Without the mind to contain the loss and subsequent struggle of adjustment to new cultures and languages, the body put on an armour to avoid more blows, to hide the gaping wound from all, including myself, negating absence. I absented myself from my own reality, my own self, perpetrating disconnection forever whirling. I took care of my mother, spending hours comforting her for the loss of the child who had not consciously witnessed the rip in the fabric that sewed her couple. By attending to her needs, I neglected mine, inscribing loss even deeper on the flesh that festered.

9 En Route by New Paths

The birth of my children changed my life, opening new horizons. I could restore life in its bounteousness, if not for myself at least for my children. Even with my non-biological daughter, I could better the deal; true I could not resuscitate her mother, but I could give her the family she had not had. Friends could not understand that I could bear her sitting between her father and myself; I knew she needed to feel included in our love. My own loss of a father helped me acknowledge her needs and not sense them as detrimental to my own happiness. I remember that David's birth and care came naturally, so much so that the nurses at the hospital believed I had other children. A new me was born with David; in hindsight I see I set out to redress the lack of emotionality and physicality in my own childhood, even if I failed otherwise in the eyes of the child now grown adult. Maya was born when my grandmother died. The gynaecologist asked me if my grandmother had not rather I stayed with my newborn baby than go to her funeral the next day. I did not go and put aside her death, carrying her in me. I then cherished raising two young children and creating a family for our eldest daughter. For a long time, though, funerals allowed me to cry over my lost ones, but only funerals not involving my family. At family funerals, the old need for distance from the distress made me keep a stiff upper lip. Death masks, on the other hand, I still fear like the plague, for they spell absence in such devitalising force that I cannot sleep for days, lest the ghost of the dead would visit me, perhaps even infiltrate my soul.

When my mother died I already lived in Israel. With her, I managed to start the mourning process before her death, probably on account of therapeutic work on myself. Three months before her death, I visited her on my way back from Canada and told her that countless times I had wanted to say to her, 'I can see you're not in the right mood for a real conversation. I'll call you back when you are.' I had felt cheated from childhood on, for from the age of ten, if not earlier, I had been a parent, not a child. She made no space for my emotional needs and because she blew everything out of proportion on account of anxiety, I had soon stopped confiding in her or showing emotions that could arouse her anxiety. The receptacle of her ups and downs, I did not expect her to contain my own distress or worries. I would call to listen to her experiences and say virtually nothing about myself. So when I anguished over my partner's betrayal because his debt to Belgium went over and above his responsibility to his nuclear family (he had transferred his debt to those Belgians who had hid him during World War II on to the university – his *alma mater* in Brussels – and accepted a full teaching and administrative load for three years in alternation with his full position in Israel, becoming a 'suitcase professor' as we called him), I could not find solace in my mother. She would bombard me with her mood swings and not be there for me. But after telling her that I had missed a mother, she changed attitudes instantly and a new channel of communication opened. I had started preparing the mourning process. After her death, I spent about six months mourning her and my father by going over their correspondence, quite a difference from the past lack of mourning for my father and my brother.

My family story has taken me through many traumas so that once and for all I can put them behind and focus on the present and the future without dwelling on past wounds any longer, or even feeling them. In many ways, my reaction to the traumas endured reflects Monica Hinton's discussion of resilience, though my traumas did not relate to childhood sexual abuse.[26] The pattern followed stems from a desire to leave the past behind and reinforces the ability to cope with future adversity. While I recognise putting up a brave face in front of other hardships, I nonetheless admit that certain situations trigger responses recalling those in past stressful circumstances. Once I realise that I rely on unproductive past reflexes, I readjust and feel better. Today I have healed the wounds by exorcising the pain of the child lost between worlds, between cultures, between languages, between life and death thanks to my own therapeutic process and personal biblio-/scripto-/phototherapy as well as thanks to my ability to help children and adults heal their own wounds.

10 Creative Empowerment

By writing and photographing, I have managed to examine some of my traumatic experiences in a scripto- and phototherapeutic fashion. Like Marie France Forcier through her choreographic work allowing her to internalise her intense dissociative response after the trauma she endured, I have identified some of the processes followed on account of pre-conceptual and conceptual traumas and feel equally transformed.[27] While trying to recapture the feelings of anxiety generated by traumatic circumstances and events, I worded the experiences that gnawed my heart and mind, airing them in ways that de-fouled them. From un-breathable and 'uncapturable,' they started taking shape and losing their nauseating feel. The project has had an impact similar to that afforded by Holotropic breathwork as delineated by Peter Bray; his working through his father's death inevitably bears a resemblance with my narrative experience of my own father's death, a resemblance enhanced by his describing the process taken and recording the multiple emotional responses and sensations as though writing a short story.[28] His creative act reflects Pat MacEnulty's consideration that scripting trauma has a therapeutic effect that leads to healing.[29] Just as with Forcier's choreographic work, Bray's

26 Monica Hinton, 'What enables Resilience after Traumatic Childhood Experiences?' in this volume.

27 Marie France Forcier, 'Investigating the Post-Traumatic Lens in the Choreographer's Work,' in this volume.

28 Peter Bray, Holotropic Breathwork as a Therapeutic Intervention for Survivors of Trauma: An Autoethnographic Case Study,' in this volume.

29 Kate Burton, 'Shaping Personality Through Suffering: The Transformative Writing of Pat MacEnulty,' in this volume.

breathwork and MacEnulty's scripting work analysed by Burton, my own scripto-, photo- and bibliotherapeutic work has inscribed marked liberating changes on the traumatised self.

Eventually, my poetry has also started recording transformation. For instance, 'turning,' suggests the immersion in the inebriating sights of autumn trees and the inscription of magic sensual feelings on memory so as to prepare the body for tougher winter realities.[30] Even when revealing what had shaped me and burdened me with a heavy weight as in 'I asked the sea,'[31] the lines manifest an ability to move on and rejoice in the new, lifting experiences that life has graced me with. Similarly, 'reading myself and worlds' reflects on the horizons opening up to liberating spheres.

turning

brush strokes glide
swiftly over my head
parade
like turning leaves
on a Fauve painting
light sprinkles and dabs colour
shivering to bob
like children
playing
hopscotch

speckled evening dress
with velvet silk and taffeta merging
descends in
softness and sheen
to capture aching eyes
slow paced yet joyful
old rays alter landscape
mirage of changing colours
in fluid movement

soft breeze gentle applause

30 Danielle Schaub, *Interior Views*, 35.
31 Ibid., 33.

assails the nose
whirls ancient dust
into freshened scents
tilts the drunken
sights brushing over skin
warm & cool
wind titillate
an erratic dance

the tree swirls into
me bewitching me to join
its kaleidoscopic dancing song
seductive fluidity captures its melody
immersing landscape
to engulf fever
in glistening fragrant touches
weaving the canvas of memory
fueling the vessel about to sail
the blanketing sea of rigour

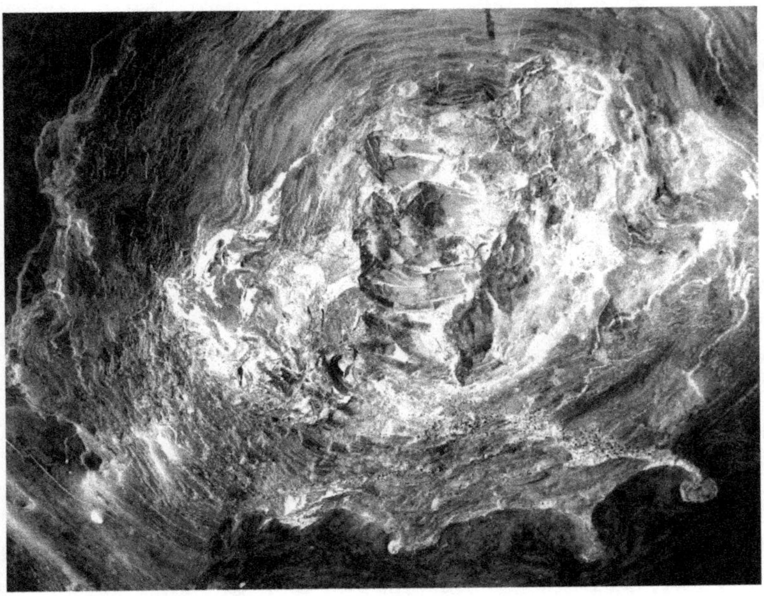

ILLUSTRATION 9.5 Turning.

I asked the sea
A poem after Zelda's 'A name for each'

I asked the sea to give me a new name
For it has witnessed all the changes
That happened in me
In the past years of lonely walks
Pondering over life, the world and me.

Both my mother and father no longer are
To turn to them and ask a new name
But if they were would they see the new me?
Would they know what I went through
With the name they once bestowed on me?

God and the whole world judged me
Tying a noose around my neck
Tighter and tighter
To the point I couldn't breathe any more
Couldn't feel, couldn't love, couldn't live

Neighbours who knew me not
Saw in me a symbol
Of the cultures informing me
For speech, posture, relentless toil,
Even my house fought an endless war

Sinless in the eyes of others
But oh so imperfect in mine
I competed with the mountains
Forever yearning more
Plucking antagonism like flowers

Today the sea gave me three names
Joy, Zoe and Ciel
Fairy grandchildren
Whose joy and zest of life
Play in the sky's playground

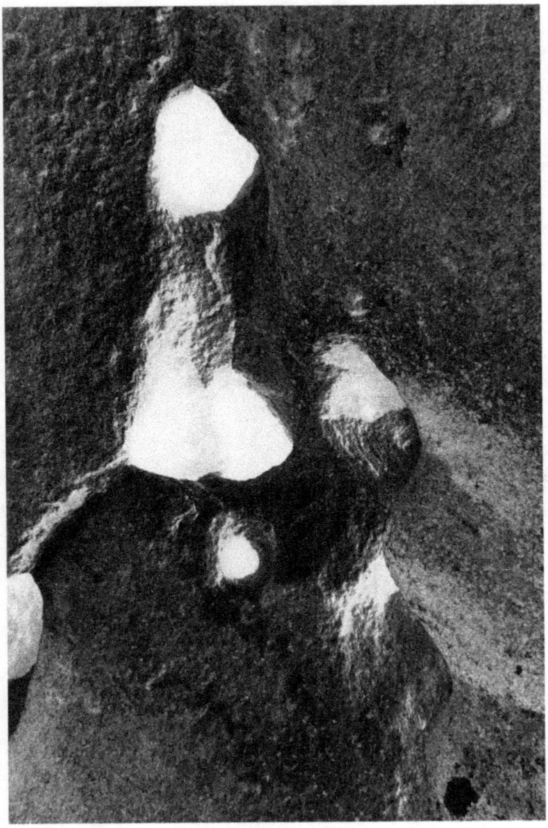

ILLUSTRATION 9.6 I asked the sea.

Today devoid of the uninvited guest
That once weighed on my chest
Haunting me day and night
I walk burdenless
Leaving no trace, featherlike

reading myself and worlds

words storm me to other
worlds into which I clothe
bodies or tread spheres
while away times

of others whose lives
breathe mine

images swirl around
new meanings for life
share feelings to
feed from
expand at will

lying down on a narrow
wooden bench
in an abandoned
changing room
masquerading olden times
you read by the clothes
and shoes of those
peopling your world

oblivious of real
smells and sounds
you steal away
from duties
live the page

though miles apart you and
I share a common thread
as if born of the same egg
you a man, I a woman
bound by the same leap

two beings gender
cannot part read
their lives into being
you stretched out
I curled up
conceived anew among
words enlivened in
magic spells
dreaming horizons

ILLUSTRATION 9.7 Reading myself and worlds.

Releasing all the childhood bravery and repression in the flow of words and imagistic constructions, the writing and picturing of trauma in fragmented cadences on the page echo the snippets of haunted memories, of pain long held and discharged. The glimpsed images of frail humanity, always failing to uphold the glorious immortality of the child's assumed world peopled by the beloved emerge in a linguistic whirl. With the wounds healed, these languages at once allow and contain an unstoppable flow of emotion, making way for renovations and reinvigorating realities.

Bibliography

Amir, Dana. *Cleft Tongue: The Language of Psychic Structures*. Trans. Mirjam Hadar. London: Karnac, 2014.

Cyrulnik, Boris. *Un merveilleux malheur*. Paris: Odile Jacob, 1999.

Freud, Sigmund. 'Screen Memories.' *The Standard Edition of the Complete Psychological Works of Sigmund Freud, Volume III (1893–1899): Early Psycho-Analytic Publications*, 299–322.

Hirsch, Marianne. *Family Frames: Photography, Narrative and Postmemory*. Cambridge, MA: Harvard University Press, 1997.

Hoffman, Eva. *Lost in Translation: A life in a New Language*. New York and London: Penguin, 1989.

Kristeva, Julia. *Strangers to Ourselves*. Trans. Leon S. Roudiez. New York: Columbia University Press, 1991.

López-Corvo, Rafael E. *Traumatised and Non-Traumatised States of the Personality: A Clinical Understanding Using Bion's Approach.* London: Karnac, 2014.

Maracle, Lee. *Bobby Lee: Indian Rebel – Struggles of a Native Canadian Woman* Richmond, BC: LSM Press, 1975.

Pontalis, Jean-Bertrand. 'Mélancolie du langage.' *Perdre de vue*. Paris: Gallimard, 1988. 249–254.

Rugg, Linda Haverty. *Picturing Ourselves: Photography and Autobiography*. Chicago: University of Chicago Press, 1997.

Sarkar, Mustafa, and David Fletcher. 'Ordinary Magic, Extraordinary Performance: Psychological Resilience and Thriving in High Achievers.' *Sport, Exercise, and Performance Psychology* 3:1 (2014), 46–60.

Sayings of the Jewish Fathers. Trans. Charles Taylor. Internet Sacred Text Archive, 2011. Viewed 27 May 2015. http://www.sacred-texts.com/jud/sjf/sjf03.htm.

Schaub, Danielle. 'Images of Those Who Dream Us: Canadian Authors' Reflections.' In Danielle Schaub, ed., *Reading Writers Reading: Canadian Authors' Reflections.* Edmonton: University of Alberta Press and Jerusalem: Magnes Press, 2006a. xvi–xxii.

Schaub, Danielle. *Interior Views: Photopoetry*. Edmonton: Rubicond, 2009.

Schaub, Danielle. 'Michel Deville's *La Lectrice*: Honouring or Deriding Freud's Theories Through Bibliotherapy?' *International Journal of Psycho-Analysis* 89 (2008): 1237–1250.

Schaub, Danielle. 'Night Travel.' *Open Letter: A Canadian Journal of Writing and Theory* 10:8 (Spring 2000) [Part Two of a special issue on 'The Body Chronic']: 53–59.

Schaub, Danielle, ed. *Reading Writers Reading: Canadian Authors' Reflections.* Edmonton: University of Alberta Press and Jerusalem: Magnes Press, 2006b. xvi–xxii.

So-un, Kim. 'The Story-Bag.' *The Story-Bag: A Collection of Korean Folk Tales.* Translated by Setsu Higashi. Rutland, Vermont: Charles E. Tuttle Co., 1955. 3–10.

van der Kolk, Bessel A. 'The Compulsion to Repeat the Trauma: Re-enactment, Revictimization, and Masochism.' *Psychiatric Clinics of North America* 12:2 (June 1989), 389–411.

Van Herk, Aritha. *The Tent Peg*. Toronto: McClelland and Stewart, 1987.

Winnicott, Donald. W. 'Mirror Role of Mother and Family in Child Development.' In Donald W. Winnicott, *Playing and Reality*. Harmondsworth: Penguin, 1971a. 130–138.

Winnicott, Donald. W. *Playing and Reality* (Harmondsworth: Penguin, 1971b).

Winnicott, Donald. W. 'The Theory of the Parent-Infant Relationship.' *International Journal of Psycho-Analysis* 41 (1960): 585–595.

CHAPTER 10

Holotropic Breathwork as a Therapeutic Intervention for Survivors of Trauma: An Autoethnographic Case Study

Peter Bray

1 Introduction

In June, 2010, I was presenting a paper at an international transpersonal psychology conference in Moscow.[1] As part of the experience I had elected to attend a two day Holotropic Breathwork (HB) workshop led by Stanislav Grof, one of the founders of transpersonal psychology.[2] As a simple ritualised process, HB harnesses the innate capacity for individuals to realise their potential for deep inner healing through the expression of energies that lead to the realignment and/or correction of trauma.[3] Paralleling the humanistic concept of self-actualising, it assumes that willing participation in breath work will permit access to a heightened state of consciousness allowing a spontaneous response to 'the wisdom of whatever emerges.'[4] HB is often facilitated in large groups sub-divided into paired participants alternating between the roles

---

* PhD, Senior Lecturer and Programme Leader for Counsellor Education at the University of Auckland. Peter has recently edited a number of interdisciplinary volumes and articles that reflect his developing interest in spirituality, heroic identity and the transformational aspects of loss and trauma.

1 Peter Bray. 'Consciousness Revolution: Transpersonal Discoveries That Are Changing the World' (Paper presented at the 17th International Transpersonal Conference, Moscow, June 23–27, 2010).

2 Miles A. Vich, 'Some Historical Sources of the Term "Transpersonal,"' *Journal of Transpersonal Psychology* 20 (1988): 107–110. In this article Vich notes that Abraham Maslow began using the word 'transpersonal' which means 'across or beyond the individual person or psyche' – to describe his new approach to psychology in his correspondence with transpersonal psychology's co-founder Stanislav Grof in the mid 1960s.

3 Sharon G. Mijares, ed., *The Revelation of the Breath: A Tribute to Its Wisdom, Power, and Beauty* (New York: SUNY, 2009), 105.

4 Stan Grof, 'Holotropic Breathwork: New Perspectives in Psychotherapy and Self-Exploration,' viewed 4 February 2018, https://www.wisdomuniversity.org/grof/module/week3/pdf/Holotropic%20Breathwork.pdf.

 | DOI:10.1163/9789004385931_011

of active 'breather' and caring 'sitter.'[5] Since the technique aims at the achievement of 'wholeness, healing, and wisdom,' the effectiveness of the session rests fundamentally upon the individual's readiness to trust in the process and embrace the potential for personal transformation.

As a scholar of Grof, I had some idea of what the experience of a self-subscribed, rather than 'prescribed,' session might be like.[6] However, prior to my first HB encounter I found myself becoming so distracted by intrusive thoughts concerning my father's rapidly deteriorating health and my family in England that I nearly abandoned it as a frivolous waste of my time. A few months earlier I had spent what I had supposed was our final Christmas together. Dad had just turned 89, and in the first wheezing hug he ominously and prophetically alerted me to his breathlessly short timeline, 'I won't make 90,' he rasped. Whilst his intellect remained cynical and obstinate, a persistent and debilitating frailty pressed upon him and, in only a few months, he was admitted to a local cottage hospital where he painfully lingered until he died.

This chapter will consider HB as an adjunct to trauma therapy and outline how this method of guided, accelerated therapeutic breathing and body work may relieve and release energy caused by experiences that, as Danielle Schaub notes, are pre-conceptual traumas laid down in the body like the 'scribbled layers of anxiety over loss and abandonment'[7] and etched onto the psyche. It will present the process, theoretical principles, and expected outcomes of HB while examining some of the common questions put to its practitioners. A final section provides an autoethnographic case account that describes the experience of controlled breathing combined, with the hyper-stimulation of the auditory system, in a typical session to 'access repressed memories, perinatal experiences, and archetypal imprinting.'[8]

---

5 Kylea Taylor, *Considering Holotropic Breathwork* (Santa Cruz, C.A.: Hanford Mead Publishers, 2007), 10.

6 Over the last half century Stanislav Grof has written a number of books that have outlined his cartography of the psyche such as: *Beyond the Brain: Birth, Death and Transcendence in Psychotherapy* (Albany: State University New York Press, 1985); and *The Holotropic Mind: The Three Levels of Human Consciousness and How They Shape Our Lives* (New York: Harper Collins, 1993). However, *Holotropic Breathwork: A New Approach to Self-Exploration and Therapy* (New York: SUNY, 2010), written with Christina Grof, provides a rationale and a description of the intervention in practice.

7 Danielle Schaub, 'Reading myself and worlds: Coping strategies in the face of cumulative trauma' in this volume.

8 Mark C. Kasprow and Bruce W. Scotton, 'A Review of Transpersonal Theory and its Application to the Practice of Psychotherapy,' *The Journal of Psychotherapy Practice and Research* 8 (1999): 20.

Presently the therapeutic potential of HB as a 'professionalised' psycho-spiritual intervention is still regarded as apocryphal, in the sense that it has yet to be fully validated by empirical studies. However, Joseph Rhinewine and Oliver Williams argue that 'prolonged, deliberate overbreathing … capitalize upon the effects of hyperventilation on the central nervous system to facilitate development of a temporary, benign, and potentially therapeutic state of altered consciousness,' which may be 'a useful therapeutic modality in treatment of psychiatric disorders.'[9] Similarly, even as this account of the HB experience is limited by its personal perspective, there is also a place here to valuably consider the positive post-traumatic growth potential of HB for survivors of trauma.[10]

2 Principles of Accelerated Breathing, Trauma Release, and Integration

Devised as a largely pre-verbal, experiential, and client-centred psychotherapeutic method of self-exploration in the mid-1970s, and first offered as a structured training programme in 1987, Stanislav and Christina Grof's version of breath work draws upon spiritual practices that include yoga, meditation and the Indian practice of Pranayama, Buddhist Vipassana and Zen techniques, and incorporate Alexander Lowen's bioenergetics, Arthur Janov's primal therapy, and Wilhelm Reich's bodywork.[11] However, HB does not focus primarily upon trauma recovery. Curiously described as 'industrial strength meditation,' HB is practiced equally by survivors of trauma and by people with no known history of it. 'The primary injunction in Holotropic Breathwork is not to "go into the trauma" but "do the breathing until you are surprised by what emerges."'[12]

---

9 Joseph Rhinewine and Oliver Williams, 'Holotropic Breathwork: The Potential Role of a Prolonged, Voluntary Hyperventilation Procedure as an Adjunct to Psychotherapy,' *Journal of Alternative and Complementary Medicine* 13.7 (2007): 772.

10 Ibid., 773; according to Rhinewine and Williams, 'Only three studies appear to meet commonly accepted minimum criteria of methodological sophistication to be considered as constituting reliable empirical evidence … and only one of these has been published in a peer-reviewed journal.'

11 Nicola Crowley 'Holotropic Breathwork™ – Healing Through a Non-Ordinary State of Consciousness,' Royal College of Psychiatrists website, 6, viewed 4 February 2018, http://www.rcpsych.ac.uk/pdf/crowleyholotropic1.6.05.pdf; Grof and Grof and Grof, *Holotropic Breathwork: A New Approach.*

12 Martin Boroson, et al., 'Twelve Things You Should Know about Holotropic Breathwork™,' 55 *Inside Out* (2008): 1–5.

A Principles and Theory

Traditional models of psychology tend to limit the psyche to the largely consensus reality narratives of the biological and postnatal construct of the Freudian unconscious. Psychoanalysis stresses content over process and the interpersonal over the intrapsychic. However, based upon an assumption that what is already happening in a person's process is self-healing, HB seeks to directly connect the client to these internal processes as they are happening in the here and now.[13] Originating in the philosophical and mystical traditions of the East, Carl Jung's 'collective unconscious,' and data collected from his own clinical observations and experiences of non-ordinary states of consciousness, Stan Grof draws upon an expanded cartography of the psyche that adds the perinatal and transpersonal domains to the standard biographical realm of experience.[14] He suggests that it is from within these three dimensions of human consciousness that one fully appreciates the experience of HB. 'Phenomena from all these domains are seen as natural and normal constituents of the psychological process; they are accepted, and supported without preference.'[15]

Representing a form of psychic radar, or Jung's concept of the Self, Grof and Grof locate agency within the individual's 'inner healer,' whose sole purpose is to serve the integration of the whole person by bypassing the intellect.

> As the process is unfolding, this 'inner healer' manifests therapeutic wisdom which transcends the knowledge that can be derived from the cognitive understanding of an individual practitioner or from any specific school of psychotherapy or body work.[16]

As a unifying principle the inner healer has an innate capacity to access different dimensions of experience and intelligently prioritise and attract those unconscious materials that have the greatest emotional charge, and are most available for conscious processing and integration. Thus, in order for healing processes to occur and be truly effective, the breather allows the inner healer

---

13 Gilles Brouillette, 'Reported Effects of Holotropic Breathwork: An Integrative Technique for Healing and Personal Change,' viewed 4 February 2018, http://www.grof-holotropic-breathwork.net/page/doctoral-dissertations.

14 Peter Bray, 'A Broader Framework for Exploring the Influence of Spiritual Experience in the Wake of Stressful Life Events: Examining Connections between Posttraumatic Growth and Psycho-Spiritual Transformation,' *Mental Health, Religion and Culture* 13.3 (2010): 293–308.

15 'Association for Holotropic Breathwork™ International,' Viewed 4 February 2018, http://www.grof-holotropic-breathwork.net/page/2182480:Page:678.

16 Ibid.

to take command. It is an act of immense trust and, similar to the concept of resilience identified in Monica Hinton's scholarly chapter, its conscious activation reinforces the individual's capacity to positively use it to cope in the future.[17] Thus, experienced over a number of sessions, the breather develops a confidence, trust, and belief in the process and in the autonomous healing of the Self.[18]

> Grof (1985, 1996, 2000) has demonstrated that disturbances and experiences at any stage of the intrauterine and birth processes may be reactivated by psychological trauma which prompts the unconscious to reveal events from this foundational memory system and reactivate and focus them through biographical, perinatal and transpersonal lenses.[19]

Stan Grof's assertion that the birth process has the potential to leave a traumatic scar in the perinatal domain of the psyche suggests that the foetus is conscious and forms memories that constellate around corresponding systems of condensed experience. Organised around the four consecutive periods of delivery in childbirth, this process describes dynamic experiential patterns of the deep unconscious called the Basic Perinatal Matrices.

The perinatal domain creates an experiential bridge between the other domains and provides a rich source of illustrative material for the subsequent creation and sharing of mandala art in the group work that follows the session. In the second biological, postnatal domain of experience, participants may effectively resolve past conflicts, confront repressed memories, and reintegrate and clear traumas. Whilst, in the third, transpersonal domain, information is accessed outside of the normal boundaries of the ego and body, space and time. In this Jungian domain HB participants may have conceptually challenging spiritual, mythological and archetypal encounters that include out-of-body experiences and past life memories, identification with other life forms and a sense of oneness and connection with the collective unconscious.

As the therapeutic design of HB is to make contact with stored core memories and their attendant affect and/or connect with the collective transpersonal universe, unsurprising in any one session the breather might encounter a spectrum of archetypal materials with themes related to death and rebirth,

---

17 Monica Hinton, 'What Enables Resilience after Traumatic Childhood Experiences?' in this volume.

18 Caitriona Jackson, 'Holotropic Breathwork™: An Experiential, Theoretical Account,' *Inside Out* 29 (1997).

19 Bray, 'A Broader Framework for Exploring the Influence of Spiritual Experience,' 298.

the struggle toward transcendence and transformation, and experience a deep sense of connectedness to others and the cosmos. One of the advantages of HB is the autonomous nature of the healing. Individuals are encouraged to freely express and interpret their experiences 'without any specific language or worldview.'[20] Thus, HB participants may remember and relinquish their own birth trauma and any associated negative beliefs about themselves or the world.

B *Breathing*

In their practice Stan and Christina Grof validate the almost universal importance of breath and breathing from ancient and pre-industrial societies and their use of breathing techniques in religious ritual and healing practices. They note that these techniques 'cover a very wide range from drastic interference with breathing to subtle and sophisticated exercises.'[21] The language of breath and breathing, they suggest, reflects human beings' intimate and evolving relationship with breath and breathing practices that provide access to, and linkage between, the human body, nature, the psyche, and the spirit.[22]

The practice of focused breathing, like breath meditation, is a universal method of awakening the spirit or soul.[23] Equally, the ancient Greek and Indian words *pneuma* and *prana*, like *chi* in Chinese medicine, describe both air, breath, spirit, and the essence of life and the Japanese word *ki* is a central principle in martial arts and spiritual practices. Similarly, the Hebrew word *ruach*, encompasses breath and creative spirit, and New Zealand Māori use the word *hau* to explain the presence of air, breath, and the essential spiritual ingredients of life. Unsurprisingly, the Grofs propound that, throughout time, human beings have efficiently used breath work to create multi-consciousness states that have provided essential pathways inward to the Self. They describe this psychologically rich experience as 'holotropic,' an experiential and actualising phenomenon that impels the organism toward wholeness.[24]

20 Boroson, et al., 'Twelve Things You Should Know,' 55.

21 Grof, 'Holotropic Breathwork: New Perspectives.'

22 Rubye Lee Cervelli, 'An Intuitive Inquiry Into Experiences Arising Out of the Holotropic Breathwork™ Technique and its Integral Mandala Artwork: The Potential for Self-Actualization' (PhD diss,. Institute of Transpersonal Psychology, 2009), 20–21.

23 The Latin word *spiritus* means: soul; courage; vigour; and breath, and is related to the word *spirare*: to breathe.

24 A central principle in the theories and practice of humanist psychologists Abraham Maslow and Carl Rogers, 'self-actualisation' also provides both motive force and an explanation for benefit-finding in the wake of traumatic experiences. Peter Bray, 'Trauma and Growth: The Psychology of Self-Actualisation and Positive Post-Traumatic Processes,'

Originally modified by Stan Grof from his psychedelic therapy with Vietnam veterans, HB employs a traditional pattern of accelerated deep breathing that synchronises continuous circular inhalation and exhalation. Employing evocative music, breathers are brought into a receptive trance-like state of consciousness in which they access a broad spectrum of controllable consciousness experiences without the use of drugs.[25] Once the goal of reaching an altered consciousness has been achieved the breathing technique is no longer required, or indeed relevant.[26]

'Holotropic breathing is associated with biochemical changes in the brain that make it possible for the contents of the unconscious to surface,'[27] and much of that content is stored as energy in different parts of the body. It has deep roots in the archetypal architecture and historical domains of the collective unconscious and in 'ancestral, racial, collective phylogenetic, and karmic memories.'[28] Put simply, whilst the components of HB may create similar conditions for each session group, each participant will have unique 'highly specific and personally relevant'[29] experiences. Thus, HB positively and constructively reframes hyperventilation syndrome from a pathological phenomenon associated with involuntary and benign contractions of the muscles in states of extreme hypocarbia, to a form of over breathing that contacts an organismic healing mechanism that assists the body to process 'unconscious material with [a] strong emotional charge.'[30] Indeed, voluntary hyperventilation could be useful in 'standard treatments for anxiety disorders.'[31]

In the moment, this combination of controlled over breathing, physical and emotional intensification, and relaxation is claimed to change an individual's chemistry in such a way that the blocked 'energies associated with various traumatic memories ... emerge into consciousness and [can] be integrated.'[32] This implies that exposure to transpersonal material and a 'willingness to express fully the emerging emotions and physical energies are prerequisites for

---

Trauma and Meaning Making, eds. Danielle Schaub and Elspeth McInnes (Oxford, England: Inter-Disciplinary Press, In Press).

25 Stanislav Grof and Christina Grof, *The Stormy Search for Self* (Los Angeles: J.P. Tarcher, 1990), 144.

26 Wilfried Ehrmann, 'Some Critical Issues in Holotropic Breathwork,' viewed 16 March 2013, http://www.stanislavgrof.com/pdf/Critical%20Issues%20in%20HB_Grof.pdf.

27 Grof and Grof, *The Stormy Search for Self*, 269.

28 Grof and Grof, *Holotropic Breathwork: a New Approach to Self-Exploration and Therapy*, 69.

29 Ibid., 67.

30 Ibid., 168–169.

31 Rhinewine and Williams, 'Holotropic Breathwork: The Potential Role of a Prolonged, Voluntary Hyperventilation Procedure,' 771.

32 Grof, 'Holotropic Breathwork: New Perspectives,' 16.

good integration,' which then reduces the power of the subconscious to influence subsequent behaviours.[33]

> Once the subconscious material is consciously experienced in a benevolent and welcoming environment, previously held ideas, self-limiting definitions and self-destructive impulses can cease to hold with the same power. Thus we become freer to define ourselves more by our possibilities and less by our limitations.[34]

C *Body Work*

In their review of transpersonal theory and practice, Mark Kasprow and Bruce Scotton suggest that the application of altered breathing patterns provides opportunities for 'alternative state changes to occur' that through therapeutic bodywork 'powerfully release the energy that is raised and thus influence deeper changes in the body and personality/psyche.'[35] In this context they employ Ralph Metzner's definition of an altered state of consciousness 'as a change in thinking, feeling, and perception, in relation to one's ordinary, baseline consciousness that has a beginning, duration, and ending.'[36] Thus breathing, accompanied by auditory stimuli, prepares the individual to sideline psychological defences permitting the Reichian 'character armor'[37] of unassimilated and unintegrated physical traumas to find profound release.[38] In her powerful chapter, Schaub's describes how, in her distress, the body/mind connection was severed so that the body might simultaneously hold the trauma and armour itself 'to avoid more blows' and 'hide the gaping wound to everyone ....'[39] According to Reich, as psychosomatic symptoms originate

---

33 Ehrmann, 'Some Critical Issues in Holotropic Breathwork.'

34 Oliver Williams, 'The Healing Potential of Holotropic Breathwork,' viewed 4 February 2018, http://rebecoming.org/healing-potential-of-holotropic-breathwork/.

35 Kasprow and Scotton, 'A Review of Transpersonal Theory,' 20.

36 Ibid., 17; Paraphrasing Ralph Metzner, 'Therapeutic Application of Altered States of Consciousness (ASC),' *Worlds of Consciousness, Vol. 5*, eds. M. Schiliclitiny and H. Leunes (Berlin:VWB, 1995).

37 Grof and Grof, *Holotropic Breathwork: a New Approach to Self-Exploration and Therapy*, 68, 173.

38 Citing, Wilhelm Reich (1949, 1961), Grof states that HB confirms Wilhelm Reich's observation that psychological resistances and defences are associated with restricted breathing' and that faster 'breathing typically loosens psychological defences and leads to a release and emergence of unconscious (and superconscious) material.' Grof, 'Holotropic Breathwork: New Perspectives.'

39 Schaub, 'Reading myself and worlds' in this volume.

in old physical insults – such as memories of painful operations, accidents, diseases, childbirth or a past life injuries or death – the physical tensions that they create can be released as muscular bioenergetic discharges in the body, or by the cathartic release of blocked emotional processes. Thus, in post breath work, if the breathing has not resolved all of the emotional and physical tensions activated during the sessions, a technique of 'bodywork,' often referred to as 'focused energy release work,'[40] is employed to intensify and then release any uncomfortably trapped emotional material that has emerged during the session. Energy release work is an essential part of HB and 'plays an important role in the completion and integration of the experience.'[41]

However, even as energy release work may assist participants to become less stuck, more grounded, and finished in the session they may still have to integrate memories 'of that situation ... in which the repression of the instinct occurred.'[42] Martin Boroson, Jean Farrell, Nienke Merbis, and Dara White suggest that body work is effective because it employs sympathetic physical contact.[43] As the profound psychosomatic structure and psychological meaning of past traumas intensify everyday tensions and pains, immediate physical and psychic relief is achieved simply by repeatedly amplifying the blockages physically, by vocalising emotions as they arise, and then relaxing:

> A client might also want physical resistance for a particular gesture in order to intensify the feeling in it. But this physical resistance does not involve *doing something to* the client, and it is never ever intended to overwhelm the client. It is simply meeting the client where she is, and encouraging her to go a bit further, if she wishes.[44]

The issue of re-emerging traumatic memories and experiences, however, does raise the spectre of re-traumatisation. Citing psychiatrist Ivor Browne's article 'Unexperienced Experience'[45] the Grofs respond to this important issue by advancing that the breather does not re-experience the actual trauma, but only their original emotional and physical reaction to it. Thus, traumatic events 'recorded in the organism, but not fully consciously experienced, processed, and

40 Kylea Taylor, *The Breathwork Experience* (Santa Cruz: Hanford Mead Publishers, 1994), 9.
41 'Association for Holotropic Breathwork™ International.'
42 Wilhelm Reich, *The Function of the Orgasm* (New York: Touchstone, 1973), 300.
43 Boroson, et al., 'Twelve Things You Should Know,' 55.
44 Ibid.
45 Grof and Grof, *Holotropic Breathwork: a New Approach to Self-Exploration and Therapy*, 150–151.

integrated'[46] are responded to simultaneously in their original form in full age regression and are rationally accounted for and understood from the maturity and experience offered by an adult perspective in the here and now. HB trainer Kylea Taylor observes that because HB allows the trauma to emerge unhindered it can be correctively experienced and metabolised through the healing connections of the anaclytic process.[47] It should be noted that HB only induces the experience of trauma if it is there to begin with.[48] Furthermore it is suggested, breathers in the process of reliving traumatic memory are not suffering as much as experiencing and vocalising the relief of purging the emotional and physical pain from their bodies.[49]

D *Safety and Effectiveness*

> There are wide differences of opinion within the transpersonal community as to the appropriateness of doing transpersonal work with psychotic individuals. Jung, Wilber, and Grof and Grof have argued that transpersonally oriented therapies are not appropriate for psychotic individuals, whereas Lukoff and others suggest that transpersonal psychotherapy may be particularly appropriate for psychotic disorders, even serious ones.[50]

To establish a level of safety in which to access holotropic experiences, HB self-referring participants are asked to 'voluntarily' screen themselves pre-session for contraindicating physical and psychological conditions such as pregnancy, epilepsy, glaucoma, hypertension, stroke and heart problems, psychosis, severe personality or panic disorders, and known sensitivity to the sudden emergence of repressed material and/or the effects of mild hyperventilation.[51] The literature suggests that similar screening tools are used with mandated clients but presumably these are used in close consultation with a trained professional. It is also assumed that as most participants are self-selected they are more likely to be able to safely predict their positive capacity to manage their own internal processes and are consequently more forgiving and/or effective in their self-healing.[52] Kasprow and Scotton note that any informal screening or

46 Grof, 'Holotropic Breathwork: New Perspectives.'
47 Taylor, *Considering Holotropic Breathwork,* 19.
48 Boroson, et al., 'Twelve Things You Should Know,' 6.
49 Grof, 'Holotropic Breathwork: New Perspectives.'
50 Kasprow and Scotton, 'A Review of Transpersonal Theory,' 17.
51 Ibid., 20.
52 Kylea Taylor, in consultation with Tav Sparks, suggests that the low failure rates of HB may result from most participants having histories of secure attachment. Kylea Taylor, *Considering Holotropic Breathwork,* 140–141.

evaluation should also include an assessment of the breather's 'spiritual experiences, developmental level, premorbid functioning, and interest in exploring the symptoms.'[53] This information identifies and locates psychotic symptoms so that appropriate 'education, reassurance, psychotherapy focusing on biographical issues that may arise, and mental training such as meditation can help the patient move through and eventually integrate the psychotic state.'[54]

Even with the possibility that individuals may be exposed to a 'dangerous layer of existence best permanently avoided,' or that 'neither the inner healer, nor the best facilitator can guarantee that no problems will ever arise,'[55] the final outcome still largely rests with the participant's ability, sympathy, and willingness to surrender to the process, the setting, arrangements of the session, and the quality of its facilitation and support. That said, James Eyerman's study of more than 11,000 HB in-patients over 12 years impressively concludes that there was not 'one single reported adverse sequelae,' making it 'a low risk therapy' for 'patients with an extremely broad range of psychological problems and existential life issues.'[56] An earlier study concurred that as an experiential oriented psychotherapy, HB may be useful 'particularly with long term psychotherapy patients,' because it reduces death anxiety and increases self-esteem that may be at 'the root of sometimes seemingly intractable psychological problems.'[57] Similarly, others like Michael Weir and Christine Perry who have used HB for patients with chronic histories of recurrent depression, PTSD, alcohol dependence and anxiety, and panic disorders, and whose conventional treatments had been previously unsuccessful, found that, although not a 'cure-all' for 'treatment focused on symptom resolution,' it can be 'a powerful tool for self-exploration and personal growth.'[58]

It is perhaps because of Stan Grof's longstanding commitment to transpersonal psychology and research into holotropic states of consciousness that he has increasingly distanced his practice from others that claim empirical therapeutic success without the support of a rigorous theory. He is, for example, particularly scathing of Leonard Orr's respiratory methodology of 'rebirthing,'

53 Kasprow and Scotton, 'A Review of Transpersonal Theory,' 8.

54 Ibid., 17.

55 Kate Thomas, 'Transpersonal Experiences – A Need for Re-evaluation?' *Network* 81 (2003): 15–18; Wilfried Ehrmann, 'Some Critical Issues in Holotropic Breathwork.'

56 James Eyerman, 'A Clinical Report of Holotropic Breathwork in 11,000 Psychiatric Inpatients in a Community Hospital Setting,' *MAPS Bulletin*, Special Edition (2013): 26.

57 Sarah W. Holmes, et al., 'Holotropic Breathwork: An Experiential Approach to Psychotherapy,' *Psychotherapy* 31.1 (1996): 120.

58 Michael Weir and Christine Perry, 'Non-Ordinary States of Consciousness in Healing and Health: The Work and Techniques of Stanislav Grof,' viewed 4 February 2018, http://www.rcpsych.ac.uk/PDF/weir-perry.pdf.

which he claims has a 'painfully incomplete'[59] conceptual framework and whose theory is speculative and simplistic. Yet even as his controversial trade marking of HB therapy may safeguard clients and guarantee a quality service, it also appears to promote a message that HB is an exclusively Grofian discipline. Sadly, it is a message that appears at odds with the philosophical and humanistic roots of transpersonal psychology, the altruistic concepts of healing, and the philanthropic and free spirited practices of immaterialist cultures from which HB derives its energy.

3 The Elements and Course of a Typical Holotropic Breathwork Session

Five, or six, fundamental elements contribute to a typical two to four hour session of HB. These include a pre-session presentation of Stan Grof's holotropic theory and the HB method, the use of accelerated breathing, music, body work, and subsequent creative expression through mandala painting, and supportive group discussion. Taylor intimates that the reassuring linear progression of this method helps trauma survivors to more effectively process the timeless and fragmentary contents of painful traumatic memories as they emerge.[60]

The first element of HB involves practical and psychological preparation to participate. Before the breathing experience, *en masse* participants receive a briefing on transpersonal psychology's conceptualisation of the HB experience, the validity and potential of non-ordinary states of consciousness and, framed by Grof's cartography of the psyche, a generic description of how they might uniquely encounter the unfolding of the psyche. This brief, largely theoretical tour of the biographical, perinatal and transpersonal dimensions of experience requires listeners to readjust their existing world-views and signals the need to willingly submit to authorities both within and beyond the Self. This is also an opportunity to technically instruct the participants in their symbiotic roles as sitters and breathers, to highlight their responsibilities to each other, and to raise any physical and emotional concerns related to real or potential contraindications.[61]

---

59 Grof and Grof, *Holotropic Breathwork: a New Approach to Self-Exploration and Therapy*, 200; Leonard Orr and Sondra Ray, *Rebirthing in the New Age* (Berkeley, CA: Celestial Arts, 1977). For an irreverent critique of rebirthing see: Margaret Thaler Singer and Janja Lalich, *Crazy Therapies: What are they? Do they work?* (San Francisco: Jossey Bass, 1996).

60 Taylor, *Considering Holotropic Breathwork*, 19–127.

61 'Association for Holotropic Breathwork™ International.'

Applying anthropologist Victor Turner's concept of ritual as a vehicle for social transformation, Taylor specifically conceptualises the sessions for survivors of trauma as having three stages of experiential ritual: a 'pre-liminal' preparatory stage; a 'liminal' participatory stage that explores the dynamic of liminality and communitas which facilitates protective and therefore unconstrained group submission to the authority of the ritual and connective healing; and, a 'post-liminal' stage which offers integration and 'aggregation.'[62]

On entering the session the pre-liminal stage foreshadows the experience and grounds the participants in the practical and social tasks of preparing their spaces with bedding, negotiating with their sitters, and settling to the threshold experience of guided relaxation and breathing. As trained facilitators oversee the group, each breather lies on their backs on mats with their eyes closed, carefully watched over by their sitter. The second or liminal stage appears in the context of a protective ritual, setting, and contained outcomes of the breath work session. Kylea Taylor proposes that the day itself creates a sense of being 'set apart from ordinary reality,' as a retreat in which a supportive empathic 'temporary relationship of intimate equals'[63] akin to communitas, occurs. This creates an intersubjective relationship, a sacred and communal space, in which to safely experience the unfolding of psychic material into personal consciousness. Although it is claimed that the HB model is protective of survivors with dissociated trauma symptoms, it still relies very heavily upon the facilitators' and participants' capacities to responsibly understand and work within their contracts. For some, given permission to explore the unknown does not always equate to their being able to trust in the process. The reality of allowing a spontaneous and unfamiliar process to expose trauma to consciousness and reconnect the self through healing guided by an inner intelligence is likely to be considerably challenging.

In the liminal stage, the key element of HB is the breathing that directly accesses the holotropic state of consciousness. Initiated by the group facilitator, intentionally open instructions allow the breather to settle into a pattern that suits both personal style and physical comfort. 'The experience is entirely internal and largely non-verbal, without interventions.'[64] Taylor observes,

> I saw some instances of severe dissociation gradually become more conscious as the body retold the story again and again ... The Breathwork

62 Victor Turner, *The Ritual Process: Structure and Anti-Structure* (Chicago: Aldine Publishing Co., 1969), 95–96; Taylor, *Considering Holotropic Breathwork*, 126–136.

63 Taylor, *Considering Holotropic Breathwork*, 132.

64 'Association for Holotropic Breathwork™ International.'

> experience would retell the abuse with the same sounds, the same movements, the same needs for support over and over, with increasing awareness, change, and integration over a period of time. The set and setting of ritual provides protection, permission, and connection which allows change to be encountered – then tolerated – and finally, metabolized.[65]

Occasionally sensitive body work may be required to focus on the amplification of emerging somatic blocks until they resolve themselves spontaneously.

Stan Grof notes that for some participants faster breathing may not always induce physical or emotional tensions or dis-ease but instead may engage with those positive states more likely to arise at the conclusion of the session such as feelings of love and relaxation and an expanded sense of well-being.[66]

A further important ingredient of the session, music brings the participants into their breathing patterns by its own very tangible and psychologically stimulating presence. Drawn from ritual and spiritual traditions of various native cultures the music is not chosen for its entertainment value or presented for distraction or analysis but for its ability to reflect the generic process of holotropic unfolding. Arranged in five overlapping phases it begins with powerfully rhythmic pieces chosen to establish evocative and stimulating responses to support the induction and accentuate the intensity of psychic opening. Breathers are encouraged to seek full immersion in the music's ebb and flow and to give spontaneous and free expression to their experiences. Half way through the session, when the experience tends to culminate, the music builds to a dramatic climax, then sacred 'breakthrough music' is introduced followed by emotionally moving 'heart music,' appropriately concluding with a set of peaceful and meditative pieces.[67]

Following their experiences participants enter a third post-liminal and integrative stage of the ritual where they are offered more conventional forms of emotional expression through physical exercise and dance to free energy accumulated in the session. Breathers are also invited to continue integrating their experiences through expressive writing and/or by painting mandalas. Although their creations may not make sense at the time this kind of work leads to realisation and subsequent psychological development.[68]

In her very personal and deeply reflective account of struggle with the long-term energetic impulses of trauma, Marie France Forcier's chapter explains

---

65 Taylor, *Considering Holotropic Breathwork*, 19.

66 Grof, 'Holotropic Breathwork: New Perspectives.'

67 Stanislav and Christina Grof 'Principles of Holotropic Breathwork,' viewed 4 February 2018, http://www.grof-holotropic-breathwork.net/page/2182480.

68 Brouillette, 'Reported Effects of Holotropic Breathwork.'

how the l accumulation of trauma in the body over time can be allowed release and healing through artistry and expression.[69] The powerful recognition that her PTSD 'had been infiltrating my creative work' and to intentionally 'let the phenomenon happen and to consciously develop it,' was wonderfully intuitive.[70] It has subsequently led her as a choreographer and artiste to the liberating and transformative notion that she has 'gained far too much insight into understanding of the power of memory-informed movement to return to my earlier choreographic dispositions.'[71]

Finally, participants are encouraged to share some of their experience within a group. This needs careful management by the facilitators to minimise interpretation or analysis at a time when the fresh experience may not have fully emerged into understanding or been reconciled. Nevertheless, the Grofs suggest that 'Jungian amplification in the form of mythological and anthropological references can be very useful in the discussion of the holotropic experiences, as well as the mandalas.'[72]

4 Holotropic Breathwork and Trauma

HB sessions tend to draw participants who have intentionally and willingly chosen to bring their addictions, neurotic and psychosomatic disorders, communication problems, and life crises to be explored in alternative states of consciousness.[73] Through a form of catharsis it offers the opportunity to relinquish physical and emotional blockages associated with prior trauma.[74] However, how survivors of trauma are served by the combination of hyperventilation and the hyperstimulation of the auditory sensory system to induce a hypocapnia that 'directly affects regional and local cerebral hemodynamics that can modify the functional state of brain structures'[75] is still something of a mystery.

69 Marie France Forcier, 'Investigating the Post-Traumatic Lens in the Choreographer's Work,' in this volume.

70 Ibid.

71 Ibid.

72 'Association for Holotropic Breathwork™ International.'

73 Crowley, 'Holotropic Breathwork™ – Healing Through a Non-Ordinary State of Consciousness'; Vladimir A. Emelianenko and A.V. Emelianenko, 'Application of the Holotropic Breathwork: Psychotherapeutic Aspects,' viewed 4 February 2018, https://www.academia.edu/14902147/Journal_of_Transpersonal_Research_Vol_6_2_._Special_Issue_Holotropic_Breathwork_and_Other_Hyperventilation_Procedures.

74 Eyerman, 'A Clinical Report of Holotropic Breathwork.'

75 P.I. Terekhin, 'The Role of Hypcopnia in Inducing Altered States of Consciousness,' *Human Physiology* 22.6 (1996): 730–735.

What distinguishes the psychology of HB from many psychotherapeutic approaches is that it bypasses verbal communication in favour of the direct expression of emotions. Also, by recognising the existence of a higher cosmic consciousness, it privileges a personal spirituality that extends beyond the purview of many organised religions.[76] In addition, unlike conventional experiential psychotherapeutic approaches and spiritual systems, HB does not use analysis or interventions based on *a priori* theoretical constructs.[77] Although an overall facilitator may 'explain the method, create the safe setting, support the process, and work with people if they experience any difficulty,'[78] the work is mainly done within the dyads and later in groups that provide the opportunity to share experiences and insights. As the trained facilitators only function as helpers, when required, the participants become their own therapists either as 'responsive and non-intrusive' sitters who 'ensure effective breathing, create a safe environment, respect the natural unfolding of the experience, and provide assistance in all situations that require it,'[79] or as breathers invited by the intervention to immerse themselves in their own intelligently guided inner processes.

In order to see just how HB intensifies the symptoms of trauma to relieve them and how it can be used as an adjunct to therapy, one must understand what Grof and Grof identify as trauma. In their work they distinguish two forms of trauma that require very different interventions in their HB sessions. The first they describe as 'trauma by commission,' which accommodates a range of frightening and personally destructive abuses and situations that they define as 'external intrusions that had damaging impact on the future development of the individual.'[80] These correspond to the widely regarded view that as unconscious 'foreign elements' traumas have the capacity to 'be brought into consciousness, energetically discharged, and resolved.'[81] However, the second manifestation of trauma they identify as 'trauma by omission' stems from a lack of physical and emotional contact 'essential for a healthy emotional development' early on in life.[82] In the latter 'Grof advocates close physical contact and the expression of care once the breathing and bodywork have been

76 Renn Butler, 'Review of Holotropic Breathwork: A New Approach to Therapy and Self-Exploration,' viewed 4 February 2018, http://www.grof-holotropic-breathwork.net/group/thereadingroom/forum/topics/review-of-holotropic.

77 'Association for Holotropic Breathwork™ International.'

78 Boroson, et al., 'Twelve Things You Should Know,' 6.

79 'Association for Holotropic Breathwork™ International.'

80 Grof and Grof, *Holotropic Breathwork: a New Approach to Self-Exploration and Therapy*, 40.

81 Ibid.

82 Ibid., 40–41.

completed.'[83] Consequently, if a participant with this form of trauma agrees to be deeply regressed to an appropriate level of holotropic consciousness they can then be offered simple, non-threatening, and ethical physical contact as a 'corrective experience'[84] to expose and melt resistance and heal this trauma of omission. In the specific context of HB these corrective experiences lead to healing connections as opposed to re-traumatisation.[85] This intervention borrows from the theory and practice of 'fusion therapy' devised by Pauline McCririck and Joyce Martins who initially used this method to meet their clients' desires for attention and satisfaction triggered by alienating therapeutic relationships that replicated earlier deficits in their object relations development.[86]

For breathers with 'a history of sexual abuse, physical contact is a very sensitive and charged issue' and it takes a while for trust in, and acceptance of, the process to build before they can totally participate in its process.[87] This may also prove problematic for sitters with their own intimacy issues or similarly unmet needs. However, Kylea Taylor remarks with Wilfried Ehrmann that, alongside its 'very strong catalytic effect,' in the group context there is a 'feeling of safety in receiving physical touch that would be difficult to achieve in a one-on-one therapy session.'[88] Taylor also notes that as the holotropic state creates a bi-modal consciousness in the breather or, as Stan Grof notes the simultaneous experience of 'two very different realities' as a witness and experiencer, the presence of a sitter provides an additional 'compassionate witness'[89] that serves to correctively balance the reliving of the trauma experience by objectively acknowledging and affirming the subjective experiences of the breather's inner witness.

Assuming that trauma is undigested or 'unexperienced experience,' Taylor endorses 'community and ritual'[90] as significant elements of HB to loosen

83 Weir and Perry, 'Non-Ordinary States of Consciousness in Healing and Health.'
84 The Association for Holotropic Breathwork International, 'Ethical Guidelines for Facilitators of Holotropic Breathwork,' viewed 18 January 2014, http://www.grof-holotropic-breathwork.net/page/ethical-guidelines-for.
85 Taylor, *Considering Holotropic Breathwork*, 133.
86 Stanislav Grof, *When the Impossible Happens: Adventures in Non-Ordinary Realities* (Boulder CO: Sounds True Inc., 2006), 14–17.
87 Grof, 'Holotropic Breathwork: New Perspectives.'
88 Ehrmann, 'Some Critical Issues in Holotropic Breathwork'; Taylor, *Considering Holotropic Breathwork*, 19.
89 Stanislav Grof, *Psychology of the Future: Lessons from Modern Consciousness Research* (Albany: State University of New York Press, 2000), 2; Taylor, *Considering Holotropic Breathwork*, 19–20.
90 Taylor, *Considering Holotropic Breathwork*, 120.

personal defence mechanisms enough to permit the recovery of trauma stored in the psyche. In practical terms, she suggests that without a relational community of sharing and support the survivor dissociates from and represses the experience without satisfactory resolution. From her experience as a HB facilitator working with trauma survivors, Taylor concludes that human beings elicit ritual to help them manage rites of passage, absorb difficult changes in their lives, and achieve closure. She advances that because the group work of HB functions as a ritual, a commitment or an invitation to enter unknown territory, it 'offers the same benefits that ritual has offered to groups of individuals from the beginning of history.'[91] She also notes that as trauma survivors already have highly developed psychic resources, or acute senses because of their need to maintain a level of hypervigilance, the safety of the ritual and the presence of the sitter and potential interpersonal support in the group make it possible to naturally harness their inner resources without becoming overwhelmed.[92] As loss and grief, two fundamental aspects of trauma recovery, are simultaneously awakened, contained, and metabolised, so survivors receive a corrective re-experiencing of the trauma and can move to a more stable and integrative state in the final stages of their work, where rituals of bereavement can have a more effective impact.

5 Unblocking Trauma: An Autoethnographic Case Account of Holotropic Breathwork

According to the work of psychiatrist Binarová Denisa, as a 'first-breather,'[93] I am likely to have an experiential style, personality properties, attitudes, and values that will, at the conclusion of the session, invite me to be more accepting of previously rejected ideas and opinions, increase my purpose in life, and enable me to have a deeper understanding and acceptance of others and my immediate world.

A *Introduction*

The following notes describe my first experience of HB. Although I had some prior knowledge of its overarching 'holotropic' theory, I did not know or have any real expectations of its facilitation or what my process might be like. Nevertheless, my privileged familiarity with the Grofs' work, not to mention my

91 Ibid., 125.

92 Ibid.

93 Binarová Denisa, 'The Effect of Holotropic Breathwork on Personality,' *Czech and Slovak Psychiatry* 99.8 (2003): 410–414.

careful completion of the self-assessment questionnaire, the pre-breathwork advertising and the briefing on the holotropic cartography of the psyche made it almost impossible not to imaginatively anticipate what was about to happen. My inner radar or 'inner healer' may not have been compromised but my conscious self was increasingly anxious about doing HB right.

As the experience responds to the unique needs of the individual, what I have recorded is consciously, to paraphrase Pat MacEnulty, an act of therapy intended to inform, entertain, heal, and communicate the possibilities of our human and divine natures.[94] Nevertheless, I am hopeful that you will regard this subjective account as a typical experience and myself as a typical participant whose struggle, retrospectively, was relatively benign. Not in itself a powerful healing process, not quite an 'unstoppable flow of released emotion,'[95] rather a witnessing, and gradual amelioration and exorcism of a shared pain, an unblocking or breakthrough – an unfolding metaphor, a becoming seed of an experience of future possibilities.[96] Or a moment, and then a memory, birthed to create change. For others the process was clearly proving more expansive, energetic, and alarming. As a sitter it takes a considerable shift in worldview to understand that, like drawing poison from a wound, the external manifestations of healing look and sound far more disturbing than the profound relief that attend the grunts, laughs, and roars towards freedom.

In the following account I have included Stan Grof's largely instructional contemporaneously noted verbatim – in the left-hand column – against my own account completed within a few days of the experience.

B *Beginning to Breathe*[97]

Day 1 – Beginning.[a]

Introducing the Experience.
The monotheistic materialism of industrial society pathologises spirituality...

Day 2 – Breathing.

Anticipation.

In a Moscow hotel conference room with 80 strangers. Scattered haphazardly across the floor perched on mats,

94 Kate Burton, 'Shaping Personality Through Suffering: The Transformative Writing of Pat MacEnulty,' in this volume.

95 Schaub, 'Reading myself and worlds' in this volume.

96 Discussing MacEnulty's 'Floating on the Darkness,' Kate Burton's examination and description of the burden and responsibility of carrying a parent's trauma deftly resonates with my own unconscious and felt experiences. Similarly, my father's trauma bound me to him right up until the end. Burton, 'Shaping Personality Through Suffering,' in this volume.

97 The following account was written on June 23 and 24, 2010. It reports the author's experience of a Holotropic Breathwork session.

Hindu experiential, spiritual exercises, like yoga, raise awareness and explore the energy that is identical to that found in the universe.
Ultimately we are all identical with that identity...Moving from body ego identification to identification with the source...sometimes small steps... sometimes breakthroughs.
These experiences have a quality of numinosity...They are the software of the psyche. Working with holotropic states it is virtually impossible to use the intellect to understand the psyche.

chattering a rainbow of languages to colleagues and new friends. There are people everywhere rearranging blankets and personal belongings to take full advantage of newly claimed spaces. I carefully pick my way through the excited bodies towards my Belgian sitter who worked with me yesterday and ready myself to experience the deep breathing and evocative music that will allow me to explore the deeper dynamics of my psyche.

Preparation.
I begin by discarding items of clothing that can obstruct the therapeutic process such as shoes, jewellery, glasses and connections to cyberspace. Thus, as an unencumbered breather I lie on my back on a thin mattress with my head resting on a small pillow.

Sitters...
Don't leave the breather.

My sitter, Carl, positions himself comfortably next to me preparing for the three hours observation that will ensue. With a box of tissues and a bottle of water close to hand, he has clear instructions not to leave me on my own.

From a strictly materialistic point of view, if you have spiritual experiences...there is something wrong with you. You are not educated and you get a diagnosis.

'What do they think I am going to do...?'

Whilst waiting, we loudly amuse ourselves with possible fantasy scenarios.

...In Brahma the questions asked are
Who are you? Who am I?
The answer given is,
You are god. You are divine.
...A divine spark!

'In a world where the dominant model of healing encourages the suppression of symptoms, it's not surprising that any technique that encourages the amplification of symptoms will be controversial'[b]

Cynicism.
The day before I had been Carl's sitter and had been impressed by his gymnastic convulsions as the breather. Later, I was more than put out when he cryptically suggested that,

'Nothing happened.'

Even to different therapies, there is a challenge in understanding the potential of 'altered states' of consciousness.

Each will tell you something different about what is wrong with you, and how you should do your therapy.

Respect your own uniquely individual authority. Holotropic Breathwork uses the power of the inner healer.

This didn't help at all.
I wasn't about to be satisfied with anything other than a fully aware, deeply penetrative and significant plunge into the inner workings of my complex psyche. I hadn't travelled half way around the globe, overcoming all sorts of personal and professional demons, to claim anything less.

Body Awareness.
On my back with my eyes closed, arms resting by my sides, palms turned up to accept the experience, I feel a level of unaccustomed anxiety and vulnerability.

The facilitator will focus the breathers on their bodies so that they become aware of aches and pains as they begin to practice and focus on mindful relaxation.

I am ready to begin but my mind is making excuses to leave the room.

Working with connected/circular breathing that is a little faster than usual...work out what suits your personal style.

Support.
Now, the slow heavy voice of the facilitator breaks my reverie forcing me to connect to reality and to the exercise...

...To aid the process of relaxation I want you to visualise a light passing slowly over your body, scanning and soothing it as it moves upwards from your toes to your head.

Supine, each wave of gently directed probing sends me deeper into a warmer and more accepting state.

Experience the deep comfort of having someone there.

Breathing.
In this place of soft consciousness I am fully aware: sensing others around me; the air conditioning; incidental noises in the building; and random thoughts that become easier and easier to resist and then put away.

As the rhythmic music…is played quite loudly the breather is encouraged to deepen and speed up their breathing above normal.

…mindful…
relaxation…

Instead of feeling uncomfortable about maintaining a slightly heavier and faster breathing routine the rhythmic rising and falling of my chest feels reassuring and natural. Simultaneously, the strong and evocative beat of aboriginal music fills the room and I am aware that my muscles are responding to the changes in my breathing.

You as the healer are kept in control – use the word stop *to get the attention and support from your sitter or trained facilitators to stop whatever they are doing for you. Any other words might be part of the healing process…part of the inner dialogue.*

Trust.
My eyes are closed in a room with 80 strangers. Yet, I am giving my body over to its own intelligence and it feels right. In the emerging inner peace I feel myself trusting my sitter and the process. I am being comfortably held by other forces – the paradoxical tension between holding on to self control and letting go.

Individuals may experience the trauma of abuse or experiences of not receiving, or being denied something.

I feel ready for anything!

What might my body do that it hasn't done before and where might my mind rove?

The breather has a right to refuse assistance.

I am a white middle aged, middle class male … surprise me!

Everything is created by consciousness; there is nothing that cannot be experienced. It can do things that the brain by itself cannot possibly do.

Like radar…the holotropic state finds the areas in the unconscious which are most relevant.

'Manifestations of altered consciousness emerging after approximately 8 minutes of hyperventilation…'visions' have been reported after periods of hyperventilation exceeding 15 minutes."[c]

As the body ego dissolves we can subjectively share in the experiences of all life forms…a very wide spectrum of experience.

The collective unconscious incorporates a record of human history… Anima mundi!

A whole record or history of experience is accessible from the Basic Perinatal Matrices.[d]

Relived through large archetypal experiences and images in the transpersonal realm of experience…

Our individual psyche contains the whole universe.[e]

The psyche is the ultimate mystery. There is no way to figure it out with the intellect.

Music.

Soon the flowing music becomes the only way to judge the passing of time. I am floating just below its surface, observing with some relish and without the need to interpret or interfere that my body, or rather the muscles, are gently rippling to their own rhythms and cadences.

My body is doing what it wants and I feel an unaccustomed sense of surrender.

With an unfolding calm in my centre and a growing trust in the process, I am able to luxuriate in the warmth of just being.

The music is deeply rhythmical like the beat of a heart, my heart. I revel in its spaciousness.

I am at once a container, a vehicle, a stage, a canvas of universal human expression and connection. United with this flowing cosmic landscape an ancient pulse begs my body to respond.

Momentarily my detached and reluctant intellect breaks loose toward the surface.

…Is this too soon, and how is this to work?

In unquestionable response my arm gently detaches itself from the mat and rises snake-like, charming my mind into silence. The intelligence

In holotropic states we can get over boundaries, we can transcend them. But there needs to be a safe context. Sitters, see to it that the breather doesn't move too far. Use soft materials to restrain him. To prevent injury or physical impact that influences the breather's or other breathers' experiences.

that guides my arm permits the other parts of my body to meet their own desires and resolve their own issues.

Inner Intelligence.
Without seeing I feel inner healing unfolding with certainty, grace and purposeful eloquence. I am opening and it is liberating as my limbs wrap around each other and dance.

The breathing causes spasms…the music induces deep tensions associated with traumatic experiences…Physical contact can be offered that will enable and unblock these experiences and help the individual understand what they mean.

My torso pulses and my legs work expansively, my arms twist and flex, swooping and gliding while it falls to my hands to articulate the subtleties of deep unexpressed emotion. I am being comfortably held by my own body, aware of its indecipherable choreography and marvelling at its effortless movements.

'By experiencing them, people are getting rid of them.'[f]

It seems counter-intuitive…rather than controlling them, the breather is asked to attend to these physical tensions… even to vocalise.

Earlier we had been asked to anchor our thoughts upon some particular source of strength. I had tried to focus on God but couldn't sustain it.

Different psychosomatic disorders can present themselves in the body. This is where the bodywork is useful.

At this moment, on this day, in my first breath work session I couldn't avoid the fact, nor remove it from my mind, that my father of 89 years was dying in a cottage-hospital bed in Norfolk, England. The unavoidable realisation held me hostage. Dad is dying and I am in Moscow.
'There is nothing you can do for him now. We just have to wait.'

One major observation or one category of experience, from thanatology, is that in certain near-death situations consciousness leaves the body.

Our individual psyche is a microcosm that contains the whole universe…

Reconciliation.

On a mat on a Moscow floor. Here is Dad.
I can see him so vividly in the early English morning. His head is buttressed by painfully large pillows. The sun patterns the bed clothes and outlines his awkward frailty caged in that vast metal bed. He has become a fraction of a man, an angular frame of translucently pale skin on bone. His chest slowly and painfully rises and falls as he fights for each rasping breath. His mouth, now permanently open, receives only extra oxygen as tubes feed and lead away to boxy machines on stands.

If you work with the holotropic model of the psyche the roots go to deep levels.

'If we have emotional problems, psychosomatic problems, or problems in relation to other people, the roots are not just in our biography but there are also additional roots connected to the trauma of birth...and even, what we call the transpersonal level.'[g]

I am engulfed by a wave of uncontrollable sadness, a dark void of extraordinary loss. My body responding to these new emotions gulps and drowns in their depths. My orientation is confused, am I descending or ascending? Is it my experience or my father's?

Relax enough to enjoy the present and leave the intellect behind.

In spite of my total absorption I am aware of the others working through their processes. They sigh and shout, make vomiting noises and cry in strange accompaniment to the seemingly permanent backdrop of evocative music.

To overcome these problems you need to work through the different levels. It must be experiential. The bad news is that there are many levels to manage.

Even as I am inexorably drawn back into my journey I join them. My vocalisations are timid at first but turn by degrees into a robust appreciation and identification with emotions of loss. I am an outpouring of wailing and tears in a womb of comfortingly soft translucent shapes.

Now, suddenly propelled through
these emotionally drenched forms
I struggle with buffeting changes of
pressure.

Tensions will build up and then there will be some relaxation…

Union.
I feel warmth and then tension in my arms. Unseen hands have gripped them and are firmly pulling them upwards. For the first time I am aware of another physical presence, an actual intelligence, and in that moment I understand. I am allowed to fully own these desperate feelings of sadness and longing and yet powerfully I identify my father's presence. How can I sufficiently describe the completeness of our delicate entwinement? My feelings are his feelings. I am experiencing his pain, his shortness of breath. I am his anger at having to leave a life unfinished, a rude severing from family and dreams.

Certain assisted body work may also be required for individuals who experience a block that needs to be worked out; otherwise individuals allow their bodies to express their needs at that time while under the supervision of a caring sitter.

In this hermetic vessel, and through the exchange of symbolic language, the intellect converses with the transpersonal and transformation can take place.[h]

Fused with him I understand that I am so much more, that there is so much more. Our hunger for life and pleasure in what we are sets us spinning in a climactic vortex and in this final movement we are the music and the players; we are their instruments and scores, the concert hall and the audience. Feeling what he feels and thinking his thoughts we glimpse a 'heaven' Dad claimed not to believe in.
Death or life beyond still summons and tugs with cruel insistence.
'We are so tired Dad.'
'How are you holding on Dad?'
I can quite clearly see my mother and my aunt sitting by the bed helplessly

witnessing and intuitively understanding Dad's unrelenting struggle. I can feel it and it fills me with dread. His life and his loss are ours and it hurts. Caught between the certainty of life and the uncertainty of death I linger with my Dad in that place that is more womb than world and feel his fear and his inertia as my own. I try to comfort him with my presence and a trickle of warmth comes back in response. I feel recognised, almost understood. Unexpectedly, this understanding is interrupted by another. A firm but kindly voice that I don't recognise at all addresses us.

'It will be alright', it says.

'Let go now. It's okay to just let go.'

Understanding.

I feel Dad relax but he is so tightly bound to the earth that he finds it hard to move; the bed, the blankets, the air line, the drip, the familiar voices all serve to bind him to the present. Then it seems that my outstretched arms find new purpose. Still raised, my hands seek the body of my father but I am myself again and recognise my extraordinary loss. I ache to hug him but I know I can't allow myself to prolong his pain by physically tying him to me. As if in acknowledgement I feel his warmth again. Tears are streaming down my face.

'So many losses, so many to lose', comes the voice but this time it is all directed at me.

I feel wracked with the grief of all humanity and it is bitter sweet.

Gift.

I feel wave upon wave of tension release itself as I give up my father to his bliss and my tears of pain turn to tears of great joy. My hands, still wishing to claim what was lost, come together as if to receive or shape something and a globe of soft light appears above me and gently floats down into them. I am surprised and at the same time receive it unquestioningly. I understand it to be something of my father that has been tenderly and lovingly formed and is at that moment being channelled into my waiting hands. Of their own volition they mirror the sphere and guide it downward as it pushes itself into my chest. I watch all this with a degree of detachment not altogether understanding its significance. It is what it is. However, as the process concludes a huge smile immediately suffuses my face and I quite literally light up with relief and joy. Dad and I have been together – we are together! We shared an extraordinary moment and he has given me something, something wonderful and inexplicable, a great treasure. It seems to me now that he is free in a way that I can only just conceive and I know with absolute certainty that he is alright – that we are alright!

'A typical result…is profound emotional release and physical relaxation… people report that they feel more relaxed than they have ever felt in their life. Continued accelerated breathing thus represents an extremely powerful and effective method of stress reduction and it is conducive to emotional and psychosomatic healing. Another frequent result of this work is connection

Dazzled.
I open my eyes in a room full of unique and precious individuals. It is as if I have entered that room for the first time. I suddenly become aware that there are people everywhere: facilitators and sitters purposefully tend to their breathers; breathers busily work with inner processes or come in to land; and the room thrums with their energy and light. I am dazzled

with the numinous dimensions of one's own psyche and of existence in general.'[i]

by the brightness and colour of the unfolding scene and the forgotten impact of the music. Momentarily my senses reel as I try to take it in, and all the time the broad grin doesn't leave my face and the warm glow suffuses my whole being.

'Are you okay?...

After a while a facilitator comes over and hunkers down...

...When you feel you have landed then go and draw a mandala and share your experiences in a group.

I can't wipe the smile from my face as I reply,

'I have never felt better'.

And I mean it.

Carl carefully assists me from the room. I have been 'breathing' for over two hours but have no notion of the time. It is only later that I look at my phone and see that my sister in England has sent me a text message. It reads quite simply,

'In the terminal stage of the session... Intimate contact with nature can also have a very calming and grounding effect and help the integration of the session.[j]

'Sorry. Dad has left us – big hug xxx'

I went outside and into the park...

---

a Unless referenced, the italicised text in this column is taken from notes made at Stanislav Grof's morning lecture, preparatory to author's holotropic breathwork session on Monday, 21 June, 2010.

b Boroson, et al., 'Twelve Things You Should Know', 6.

c Rhinewine and Williams, 'Holotropic Breathwork: The Potential Role of a Prolonged, Voluntary Hyperventilation Procedure', 772.

d Grof, The Holotropic Mind (New York: Harper Collins, 1993).

e Richard Tarnas, Cosmos and Psyche: Intimations of a New World View (New York: Viking, 2006).

f Stanislav Grof and Christina Grof, 'Christina and Stan Grof: Holotropic Breathwork, viewed 4 February 2018, http://www.youtube.com/watch?feature=player_embedded&v=YVILRQ4gHBk.

g Ibid.

h See Carl Gustav Jung on the 'individuation process' in Aniele Jaffe, ed., Memories, Dreams, Reflections, trans. Claire Winston and Richard Winston (New York: Random House, Inc., 1989), 209.

i Grof, 'Holotropic Breathwork: New Perspectives.'

j Ibid.

As the events of the session further unfolded and my father's death became a reality, I returned to my world disoriented and dreamy. I didn't draw a mandala to help me understand myself or integrate the experience. I didn't want to be busy or overly analytical, and I did no further work at the session. I sought my sitter and our small group and reassuringly moved off from the claustrophobic hotel interior into the lush exterior of a Moscow park. Sitting on the grass surrounded by laughing company I was grounded and felt a sense of my own 'realness.' Aware that I could not integrate what had happened to me by relying on intellectual verification alone, I became cognisant of the session's solace and its support in the management of the difficult events that surrounded my father's death. I had allowed my process to lead me and it was only later that my need to really confirm dad's death and talk to my family anxiously asserted itself. However, in the intervening hours I was deeply peaceful and in my tenuous connection to dad I was sufficient.

6 Endnote: Breathe-Through

Concluding their article, 'Twelve Things You Should Know about Holotropic Breathwork™,' Grof certified facilitators Martin Boroson, Jean Farrell, Nienke Merbis, and Dara Whitemost summarise the benefits of participation in a workshop session as follows:

> In a Holotropic Breathwork workshop, people experience a place of deep safety and profound trust, often for the first time. They learn to take time out from ordinary life for their deeper concerns and dreams. They learn how to bear witness to their own suffering and the suffering of others. They learn how to support one another through a dramatic process of unfolding. They learn that the enormous spiritual treasures of the Kosmos are available in each of us. They learn to trust their inner healer. They learn that experiencing their truth is the quickest way to wholeness. They learn to be compassionate to themselves and others. They learn to celebrate their uniqueness and respect other peoples' differences. They learn that it's okay to feel little and vulnerable, and that it's okay to feel big and powerful. They learn to empathize with everything in the created universe as part of themselves, and they learn that they too are part of everything. They learn how to trust the deep wisdom of their own psyche, and to stay open to its ever-evolving story.[98]

98 Boroson, et al., 'Twelve Things You Should Know,' viewed 19 August 2018 https://iahip.org/inside-out/issue-55-summer-2008/twelve-things-you-should-know-about-holotropic-breathwork.

Bibliography

Binarová, Denisa. 'The Effect of Holotropic Breathwork on Personality.' *Czech and Slovak Psychiatry* 99.8 (2003): 410–414.

Boroson, Martin, Jean Farrell, Nienke Merbis and Dara White. 'Twelve Things You Should Know about Holotropic Breathwork™.' *Inside Out* 55 (2008) viewed 19 August 2018 HYPERLINK https://iahip.org/inside-out/issue-55-summer-2008/twelve-things-you-should-know-about-holotropic-breathwork.

Bray, Peter. 'A Broader Framework for Exploring the Influence of Spiritual Experience in the Wake of Stressful Life Events: Examining Connections between Posttraumatic Growth and Psycho-Spiritual Transformation.' *Mental Health, Religion and Culture* 13.3 (2010): 293–308.

Grof, Stanislav. *Beyond the Brain: Birth, Death and Transcendence in Psychotherapy*. Albany: State University New York Press, 1985.

Grof, Stanislav. *The Holotropic Mind: The Three Levels of Human Consciousness and How They Shape Our Lives*. New York: Harper Collins, 1993.

Grof, Stanislav. *Psychology of the Future: Lessons from Modern Consciousness Research*. Albany: State University of New York Press, 2000.

Grof, Stanislav. *When the Impossible Happens: Adventures in Non-Ordinary Realities*. Boulder CO: Sounds True Inc., 2006.

Grof, Stanislav and Christina Grof, eds. *The Stormy Search for Self*. Los Angeles: J.P. Tarcher, 1990.

Grof, Stanislav and Christina Grof, eds. *Holotropic Breathwork: A New Approach to Self-Exploration and Therapy*. New York: SUNY, 2010.

Holmes, Sarah W., Robin Morris, Pauline Rose Clance and R. Thompson Putney. 'Holotropic Breathwork: An Experiential Approach to Psychotherapy.' *Psychotherapy* 33.1 (1996): 125–138.

Jackson, Caitriona. 'Holotropic Breathwork™: An Experiential, Theoretical Account.' *Inside Out* 29 (1997).

Jaffe, Aniele, ed. *Memories, Dreams, Reflections*. Translated by Claire Winston and Richard Winston. New York: Random House Inc., 1989.

Kasprow, Mark C. and Bruce W. Scotton. 'A Review of Transpersonal Theory and its Application to the Practice of Psychotherapy.' *The Journal of Psychotherapy Practice and Research* 8 (1999): 12–23.

Mijares, Sharon G. ed. *The Revelation of the Breath: A Tribute to Its Wisdom, Power, and Beauty*. New York: SUNY, 2009.

Rhinewine, Joseph and Oliver Williams. 'Holotropic Breathwork: The Potential Role of a Prolonged, Voluntary Hyperventilation Procedure as an Adjunct to Psychotherapy.' *Journal of Alternative and Complementary Medicine* 13.7 (2007): 771–776.

Tarnas, Richard. Cosmos and Psyche: Intimations of a New World View. New York: Viking, 2006.

Taylor, Kylea. *The Breathwork Experience*. Santa Cruz, C.A.: Hanford Mead Publishers, 1994.

Taylor, Kylea. *Considering Holotropic Breathwork*. Santa Cruz, C.A.: Hanford Mead Publishers, 2007.

Terekhin, P.I. 'The Role of Hypcopnia in Inducing Altered States of Consciousness.' *Human Physiology* 22.6 (1996): 730–735.

Thomas, Kate. 'Transpersonal Experiences – A Need for Re-evaluation?' *Network* 81 (2003): 15–18.

Vich, Miles A. 'Some Historical Sources of the Term "Transpersonal."' *Journal of Transpersonal Psychology* 20 (1988): 107–110.

Index of Modern Authors

Index of Subjects

www.ingramcontent.com/pod-product-compliance
Lightning Source LLC
Chambersburg PA
CBHW071439230926
51846CB00001B/287
9789004383197